The Yachting Gourmet

Easy Gourmet Cooking On Board!

Mary Maskal

The Yachting Gourmet

Published by Author, Inc.
www.cookspalate.com

Copyright © 2007 by MEM Publications, St. Pete Beach, FL

ISBN: 978-0-9779321-2-2
Printed in the United States of America.
First printing: 2007

Editorial and production: MEM Publications
www.theyachtinggourmet.com

This title is distributed by MEM Publications, St. Pete Beach, FL. To order additional copies, please visit our website, www.theyachtinggourmet.com or see the order form in the back of the book.

Table of Contents

Introduction

Nothing is more relaxing than spending a few hours or a few days on the water! For those of us that love boating, it 's the ultimate escape from busy lives. And, for many, spending time preparing a great meal for family and friends can also be a relaxing activity. With *The Yachting Gourmet* you will be able to do both! With this cookbook, you can combine your love of boating AND your love of cooking and create gourmet meals on board with a minimum of preparation.

No matter what size your boat, the galley is just not the same as that fully appointed gourmet kitchen you have at home. *The Yachting Gourmet* method of preparation combines the functionality of your home kitchen and your galley through a two step preparation process.

What makes this cookbook unique? Each recipe has been modified from its original version to be a two-step process; *At Home Preparation* and *On Board Preparation*. By completing some of the preparation steps at home, you will cut down your on board cooking time, the space you will need to prepare meals, and the amount of garbage you will generate on board.

What is your most important item besides this cookbook? The greatest asset you can have when using this cookbook and preparing to make wonderful meals on board your yacht is a food saver system. Select one that gives you a variety of container sizes, both bags and hard sided plastic. This is key to keeping your food as fresh as possible from the time you do your at home preparation until you are ready to complete the recipes on board.

How to Use This Cookbook

Not all galleys are created equal! Therefore, there are recipes in this cookbook for virtually all galleys. Many of the recipes assume you have certain equipment on board such as a refrigerator, cook top, microwave, oven and stern rail grill. If your boat doesn't have this full complement of equipment, there are still plenty of recipes you will be able to prepare.

All of the recipes have been selected with care and consideration for the unique environment of a galley, and been modified to make cooking on board easier and less time consuming. You will see that the recipes are modified to minimize the cooking tools needed on board, the amount of space to prepare on board, and to minimize garbage. Most recipes require only one or two pans or bowls for the on board preparation. You will also see that there is a common thread of many herbs and spices used in the recipes, making stocking your galley pantry even easier.

This cookbook is designed for the casual boater. Extended cruising requires a great deal more preparation and provisioning, however, you can certainly incorporate many of the recipes into an extended cruise menu planning. The recipes vary in their difficulty, giving you a selection that can be prepared on a broad range of yacht types and sizes. Many of the recipes can be prepared while under way, or are designed for a relaxed preparation and serving environment while at anchor in your favorite spot.

Selecting Your Ingredients

Cooking with the freshest and highest quality ingredients is always and plus. The fresher the perishable ingredients when you purchase them, the longer they will last on your yacht. By purchasing high quality pre-prepared ingredients indicated in some of the recipes, you can minimize your preparation time while maintaining the best possible flavor for your meals. Pre-prepared product such as sliced mushrooms, pre-washed greens, etc. are also a time saving plus.

The ingredients in the recipes, for the most part, lend themselves well to pre-preparation. There are a few ingredients that are always best handled at the last minute to maximize freshness. (Such things as bananas, avocados, etc.) In those cases, the preparation of that ingredient will not be done ahead of time. However, many ingredients carefully prepared and treated with an anti-oxidant such as lemon juice, can be done ahead. And, that food saver is really a key to keeping things fresh!

Equipment

Whatever equipment you may add to your yacht, always shop the marine supply vendors first. They understand the boater's unique needs and have equipment designed specifically for the galley. However, you can also find many of the preparation items in the same stores where you purchase items for your home kitchen.

Most yachts come equipped with:
Refrigerator/Freezer
Cooking Stove
Microwave
Oven

Adding a **stern rail grill** if your boat does not come equipped with one is a great addition. Many of the recipes are prepared using a grill, and the grill can also substitute for a cook top. Consult your yacht manufacturer for suggestions on the best grill to fit your particular craft.

Beyond this basic equipment, the single most important item to purchase is a **food saver system**. Be sure to get a good one that combines both bags and plastic containers. You will use this piece of equipment mostly at home but having a second one on board is a great addition too. **This is the most important piece of equipment to use with this cookbook.**

Other Appliances

If space is limited, a **food processor** can function as a multi-purpose piece of equipment for blending, chopping, slicing, etc. If space permits, you might want to have both a food processor and **blender** as well as a good **hand mixer**. And of course, don't forget the **coffeemaker**!

Cook Ware

The key here is to equip your galley with non-corrosive nesting cookware sets. Most marine supply stores have sets designed specifically for boats. Think compact and easy to store. The basic pieces are:

Stockpot or Dutch oven
Large saucepan
Small saucepan
Double boiler insert
Large skillet (preferably non-stick)
Small skillet (preferable non-stick)
Vegetable steamer insert

Additional pieces to consider, space permitting:

Wok
Griddle
Toaster
Warming tray

Knives

No cook can function without a good set of knives! Once again, this is not a place to pinch pennies, however, you do not need the full set you might have at home. The basics are:

Paring knife
Large serrated edge
Large broad bladed
Sharpening steel

Space permitting, you might want to add a **filet knife**, a **large narrow blade** and an additional paring knife or two.

Suggested Equipment List

Be sure all the equipment you have on board is a non-corrosive material. Wherever possible, purchase plastic versions and collapsible versions of items for your galley. Avoid glass if at all possible! And be sure any metal pieces will not rust.

Measuring cups, both liquid and dry (collapsible)
Measuring spoons
Flat grater
Mixing spoons

Spatula
Colander (collapsible)
Vegetable peeler
Can opener
Bottle opener/Cork screw
Whisk
Spatula
Slotted spoon
Tongs
Potholders
Mixing bowl set
Cutting board
Soup ladle
Meat thermometer

Other optional pieces that are great to have on board are:

Small cooler (to keep ice in on deck)
Barbecue tools
Crab/lobster crackers
Cookie sheet
Cake pan

Serving Pieces

Space permitting, you will want to have a few pieces on board. Your mixing bowls can substitute for serving pieces. In addition, you might have:
> **Salad Bowl**
> **Platter**
> **Tray**
> **Bread basket**

Storage Items

Besides that critically important food saver system, you will need a few additional items for storage on board. Although you want to minimize leftovers as much as possible, you will need a few basic pieces for leftovers. A small assortment of **plastic containers** that nest together or are collapsible as well as **zip tops bags** in assorted sizes should cover all your needs. Reuse containers you brought on board as much as possible.

Cleaning Up
Dish soap (keep some coconut oil based soap on board in case you need to use salt water for washing dishes.)
Dish towels
Dishcloth
Sponge
Degreaser (keep a dish soap such as Dawn on board to use for several clean up needs.)
Paper towels

Garbage bags
Cleanser

Space permitting, you may also want a **dish pan** and **dish drainer.**

Dishes and Flatware

After preparing those fabulous meals, you will need something to serve them on! Purchasing dishes and flatware from a marine supply house is always the best because they are compact, stacking, and have non-skid rings on the bottom. Have enough to serve the number of people you typically have on board, and space permitting, a few extras. You can always keep extras in your dock storage or at home for those occasions when you have more people. When selecting flatware, it is best to choose a set with **serrated knives** that can double as steak knives.

Glassware

Plastic or acrylic is a must! As with the dishes, keep enough on board to go around for a typical outing and extras in storage. **Tumblers** are a must as they can serve multiple purposes. Space permitting, smaller **rocks glasses** can serve juice as well as cocktails. If you have the room, some nice stemmed pieces such as **wine glasses** and/or **martini glasses** are great to have on board.

Stocking the Pantry

The easiest way to stock your pantry is to combine the effort with your recipe pre-planning. Ingredients you know you will be using frequently such as flour, sugar, some spices, etc. can be stored in small quantities on board in airtight containers. Otherwise, take a little extra spices and commonly used ingredients that will store well on board then replenish as needed. Because the recipes in *The Yachting Gourmet* have many common ingredients, your pantry will be stocked before you know it!

Airtight containers are essential for staples such as flour and sugar. Be sure to select ones that are easily opened and closed with frequent use. When leaving these items on board, be sure they are protected against insects and vermin. (Bay leaves make a great natural bug repellent.) For spices, either purchase small containers or re-package into small zip top bags for easy storage. Be sure to label everything!

Conclusion

Now that you have outfitted your galley you are ready to try this collection of unique and wonderful recipes. *Bon Voyage* and *Bon Appetit!!*

Appetizers

A Different Guacamole

            5 slices bacon
            2 cups sour cream
            1 teaspoon seasoned salt
      1 1/2 teaspoons chopped chili pepper
            1 medium avocado
            1 medium tomato
               tortilla chips

Instructions

At Home Preparation: Cook the bacon until crisp, drain, cool, finely chop and place in a container. Peel and chop the tomato and place in a container.   Chop the chili pepper and place in a container.

On Board Preparation: Peel and chop the avocado and sprinkle with a little lemon juice to prevent oxidation. Combine the sour cream, seasoned salt and chili pepper in a medium bowl. Add the bacon, avocado and tomato and fold gently until blended. Serve with tortilla chips for dipping.
Serves: 6.

Black Bean Dip on Fresh Corn Tortilla Chips

            1 package corn tortillas
          16 ounces canned black beans
        1/2 cup salsa
            2 tablespoons lime juice
            2 tablespoons chopped fresh cilantro
        1/4 teaspoon ground cumin
        1/2 teaspoon salt
        1/4 teaspoon pepper

Instructions

At Home Preparation: Lightly brush one side of the tortillas with corn oil and sprinkle with salt. Cut into 8 wedges and arrange in a single layer on a baking sheet. Bake at 400° about 8-10 minutes or until crisp. Cool completely and place in a container. Drain and rinse the canned black beans. Place the black beans and the remaining ingredients in a food processor and process until smooth.   Correct seasoning as needed. Place in a container.

On Board Preparation: Bring dip to room temperature. Arrange in the middle of a tray or platter surrounded with the tortillas chips.
Serves: 4.

Blue Cheese Spread

10 ounces blue cheese
3 ounces cream cheese
1 cup cashews
1 loaf French bread, or crackers

Instructions
At Home Preparation: If using the French bread, slice into 3/8 inch slices and place in a container. (Can also be toasted.) Finely chop the cashews. Soften the cream cheese by letting it sit at room temperature for about an hour. Combine the blue cheese and cream cheese until well blended. Add 2 teaspoons of the chopped cashews and mix. Shape into a ball or log and roll in the remaining cashews until well coated. Place in a container and chill until firm, or freeze.

On Board Preparation: Remove the cheese ball from the refrigerator and let come to nearly room temperature. Serve with crackers or slices of French bread.
Serves: 8.

Broccoli Soufflé Squares

16 ounces refrigerated crescent rolls
21 ounces frozen chopped broccoli
2 whole eggs, beaten
1 cup mayonnaise
10 1/2 ounces canned cream of mushroom soup
1 medium onion, diced
8 ounces grated sharp Cheddar cheese
1 dash Tabasco sauce
1 dash salt

Instructions
At Home Preparation: Cook the broccoli according to package directions; drain very thoroughly, cool and place in a container. Dice the onion and place in a container. Grate the Cheddar and place in a container.

On Board Preparation: Preheat the oven to 375°. Spread the crescent rolls out on a jelly roll pan, pinching seams together. In a bowl, combine the broccoli, eggs, mayonnaise, soup, onion and 5 ounces of the cheese. Pour over the crescent rolls spreading evenly. Top with the remaining cheese. Bake about 20-25 minutes or until golden brown. Cool slightly then refrigerate until cold. Cut into bite-size squares. Cover with foil and reheat for 20 minutes at 375° before serving.
Serves: 8.

Carmelized Onion Dip

        1   teaspoon olive oil
    1 3/4   cups chopped onions
        1   clove garlic, minced
      1/3   cup cider vinegar
        3   tablespoons honey
      1/4   teaspoon white pepper
      1/3   cup mayonnaise
      1/3   cup sour cream
      1/4   cup plain yogurt
      1/8   teaspoon salt

Instructions

At Home Preparation: Heat oil in a large skillet over medium heat. Add onion and garlic; cover and cook 8 minutes or until tender. Add vinegar, honey, and white pepper; stir well. Bring to a boil over medium-high heat, and cook, uncovered, 10 minutes or until onion is deep golden and liquid evaporates, stirring occasionally. Cool completely and place in a container.

On Board Preparation: Combine the onion mixture, mayonnaise, and remaining ingredients in a bowl; stir well. Place in a container or serving dish, cover and chill until ready to serve. Serve with crackers, bagel chips or garlic toast.
Serves 8.

Recipe Notes
This dip is great on bagel chips or garlic toast. You will also like it on bagels in the morning.

Cheese Crisps

        4   cups shredded sharp Cheddar cheese
        2   cups flour
        2   cups Rice Krispies cereal
        2   teaspoons sugar
      1/2   teaspoon salt
      1/8   teaspoon cayenne pepper
      1/8   teaspoon mustard powder
        2   sticks butter
        1   dash Worcestershire sauce

Instructions

At Home Preparation: Shred the Cheddar and place in a container. Combine the flour, Rice Krispies, sugar, salt, cayenne and dry mustard and place in a container.

On Board Preparation: Preheat the oven to 350°. Melt the butter. In a large bowl, combine the cheese with the flour mixture, melted butter and Worcestershire. Mix thoroughly. Form into 1-inch balls and place about 1-inch apart on an ungreased baking sheet. Using a fork, press lightly in a criss-cross pattern to about 1/4 inch thick. Bake for about 10-12 minutes or until golden brown.
Serves: 6.

Cheese Spread

  8 ounces cream cheese, softened
  2 cups shredded sharp Cheddar cheese
  2 tablespoons dry sherry
  1 teaspoon curry powder
1/4 teaspoon salt
  1 dash pepper sauce
1/2 cup finely chopped mango chutney
1/4 cup chopped scallion

Instructions

At Home Preparation: Shred the Cheddar and place in a container. Chop the scallions and place in a container. Chop the chutney and place in a container.

On Board Preparation: Soften the cream cheese at room temperature. In a bowl, combine the cream cheese, Cheddar, sherry, curry powder, salt and hot sauce. Stir until well blended. Shape into a round "cake" about 1/4-inch thick on the serving plate. Cover and refrigerate until firm, about 2 hours. Just before serving, spread with the chutney and sprinkle with the chopped scallions. Serve with crackers.
Serves: 8.

> ### GALLEY TIP
> *Wrap cheese in aluminum foil and store in the refrigerator.*
> *The foil is moisture proof while allowing the cheese to breathe.*

Clambake in a Crust

     1 large Italian bread loaf, round or oval
19 1/2 ounces canned clams
     1 pound cream cheese, softened
     3 tablespoons dry white wine
     2 medium scallions, chopped
     1 teaspoon lemon juice
  1/2 teaspoon salt
  1/2 teaspoon hot sauce

Instructions

At Home Preparation: Chop the scallions and place in a container. Wash and dry the raw vegetables and place in a container. Using a long serrated knife, slice the bread in two horizontally to remove the upper third. Set top aside. Using your hand or a serrated knife, remove the center from the loaf to form a hollow shell about 1/2-inch thick. Cut the center into bite-size cubes and place in a container. Place the hollow loaf and top in a container. Drain the clams reserving the liquid and place the clams in a container. Measure 1/4 cup of the reserved liquid and place in a container. (Discard the remaining liquid or save for another use.)

On Board Preparation: Preheat oven to 250°. Soften the cream cheese. Combine the clam juice with the cream cheese, wine, scallions, lemon juice, salt and hot sauce. Beat until well blended. Fold in the clams and pack into the bread shell, covering with the top. Wrap tightly in aluminum foil. Bake for 3 hours and serve with the bread cubes for dipping.
Serves: 12.

Cocktail Crab Cakes with Chili Mayonnaise

  1/3 cup fresh parsley leaves
     1 stalk celery, cut into 1" thick pieces
     2 medium scallions, cut into 1" thick pieces
  1/2 pound crab meat
     1 large egg
  1/3 cup bread crumbs
     2 tablespoons bread crumbs
     2 teaspoons lemon juice
     2 teaspoons chili powder
     1 teaspoon ground cumin
  1/8 teaspoon cayenne pepper
  1/2 cup mayonnaise

Instructions

At Home Preparation: Make the Chili Mayonnaise by combining the 2 teaspoons lemon juice, 2 teaspoons chili powder, 1 teaspoon cumin and 1/8 teaspoon cayenne until well blended. Add the 1/2 cup mayonnaise and stir to blend thoroughly. Place in a container. Cut the celery and scallions and place in a container. Clean and pick over the crab meat and place in a container.

On Board Preparation: Preheat the oven to 400°. In a blender or food processor combine the parsley, celery, and scallions. Process until finely chopped. Add the crab meat, 3 tablespoons of Chili Mayonnaise, egg, 2 tablespoons bread crumbs and salt to taste. Pulse until well mixed. Form tablespoons of crab mixture into balls and roll in 1/3 cup bread crumbs. Arrange on a generously buttered baking sheet and press down lightly to form patties. Bake about 10-12 minutes or until cooked through. To serve, top each with about ½ teaspoon Chili Mayonnaise.
Serves: 8.

Recipe Notes
To make these even easier on board, prepare the crab cakes completely at home and freeze. Thaw before baking.

Crab and Artichoke Dip

16	ounces crab meat
4	ounces cream cheese
1/2	cup mayonnaise
1/2	cup chopped onion
15	ounces artichoke hearts
3/4	cup grated Parmesan cheese
1/4	cup grated Parmesan cheese
1	tablespoon garlic powder
1	loaf French bread, or crackers

Instructions

At Home Preparation: Chop the onion and place in a container. Drain and chop the artichokes and place in a container.

On Board Preparation: Soften the cream cheese to room temperature. Preheat the oven to 375°. Mix together the crab meat, cream cheese and mayonnaise until well blended. Add the onion, artichoke hearts, ¾ cup Parmesan, and garlic powder mixing well. Pour into an 8-inch baking pan or pie plate and bake for 20-25 minutes, adding the additional Parmesan for the last 5 minutes, until lightly browned.
Serves: 4.

Crab Salad Bites on Endive

       6 ounces lump white crab meat
     1/4 ounce finely chopped red bell pepper
       1 ounce finely chopped shallot
       1 ounce orange zest
       3 ounces grated radishes
     1/4 cup mayonnaise
       3 tablespoons chopped celery greens
       2 teaspoons freshly-ground black pepper, or to taste
     1/4 cup mayonnaise
       3 tablespoons heavy cream
      24 large endive leaves
       2 tablespoons chopped parsley
       2 teaspoons salt, or to taste

Instructions
At Home Preparation: Clean and pick over the crab meat and place in a container. Chop the bell pepper and place in a container. Zest the orange and place in a container. Grate the radishes and place in a container. Chop the celery and place in a container. Separate and clean the endive leaves, gently patting dry. When thoroughly dry, place in a container. Chop the parsley and place in a container.

On Board Preparation: To the crab, add the bell pepper, shallot, orange zest, grated radish, celery greens, salt, and pepper. Combine the mayonnaise and heavy cream in a small bowl. Add the dressing to the crab and mix well. Using a rounded spoonful, mound the crab salad onto the root end of the endive and fill the leaves half the length of the endive. Arrange the stuffed endive on a platter and garnish with chopped parsley or chives.
Serves: 8.

Crudités and Curry Dip

       1 pint mayonnaise
       3 tablespoons chili sauce
       1 tablespoon curry powder
       1 tablespoon garlic powder
     1/4 teaspoon salt
     1/4 teaspoon pepper
       1 tablespoon grated onion
       1 tablespoon Worcestershire sauce
          assorted crudités

Instructions

At Home Preparation: Combine all ingredients except crudités. Place in a container and refrigerate at least 24 hours before serving. Wash vegetables and prepare as desired into bit size pieces. Place each in a separate container.

On Board Preparation: Blanche any vegetables you desire, or serve raw. Place the dip in the center of a platter and surround with crudités.
Serves: 8.

Recipe Notes
This dip can be refrigerated for up to 3 weeks.

Favorite Tapenade

1 1/2	cups oil-cured black olives, pitted
1/4	cup extra virgin olive oil
6 1/2	ounces oil packed tuna, drained
3 1/4	ounces capers, drained
2	tablespoons lemon juice
2	tablespoons brandy
1 1/2	teaspoons mustard powder
4	whole anchovy filets
1	clove garlic, minced
1/2	teaspoon pepper
1	pinch ground cloves
1	pinch ground ginger
1	pinch grated nutmeg

Instructions

At Home Preparation: Drain the tuna and capers and place in a container. Drain the anchovy fillets, and place in a container. Mince the garlic and place in a container.

On Board Preparation: In the blender, combine the olives and olive oil. Pulse 3 or 4 times to coarsely chop. Add the tuna, capers, lemon juice, brandy, mustard, anchovies, garlic, pepper, cloves, ginger and nutmeg. Process until it becomes a smooth paste. Place in a container and refrigerate up to 5 days.
Serves: 6.

Goat Cheese and Marinara Dip

    15 ounces marinara sauce
     4 ounces goat cheese
     1 loaf French bread, sliced
     2 tablespoons olive oil
    1/2 teaspoon garlic powder
    1/2 teaspoon oregano
    1/2 teaspoon basil
    1/4 teaspoon sea salt
    1/4 teaspoon freshly ground pepper

Instructions

At Home Preparation: Slice the French bread into 1/2-inch slices and place the slices in a zip top plastic bag. Drizzle with the olive oil and add the spices. Seal the bag and toss to coat the bread slices. Place on a baking sheet and bake at 400° until lightly browned. Cool and place in a container.

On Board Preparation: Pour the marinara sauce into an oven proof flat dish. Place the goat cheese in the center. Broil until bubbly and the cheese is slightly browned. (Can also be heated in the microwave but the cheese will not brown. Be careful not to overheat, about 2 minutes on high.) Serve with the French bread slices. *Serves: 8.*

Recipe Notes
Use a good quality gourmet marinara sauce or your own home made.

Goat Cheese Snack

     1 whole French bread baguette, sliced
     2 cloves garlic, lightly crushed
    1/4 cup olive oil
     2 medium tomatoes, seeded & chopped
  6 1/2 ounces artichoke hearts, chopped
    12 ounces goat cheese

Instructions

At Home Preparation: Cut the bread into 1/4-inch slices (on an angle) and place in a container. Seed and chop the tomatoes, drain and chop the artichoke hearts, mix well and place in a container. Cut the goat cheese into slices about 1/4- inch thick and place in a container.

On Board Preparation: Heat a large skillet over medium-high heat. Rub each slice of bread with the garlic and brush lightly with olive oil. Brown in the skillet on both sides. Remove from the heat and top each slice with some of the tomato-artichoke mixture and top with cheese. Drizzle with a little olive oil. Return to the heat set at low, cover, and warm just until the cheese begins to melt. *Serves: 4.*

Gorgonzola Cream Stuffed Endive

  1/4 cup sliced almonds
    1 cup crumbled gorgonzola cheese
    3 ounces cream cheese, softened
    2 teaspoons brandy
    4 medium endive heads

Instructions

At Home Preparation: Preheat the oven to 325°. Spread the almonds on a baking dish and toast until lightly golden, about 8-10 minutes. Let cool completely. Coarsely chop the almonds and place in a container. In a bowl, combine the gorgonzola, cream cheese and brandy, mixing well, and place in a container. Cut the root from the endive and separate the leaves. Wash, thoroughly dry and place in a container.

On Board Preparation: Place 1 heaping teaspoon of the filling on the base of each endive leaf. Top with the chopped almonds.
Serves: 4.

Hot Beef Dip

    6 ounces dried chipped beef, chopped
  16 ounces cream cheese
    1 tablespoon minced onion
1 1/2 teaspoons Worcestershire sauce
1 1/2 cups sour cream
  1/2 teaspoon garlic salt
  1/4 teaspoon freshly ground black pepper
      wheat crackers or toast points

Instructions

At Home Preparation: Coarsely chop the chipped beef into pieces about 1/4 inch in size and place in a container. Mince the onion and place in a container.

On Board Preparation: Preheat the oven to 350°. In a bowl, combine all ingredients and blend well. Spoon into a shallow baking dish and bake for 30 minutes. Serve hot with crackers or toast points.
Serves: 8.

Hot Swiss and Bacon Dip

8 ounces cream cheese
1/2 cup mayonnaise
1 cup shredded Swiss cheese
2 tablespoons chopped green onions
8 slices bacon
1 sleeve Ritz crackers
3 tablespoons butter
Ritz crackers

Instructions

At Home Preparation: Shred the Swiss and place in a container. Finely chop the green onions and place in a container. Cook the bacon until crisp, cool, crumble and place in a container. Crush the sleeve of crackers and place in a container.

On Board Preparation: Soften the cream cheese to room temperature. Combine the cream cheese, mayonnaise and cheese in a bowl. Add the green onions and bacon crumbles. Spread into a shallow baking dish and top with the crushed crackers. Melt the 3 tablespoons butter and drizzle over the top. Bake at 350° for 20-25 minutes. Serve with Ritz crackers.
Serves: 8.

Lemon Wings

2 pounds chicken wings
4 cloves garlic, finely chopped
2 teaspoons cumin seed
3 medium lemons
1/4 cup olive oil
1/2 teaspoon salt
1/4 teaspoon pepper

Instructions

At Home Preparation: Chop the garlic and place in a container. Slice one of the lemons and place in a container.

On Board Preparation: Preheat the oven to 400°. Put the wings, garlic, and cumin in a large plastic dish (do not use metal). Squeeze the two lemons over the wings and add the oil. Season lightly with salt and generously with pepper. Turn chicken to coat thoroughly. If you want a strong flavor, marinate overnight, or a shorter duration, to your preference. Or, for a delicate lemon flavor, proceed immediately. Place the lemon slices in a baking dish large enough to hold the wings in one layer. Arrange the wings (including all the marinade) in the dish and cover. Bake, brushing occasionally with the juices, until they are golden, about 40 minutes. Let cool to about room temperature.
Serves: 4.

Lobster Puffs

- 2 large egg whites
- 1/4 cup nonfat dry milk
- 1 cup lobster meat, cooked and chopped
- 1 medium scallion, minced
- 2 teaspoons chopped fresh parsley
- 1/2 teaspoon salt
- 1 teaspoon grated Parmesan cheese
- 1/8 teaspoon cayenne pepper

Instructions

At Home Preparation: Cook the lobster, cool, and chop fine. Place in a container. Mince the scallions and place in a container. Chop the parsley and place in a container. Separate the eggs and place the whites in a container. Reserve the yolks for another use.

On Board Preparation: Preheat the oven to 375°. Grease a baking sheet. In a bowl, beat the egg whites until frothy. Gradually add the nonfat dry milk and beat until stiff but not dry. Fold in the lobster, scallions, parsley, salt, Parmesan and cayenne. Drop by the tablespoon onto the greased baking sheet and bake 10 minutes, or until puffed and lightly browned.
Serves: 4.

Recipe Notes
These are so yummy you will want to make plenty!

GALLEY TIP
If you find anchovies a bit too salty, soak them for a few minutes in milk, then drain before adding to your recipe.

Margarita Shrimp Cocktail

    5 tablespoons olive oil
1 1/2 pounds large shrimp, peeled and deveined
  1/2 cup minced green onion
    2 large garlic cloves, minced
  1/4 cup tequila
    2 tablespoons fresh lime juice
    1 teaspoon Margarita salt
    2 small limes, cut into wedges
    1 tablespoon Margarita salt
    2 tablespoons fresh lime juice

Instructions
At Home Preparation: Peel and devein the shrimp and place in a container. Mince the green onion, including some of the green tops and place in a container. Mince the garlic and place in a container. Cut the limes into wedges (for garnish) and place in a container.

On Board Preparation: Heat the olive oil in a skillet over medium-high heat. Add the shrimp, green onions and garlic, cooking 1 minute. Remove from heat; add the tequila. Return to heat. Bring to a boil, scraping up any browned bits in the pan. Toss with the fresh squeezed lime juice and salt. If serving cold, refrigerate about 1 hour or until chilled. For garnish, dip the rims of 6 Margarita glasses or your serving bowls in the additional lime juice then into the additional Margarita salt. Divide the shrimp mixture evenly among the glasses and garnish with lime wedges.
Serves: 6.

Mussels in Black Walnut Sauce

  24 large mussels
  1/4 cup chopped black walnuts
  1/2 cup olive oil
  1/4 cup bread crumbs
    2 teaspoons red wine vinegar
    1 teaspoon balsamic vinegar
    2 dashes hot sauce
  1/4 teaspoon salt
  1/8 teaspoon pepper

Instructions
At Home Preparation: Wash and debeard the mussels. Discard any open shells that do not close when tapped; place in a container. Chop the black walnuts and combine with the remaining ingredients (except the mussels) in a food processor and puree until smooth. Place in a container.

On Board Preparation: Allow the sauce to warm until it is just slightly chilled. In a large pot with a steam rack, bring about 2 inches of water to a boil over medium-high heat. Add the mussels, cover and cook until they open, about 5 minutes. Discard any that do not open. Remove and discard the top shells. Serve with the sauce.
Serves: 4.

Olive and Almond Tapenade

4	cups Mediterranean-style green olives in oil
10	medium oil-cured anchovy fillets
1/4	pound slivered almonds
1	tablespoon minced garlic
1	tablespoon capers, drained
1	teaspoon fresh lemon juice
1/2	cup extra virgin olive oil
1	loaf French bread

Instructions
At Home Preparation: Pit the olives with a knife or olive pitting tool; set aside. Rinse the anchovy fillets in a little milk. Toast the almonds. Put the pitted olives, anchovies, almonds, garlic, capers, lemon juice, and olive oil in a food processor; process until a coarse paste forms. Place in a container and refrigerate. Slice the French bread and place in a container.

On Board Preparation: Place the Tapenade in the center of a serving platter and surround with sliced French bread.
Serves: 4.

Recipe Notes
Substitute some high quality crackers for the French bread if desired.

GALLEY TIP
A broken yolk can be removed from egg whites by dipping a wet cloth gently into the whites. The yolk will cling to the cloth for easy removal.

Olive Cheddar Snacks

2 cups shredded sharp Cheddar cheese
4 tablespoons butter, softened
1 cup flour
1 1/2 teaspoons paprika
1 dash cayenne pepper
8 1/2 ounces pimiento-stuffed green olives
1 large egg
1 tablespoon milk
1/4 cup sesame seed

Instructions
At Home Preparation: In a food processor, blend the cheese and butter until well blended. Add the flour, paprika and cayenne and process until smooth. Place the dough in a container and refrigerate. Drain the olives, pat dry, and place in a container.

On Board Preparation: Bring dough to room temperature. Preheat the oven to 350°. Wrap about 1 teaspoon of dough around each olive, pinching to seal. Roll into a ball and place on a non-stick baking sheet. In a small bowl, beat the egg and milk with a whisk. Brush over the tops of the pastries; sprinkle with the sesame seeds. Bake 15 minutes or until set and golden. Serve hot, warm or at room temperature. *Serves: 4.*

Oriental Chicken Wings

1 1/4 cups soy sauce
2/3 cup dry sherry
1 cup hoisin sauce
2/3 cup plum sauce
1 cup minced green onion
5 large garlic cloves, minced
2/3 cup cider vinegar
1/3 cup honey
5 pounds chicken drumettes
1/2 cup sesame seed

Instructions
At Home Preparation: In a medium saucepan, bring the soy sauce, sherry, hoisin sauce, plum sauce, green onions garlic, vinegar and honey to a boil over medium heat. Remove from heat and cool to room temperature. Place in a container.

On Board Preparation: In a large bowl, combine sauce and chicken drumettes. Cover and refrigerate overnight. Preheat the oven to 350°. Place the drumettes in a single layer on a baking sheet lined with foil. Bake about 1 hour until cooked through. Remove and cool to room temperature. **Serves: 8.**

Sausage Stuffed Mushrooms

6	ounces sweet Italian sausage
1	pinch red pepper flakes
1/4	cup finely minced onion
1	clove garlic, minced
1	tablespoon olive oil
1/4	cup chopped fresh parsley
1/4	cup chopped black olives
1/3	cup mayonnaise
1/4	teaspoon salt
1/8	teaspoon pepper
12	large white mushrooms
1/4	cup grated Parmesan cheese

Instructions

At Home Preparation: Remove the sausage from it's casing and place in a container. Mince the onion and garlic and place each in a container. Chop the olives and place in a container. Remove the stems from the mushrooms, wash, pat dry with a paper towel, sprinkle with a little lemon juice, toss, and place in a container. Grate the Parmesan and place in a container.

On Board Preparation: Preheat the oven to 450°. In a skillet crumble the sausage and sauté, stirring often until thoroughly done. Season with red pepper and remove with a slotted spoon, leaving the drippings in the skillet. Add the onion, garlic and the olive oil and sauté until tender and golden, about 5 minutes. Stir in the parsley and the sausage. Add the olives and mayonnaise; combine thoroughly. Season with salt and pepper to taste. Season the mushroom caps lightly with salt and pepper. Fill each generously with the stuffing and place in a lightly oiled baking dish just big enough to hold them. Sprinkle with Parmesan and bake about 15 minutes, until bubbling and browned. Let stand 5 minutes before serving.
Serves: 4.

GALLEY TIP

To store peeled garlic, cover with olive oil in an airtight container. The peeled garlic will stay fresh and you will have a nice flavored oil when the garlic is removed.

Shrimp Salad in a Cup

            2 tablespoons vegetable oil
           36 wonton wrappers
          1/2 pound shrimp
            2 medium scallions, finely chopped
            2 tablespoons finely chopped celery
            2 tablespoons chopped green pepper
            2 tablespoons mayonnaise
            2 tablespoons sour cream
            1 teaspoon curry powder
            1 teaspoon lemon juice
          1/4 teaspoon salt
            2 dashes cayenne pepper
            3 tablespoons unsweetened crushed pineapple, drained
            2 tablespoons shredded coconut
            1 teaspoon chopped parsley

Instructions

At Home Preparation: Preheat the oven to 350°. Grease 36 miniature muffin tins with the vegetable oil. Press 1 wonton wrapper into each to form a cup. Bake until just crisp and golden, about 8-10 minutes. Cool completely and place in a container. (Be sure to use a container that will protect these delicate cups.) Cook, peel and chop the shrimp, cool and place in a container. Chop the scallions, celery and green pepper and place in a container. Drain the pineapple and place in a container. Chop the parsley and place in a container.

On Board Preparation: In a medium size bowl, combine the shrimp and next 10 ingredients (through the pineapple) and gently fold until blended. Cover and refrigerate for 1 hour or up to 8 hours. Spoon into the wonton cups, then top with the coconut and parsley.
Serves: 6.

Shrimp Toast

          1/2 pound shrimp, cooked
            1 cup mayonnaise
            4 ounces shredded Swiss cheese
          1/3 cup scallion, chopped
            1 tablespoon lemon juice
        1 1/2 teaspoons chopped fresh dill
            2 dashes cayenne pepper
           42 slices French bread

Instructions

At Home Preparation: Combine the shrimp, mayonnaise, cheese, scallions, lemon juice, dill and a dash or two of cayenne. Place in a container and refrigerate.

On Board Preparation: Preheat oven to 450°. Spread each bread slice with about 1 tablespoon of shrimp mixture and place on a greased baking sheet. Bake until golden brown and bubbly, about 10 minutes.
Serves: 6.

Shrimp with Toasted Almond Dip

2	pounds large shrimp
1/2	cup sliced almonds
2	cloves garlic, chopped
1	large roma tomato, peeled, seeded and chopped
1	tablespoon red wine vinegar
1/2	teaspoon salt
1/4	teaspoon cayenne pepper
1/2	cup extra virgin olive oil

Instructions

At Home Preparation: Place the sliced almonds in a single layer on a pan and bake about 10 minutes in a 325° oven or until lightly browned. Chop the garlic. Peel, seed and chop the tomato. In a food processor, combine the almonds, garlic, tomato, vinegar, salt and cayenne. Puree until the consistency of a coarse paste. With the blender on and the small opening in the top open, slowly add the oil in a thin stream, processing until well blended. Transfer to another container and refrigerate at least 2 hours or up to 2 days. Refrigerate until ready to serve. Peel and devein the shrimp. Cook the shrimp by placing them in boiling water and cooking just until they turn pink. Cool completely and place in a container.

On Board Preparation: Remove the dip from the refrigerator and let sit about 15 minutes to warm slightly. Serve with the cooked shrimp for dipping.
Serves: 4.

GALLEY TIP
Dried spices should be discarded after six months as they lose their freshness if kept longer.

Smoked Oyster Dip

        8 ounces cream cheese, softened
        2 tablespoons mayonnaise
        1 teaspoon lemon juice
      1/4 teaspoon garlic salt
        2 dashes hot sauce
      1/2 cup chopped black olives
        9 ounces oysters, smoked, drained and chopped

Instructions
In a bowl, combine cream cheese, mayonnaise, lemon juice, garlic salt and hot pepper sauce. (Start with a dash of the pepper sauce then add one dash at a time to desired taste.) Fold in the olives and oysters. Cover and refrigerate for about 1 hour or up to 3 days.
Serves: 6.

Recipe Notes
This recipe can be prepared entirely on board or at home.

Smoked Salmon and Scotch Spread

        8 ounces cream cheese, softened
      1/2 pound smoked salmon
        2 tablespoons Scotch
        2 teaspoons lemon juice
      1/2 teaspoon horseradish
        1 dash cayenne pepper
        2 tablespoons chopped fresh chives
           crackers

Instructions
Combine all ingredients except the chives in a blender or food processor and process until well mixed. Add the chives and pulse a few times just to blend them in. Place in a container and refrigerate for 1 hour or up to 3 days. Remove from the refrigerate and let warm slightly, about 15 minutes before serving.
Serves: 6.

Recipe Notes
This recipe can be made entirely at home or on board.

Spinach Madeline

20 ounces frozen chopped spinach
4 tablespoons butter
2 tablespoons flour
2 tablespoons chopped onion
1/2 cup evaporated milk
1/2 cup liquid from cooked spinach
1/2 teaspoon pepper
3/4 teaspoon celery salt
3/4 teaspoon garlic salt
6 ounces jalapeno cheese
1 teaspoon Worcestershire sauce
2 dashes Tabasco sauce
1 cup buttered bread crumbs
   crackers

Instructions

At Home Preparation: Chop the onion and place in a container. Cut the cheese into small cubes and place in a container. Cook the spinach according to package directions. Drain reserving 1/2 cup of the liquid. Place the drained spinach in a container, and the liquid in a separate container.

On Board Preparation: Melt the butter in a saucepan over low heat. Add flour, stirring until blended and smooth but do not brown. Add the onion and cook until translucent but not browned. Add the liquid slowly, stirring constantly to avoid lumps. Cook until smooth and thick stirring constantly. Add the seasoning and cheese. Stir until melted. Add the cooked spinach and heat through if you are serving it immediately. If not, place in a casserole and top with the bread crumbs. Refrigerate overnight. (This results in the best flavor.) Serve as a dip with crackers.
Serves: 4.

GALLEY TIP
Tomatoes will peel easily if you drop them in boiling water for a few seconds.

Strawberry Cheese Ball

8 ounces cream cheese, softened
4 ounces grated sharp Cheddar cheese
1/2 medium green pepper, finely chopped
1/2 medium red bell pepper, finely chopped
3 whole green onions, diced fine
12 ounces strawberry jam
wheat crackers

Instructions

At Home Preparation: Shred the Cheddar and place in a container. Chop the green pepper and red pepper and place each in a container. Dice the green onions, including the green tops and place in a container.

On Board Preparation: The day before you want to serve, mix all ingredients except the strawberry preserves. Shape into a ball and refrigerate, covered, overnight. Place the cheese ball on a plate and shape into a doughnut shape with a center hole. Spoon the preserves into the hole or place a small dish holding the preserves in the center. Serve with the crackers.
Serves: 12.

Stuffed Mushrooms

3 ounces prosciutto, finely chopped
3/4 cup grated Parmesan cheese
1 large egg, lightly beaten
1/4 teaspoon salt
24 large mushrooms
1/2 cup finely chopped onion
1/4 cup bread crumbs
1/4 teaspoon black pepper
1 large garlic clove, minced
3 tablespoons minced flat leaf parsley
4 tablespoons olive oil

Instructions

At Home Preparation: Wash the mushrooms and dry completely. Remove the stems from the mushroom caps and chop the stems to a fine dice. Sprinkle the mushroom caps with a little lemon juice and place in a container. Sauté the stems, onion, and garlic in 2 tablespoons olive oil until very soft. Cool completely and place in a container. Chop the prosciutto and place in a container. Grate the Parmesan and place in a container. Mince the garlic and place in a container. Mince the parsley and place in a container.

On Board Preparation: Combine the onion mixture, prosciutto, bread crumbs, 1/2 cup Parmesan, egg, salt, and pepper in a bowl and stir to mix well. Place the mushroom caps on a baking sheet and divide the filling evenly among the caps. Sprinkle with the reserved Parmesan. Drizzle with 2 tablespoons olive oil. Bake in a pre-heated 400° oven for 20 minutes.
Serves: 12.

Tapenade Spread

6 1/2 ounces oil-cured black olives, pitted
2 cloves garlic
1 tablespoon capers, drained
2 teaspoons fresh thyme
2 anchovy fillets, drained
3 tablespoons extra virgin olive oil
2 tablespoons lemon juice
1/8 teaspoon freshly ground black pepper

Instructions
At Home Preparation: Rinse the olives in a colander under cold water to reduce the saltiness. Drain thoroughly and place in a container. Chop the garlic cloves and thyme and place each in a container.

On Board Preparation: Place the garlic and about 3/4 cup of the olives in a blender and process until finely chopped. Add the capers, thyme, and anchovies. Pulse on and off about 4 times or until just blended. Add the remaining olives, 3 tablespoons olive oil, lemon juice and pepper and pulse until well blended.
Serves: 4.

Recipe Notes
Place the Tapenade in a tight sealing plastic jar and cover with a thin layer of olive oil. Place the jar cover on and refrigerate until ready to serve. It will keep for several days this way.

<u>Beverages</u>

Apricot Bellinis

30 ounces canned apricot halves
23 ounces apricot nectar
1/2 cup sugar
1/2 cup crushed ice
750 milliliters Champagne
8 fresh mint leaves

Instructions

At Home Preparation: In two batches process the first 3 ingredients in a blender until smooth, stopping to scrape down the sides. Place in a container. Chill.

On Board Preparation: Put the crushed ice in 8 serving glasses. Pour equal parts of the apricot mixture in each glass. Add the champagne, garnish with mint leaves and serve.
Serves: 8.

Recipe Notes

These are great for brunch! For a non-alcoholic version, substitute ginger ale or lemon-lime soda for the champagne. It's also good with most any sparkling wine instead of champagne.

Banana Rum Punch

3 ounces rum
1/4 cup coconut cream
1 medium banana
1 cup pineapple juice
1 cup crushed ice cubes

Instructions

Combine all ingredients in a blender on high speed until smooth. Garnish with a slice of fresh coconut and a cocktail umbrella for fun.
Serves: 2.

Blood Orange Sangria

2 large strawberries, sliced
2 cups apple juice
2/3 cup triple sec
1/2 cup sugar
4 whole cloves

3 large blood oranges
1500 milliliters red wine
2 whole cinnamon sticks
1 whole lemon
1 whole lime

Instructions

At Home Preparation: Slice the strawberries and place in a container. Cut the blood oranges into 16 wedges each and place in a container. (Remove any seeds if necessary.) Cut the lemon and lime into 8 wedges each and place in a container.

On Board Preparation: Combine all ingredients in a large pitcher and stir until the sugar dissolves. Cover and chill 8 hours or overnight. Discard cloves and cinnamon sticks. Pour into individual glasses, including the fruit.
Serves: 16.

Recipe Notes
Select a fruity red wine for this sangria.

Breezy Mary

1 1/2 cups clam and tomato juice
1 1/2 cups tomato juice
1 cup pepper vodka
1/4 cup fresh lemon juice
1 teaspoon seafood seasoning
1/4 teaspoon hot sauce
1/8 teaspoon cracked black pepper
2 teaspoons Worcestershire sauce
1/2 teaspoon horseradish

Instructions
Combine all ingredients. Serve over ice.
Serves: 4.

Butterscotch Martinis

1 ounce Godiva white chocolate liqueur
1 ounce Frangelica
1 ounce Amaretto
2 ounces vodka
1 ounce butterscotch schnapps

Instructions
Combine all ingredients with crushed ice and shake vigorously. Strain into chilled martini glasses.
Serves: 2.

Champagne a'la Orange

4 ounces Champagne
1/2 ounce Grand Marnier
1 orange peel twist

Instructions
In a champagne glass pour chilled champagne. Carefully pour Grand Marnier down the inside of the glass. Garnish with the twist of orange peel.
Serves: 1.

Classic Mint Julep

3 whole mint leaves
1/4 cup crushed ice
2 tablespoons bourbon
1 sprig mint
1 teaspoon powdered sugar
1 cup sugar
1 cup water
12 sprigs mint

Instructions
At Home Preparation: Prepare Mint Simple Syrup, recipe below. Place 1 tablespoon in a container and reserve the rest for later use.

On Board Preparation: Place mint leaves and Simple Syrup in a chilled julep cup. Gently press leaves against the cup with the back of a spoon. Pack cup tightly with crushed ice; pour bourbon over ice. Insert straw, place mint sprig next to straw, and serve immediately. Sprinkle with powdered sugar, if desired. Serve in a traditional silver mint julep cup. *Serves: 1*
.

Mint Simple Syrup
Bring 1 cup sugar and 1 cup water to a boil in a medium saucepan. Boil, stirring often, 5 minutes or until sugar dissolves. Remove from heat, add mint, and let cool completely. Pour into a plastic jar or other airtight container and chill 24 hours. Remove and discard mint.

Fruit Punch

4 medium bananas
2 cups plain yogurt
2 cups pineapple juice
4 tablespoons honey
4 tablespoons fresh lemon juice
16 large ice cubes

Instructions

Combine 1/4 to 1/2 of all ingredients in a blender at high speed until smooth. Repeat until all ingredients are used.

Serves: 4.

Recipe Notes

You can also use papaya, peaches, melon or strawberries in place of the bananas.

Hot Toddy

1 1/4   cups orange juice
2   teaspoons lemon juice
2   teaspoons honey
1/4   teaspoon cinnamon
1   shot dark rum

Instructions

Mix everything except the rum in a saucepan and heat over low heat to just before boiling. Remove from the heat and add the rum.

Serves: 1.

Kiwi Colada

5   medium kiwi fruit, peeled
3   cups ice
1/4   cup rum
1/4   cup Midori (melon flavored liqueur)
8   ounces crushed pineapple, undrained
3   tablespoons cream of coconut (such as Coco Lopez)

Instructions

At Home Preparation: Peel the kiwi fruit. Cut 4 into quarters and the 5th one into slices (at least 6). Place in a container.

On Board Preparation: Place the quartered kiwi fruit and the remaining ingredients in a blender; process until smooth. Strain mixture through a sieve into a pitcher; discard the seeds. Divide evenly among 6 glasses. Garnish with sliced kiwi fruit.

Serves: 6.

Lemonade Concentrate

- 2 cups sugar
- 4 cups water
- 2 cups fresh lemon juice

Instructions
At Home Preparation: In a 2-quart saucepan, combine the sugar and water. Bring to a boil over medium heat, stirring to dissolve the sugar. Reduce the heat to a simmer and cook for about 3 minutes. Remove from the heat and cool completely. Pour the sugar syrup into a 1-1/2 quart container and stir in the lemon juice. Refrigerate or freeze. (It will keep up to 2 weeks refrigerated or for several months frozen. Freeze one cup amounts in individual containers for convenience.)

On Board Preparation: Combine equal parts of lemonade concentrate and water. For variety substitute sparkling water or club soda for the water.
Serves: 10.

Luchenbach Lemonade

- 2 cups fresh lemon juice
- 1 cup sparkling water
- 3/4 cup sugar
- 1/4 cup bourbon
- 1/4 cup vodka
- 8 sprigs mint

Instructions
Combine all ingredients except mint sprigs in a pitcher, stirring until the sugar is dissolved. Cover and chill until cold. Pour into 8 crushed ice-filled glasses and garnish with mint sprigs.
Serves: 8.

Recipe Notes
Luchenbach, Texas, home of "Waylon, Willy and the Boys" is the home of this kickin' lemonade.

Mango Champagne Cocktail

- 1 small lime, cut into wedges
- 1 tablespoon sugar
- 1/2 ounce mango puree
- 3 ounces Champagne

Instructions
Moisten the rim of champagne glass with a wedge of lime. Dip the rim into granulated sugar. Add the mango puree and champagne. Decorate with a lime wedge.
Serves: 1.

Mango Mojito

  1 medium lime, cut into 8 wedges
20 medium mint leaves
  1 cup club soda
12 tablespoons rum
  4 tablespoons mango puree
  1 cup crushed ice
  2 cups sugar
  1 cup water

Instructions
At Home Preparation: To make a Simple Syrup, place the 2 cups sugar and 1 cup water in a small saucepan over medium-high heat until sugar dissolves (about 5 minutes), stirring constantly. Place 8 tablespoons in a container and reserve the rest for future use. Cut the lime wedges and place in a container.

On Board Preparation: Squeeze 2 lime wedges into each of 4 glasses. Add the wedges and 5 mint leaves to each glass. Crush with the back of a spoon for 30 seconds. Add 1/4 cup soda, 3 tablespoons rum, 2 tablespoons Simple Syrup, and 1 tablespoon mango nectar to each glass and stir gently. Add ice and serve.
Serves: 4.

Maple Soother

  1 cup milk
  1 tablespoon maple syrup
1/2 teaspoon vanilla extract
  1 shot rum

Instructions
Heat the milk until warm in a small saucepan, being careful not to let it boil. Remove from the heat and stir in the maple syrup, vanilla, and rum.
Serves: 1.

Recipe Notes
Be sure to use pure vanilla extract for this recipe. You can use low fat milk if desired.

Margarita Punch

1 1/2 cups sugar
2 tablespoons grated lemon peel
2 tablespoons grated lime peel
1 tablespoon grated orange peel
2 cups fresh lemon juice
1/2 cup fresh lime juice
2/3 cup fresh orange juice
1 cup water
1 quart water, chilled
1/2 cup tequila
1 medium lemon, sliced
1 medium lime, sliced

Instructions

At Home Preparation: Grate the lemon, lime and orange rind and place in a container. Squeeze the lemon juice, lime juice and orange juice and place each in a container. Slice lemon and lime for garnish and place in a container.

On Board Preparation: Combine the first 8 ingredients in a saucepan. Bring to a boil; remove from heat and let cool. Pour mixture into a pitcher; add 1 quart chilled water. To serve, pour into glasses with crushed ice and add 1-2 tablespoons tequila. Garnish with lemon and lime slices.
Serves: 8.

Recipe Notes
You will need about 12 lemons, 2 limes and 3 oranges for this recipe.

Milk Punch

1/2 cup sugar
1/2 cup bourbon (do NOT use sour mash)
1/2 cup cognac
1/2 cup vodka
1 ounce vanilla extract
1/2 teaspoon freshly ground nutmeg
6 cups milk
1/2 teaspoon grated nutmeg

Instructions

In a 1/2 gallon container with a lid, combine the sugar, bourbon, brandy, and vodka, shaking well until the sugar is dissolved. Add the vanilla and nutmeg and shake well again. Add the milk, 1 cup at a time, until the container is full, shaking after each addition. Chill for at least 8 hours or up to 24. Serve over ice with fresh nutmeg grated on top.   *Serves: 8.*

Mint Bellinis

48 ounces peach nectar
2 cups sugar
1 large lemon, halved
1/4 cup firmly packed mint leaves
750 milliliters Champagne
1 small lemon, sliced

Instructions
At Home Preparation: Bring first 4 ingredients to a boil, and cook 20 minutes. Cool. Remove and discard lemon and mint; place in a container and chill. Slice the small lemon and place in a container.

On Board Preparation: Stir in the chilled Champagne or sparkling water. Serve over ice garnished with lemon slices.
Serves: 8.

Recipe Notes
Substitute 2 1/2 cups sparkling water for the Champagne for a non-alcoholic version.

Orange Spiced Cider

2 cups unsweetened apple cider
1/4 teaspoon cinnamon
1/4 teaspoon ginger
2 teaspoons honey
1 large orange
1/4 teaspoon grated orange peel

Instructions
At Home Preparation: Grate about 1/4 teaspoon orange zest and place in a container. Peel half of the orange. Squeeze the juice from the unpeeled half into a container. Cut the peeled half into slices and place in a container.

On Board Preparation: Heat the apple cider in a small saucepan over low heat. Add the cinnamon, ginger and honey, stirring well. Add the zest and juice to the cider mixture. Continue to heat the cider on low for 3-5 minutes. Place the orange slices in the bottom of serving mugs. Pour the cider into the mugs and serve.
Serves: 2.

Orange Tea Cooler

     5 tea bags
 1 3/4 cups sugar
     2 cinnamon sticks
     1 teaspoon whole cloves
     1 quart water, boiling
 2 1/2 cups fresh orange juice
     2 cups water
 1 1/3 cups cranberry juice cocktail, chilled

Instructions

At Home Preparation: Combine the first 4 ingredients; stir in boiling water. Cover and steep 5 minutes. Pour mixture through a fine wire-mesh strainer into a large container, discarding the tea bags and spices.

On Board Preparation: Stir in orange juice, 2 cups water and cranberry juice. Chill. Serve over ice.
Serves: 12.

Orange Thing

    2 cups ice cubes
 1/4 cup vodka
    2 tablespoons Grand Marnier
 1/4 cup fresh orange juice
    1 slice orange

Instructions

Combine first four ingredients in a martini shaker, cover and shake until thoroughly chilled. Strain into a chilled martini glass and serve immediately, garnished with an orange slice.
Serves: 1.

Pineapple Limeade

    4 cups pineapple juice
 2/3 cup fresh lime juice
 3/4 cup sugar
 1/2 cup tequila (optional) or, 32 ounces lime flavored sparkling water

Instructions
At Home Preparation: Stir together first 3 ingredients and tequila (optional). Place in an airtight plastic container and freeze 8 hours.

On Board Preparation: Thaw slightly. If tequila was not used, add the sparkling water.
Serves: 10.

Pomegranate Mojito

2 tablespoons raw sugar
1 tablespoon fresh lime juice
12 whole mint leaves
6 tablespoons rum
1/4 cup pomegranate juice
1 dash soda water

Instructions
Combine the sugar, lime juice and mint leaves in a tall glass; mash with the back of a spoon. Mix in the rum and pomegranate juice. Fill the glass with ice and top with a splash of soda water.
Serves: 1.

Pomegranate-Champagne Cocktail

1 turbinado sugar cube
2 tablespoons pomegranate juice
1/2 cup Champagne

Instructions
Place the sugar cube in a champagne flute; add 2 tablespoons pomegranate juice and 1/2 cup Champagne. Serve immediately.
Serves: 1.

Recipe Notes
Substitute cranberry juice for the pomegranate juice for a little different taste.

Raspberry-Orange Sunrise

4	cups fresh orange juice
1	cup frozen raspberries
1 1/2	cups semisweet sparkling wine
3	slices orange, halved

Instructions

At Home Preparation: Squeeze the orange juice. Place the orange juice and raspberries in a blender; process until smooth. Place in a container.

On Board Preparation: Combine the juice mixture and the sparkling wine. Garnish with the orange slices.
Serves: 6.

Rockin' Vodka Lemonade

12	ounces raspberry lemonade, frozen concentrate
12	ounces vodka
1	medium lime

Instructions

In a gallon pitcher prepare the lemonade concentrate according to package instructions, replacing one can of water with the vodka. Squeeze the juice from the lime into the mixture. Pour over ice and serve.
Serves: 6.

Sangria II

375	milliliters semisweet sparkling wine
7	ounces Sprite
3/4	ounce simple syrup
1 1/4	ounces Grand Marnier
1 1/4	ounces brandy
2	medium oranges, quartered
2	medium limes, quartered

Instructions

At Home Preparation: To prepare the simple syrup combine 2 cups water and 1 cup sugar in a sauce pan. Cook over low heat until clear, then boil for about a minute to thicken. Divide and place in containers. Reserve left over syrup for a later use. Quarter the orange and limes and place in a container. Slice additional citrus fruits for garnish and place in a container.

On Board Preparation: Mix all ingredients in a pitcher. Serve in glasses garnished with citrus slices and cherry if desired.
Serves: 4.

Sparkling Peach Slush

2	cups peeled & chopped peaches
1/2	cup peach schnapps
2	tablespoons fresh lime juice
750	milliliters Champagne
3	peach slices, for garnish

Instructions
At Home Preparation: Peel and chop the peaches. Combine the chopped peaches, peach schnapps and fresh lime juice in a blender. Process until smooth. Place in a container and freeze. Slice the peaches for garnish and place in a container.

On Board Preparation: Pour the champagne into a pitcher. Spoon the peach mixture in and stir to combine. Garnish with peach slices if desired. Serve immediately.
Serves: 8.

Recipe Notes
Be sure you select peaches that are ripe and sweet.

Strawberry Champagne Cocktail

1	tablespoon sweetened strawberry puree
6	ounces Champagne

Instructions
In a champagne flute, pour in the strawberry puree. Pour champagne over it to blend. It should have a pink blush to it.
Serves: 1.

Swimming Pool

- 3/4 ounce vodka
- 3/4 ounce light rum
- 3/4 ounce blue Curacao
- 2 ounces coconut cream
- 4 ounces pineapple juice
- 1 slice pineapple, cut into wedges
- 1 slice orange

Instructions

At Home Preparation: Cut the pineapple and orange slice and place each in a container.

On Board Preparation: Shake ingredients with ice. Strain into tall glass filled with ice. Garnish with pineapple wedges and an orange slice.
Serves: 1.

The Perfect Mojito

- 10 mint leaves
- 2 tablespoons sugar
- 1/2 lime, juiced
- 1 1/2 ounces rum
- 1 sprig mint
- 1 dash club soda

Instructions

Mix the 10 mint leaves, sugar, and lime juice in a small bowl; crush the mint. Add the rum and stir. Pour into a glass with ice. Add a splash of club soda, and garnish with mint sprigs if desired.
Serves: 1.

Tropical Fruit Punch

4 medium bananas
2 cups plain yogurt
2 cups pineapple juice
4 tablespoons honey
4 tablespoons fresh lemon juice
16 ice cubes

Instructions
Combine 1/4 to 1/2 of all ingredients in a blender at high speed until smooth. Repeat until all ingredients are used.
Serves: 4.

Recipe Notes
Substitute papaya, peaches, melon or strawberries for the bananas for different tastes.

<u>Breakfast and Brunch</u>

Almond French Toast

- 1 cup slivered almonds
- 3 whole eggs
- 1 cup milk
- 3 tablespoons flour
- 1/4 teaspoon salt
- 1/2 teaspoon baking powder
- 1/2 teaspoon almond extract
- 1 teaspoon vanilla extract
- 8 slices white bread, sliced 1" thick
- 3 tablespoons vegetable oil
- 3 tablespoons butter
- 3 tablespoons powdered sugar

Instructions

At Home Preparation: In a small saucepan over low heat, place slivered almonds and toast until lightly browned, about 5 to 10 minutes, tossing frequently. Cool completely and place in a container.

On Board Preparation: In a large bowl, whisk together eggs, milk, flour, salt, baking powder, almond extract and vanilla. Soak each slice of bread in the mixture until saturated. Place soaked bread slices in a shallow pan and chill for at least 30 minutes. In a large skillet over medium heat, heat the vegetable oil. Place the slivered almonds on a plate or shallow dish. Press each slice of bread, one at a time, in the toasted almonds until coated. Fry the bread slices in the skillet until golden brown. Remove to a plate and dust with powdered sugar. Serve with your favorite syrup.
Serves: 4.

Bacon Quiche Tarts

- 6 slices bacon
- 8 ounces cream cheese, softened
- 2 tablespoons milk
- 2 large eggs
- 1/2 cup shredded Swiss cheese
- 4 green onions, chopped
- 10 ounces refrigerated biscuit dough

Instructions

At Home Preparation: Cook the bacon until crisp, drain and cool. Crumble the bacon and place in a container. Chop the green onions and place in a container.

On Board Preparation: Preheat oven to 375°. Lightly grease 10 muffin cups. In a medium bowl, combine the cream cheese, milk and eggs. Using a hand mixer beat until smooth. Fold in the Swiss cheese and chopped green onions and set aside. Separate the biscuit dough into 10 biscuits. Press 1 biscuit into the bottom and up the sides of each muffin cup. Sprinkle half the crumbled bacon evenly in the bottom of the biscuit dough lined muffin cups. Spoon 2 tablespoons of the cream cheese mixture into each muffin cup. Bake for 20 to 25 minutes until filling is set and crust is golden brown. Sprinkle the remaining crumbled bacon on the top of each tart and press gently into the filling. Remove the tarts from the muffin cups and serve warm.
Serves: 10.

Bacon-Cheddar Breakfast Tarts

- 11 ounces pie crust mix
- 8 slices bacon
- 1 cup shredded Cheddar cheese
- 4 large eggs
- 1/4 cup milk
- 1/4 teaspoon nutmeg
- 1/4 teaspoon pepper

Instructions
At Home Preparation: Preheat oven to 425°. Prepare pastry for a one crust pie according to package directions. Divide the pasty into 4 equal parts and roll each into a 6" circle. Place each circle in a muffin cup or 8 ounce ramekin shaping with pleats to cover the bottom and sides. Poke the surface with a fork and bake in the oven for 8 to 10 minutes until lightly browned. Cool completely and place in a container. Cook the bacon, drain, cool completely and crumble. Place in a container. Shred the Cheddar and place in a container.

On Board Preparation: Preheat oven to 350°. Divide the crumbled bacon and shredded Cheddar evenly amongst the pastry cups. Break one egg into each pastry cup and pour 1 tablespoon milk into each. Sprinkle nutmeg and pepper over each tart and bake for 15-20 minutes, until eggs are soft cooked.
Serves: 4.

GALLEY TIP
Add one teaspoon of oil to butter when heating to keep it from burning.

Baked Orange-Pecan French Toast

- 1 cup packed brown sugar
- 1/3 cup melted butter
- 2 tablespoons light corn syrup
  cooking spray
- 1/3 cup chopped pecans
- 1 teaspoon grated orange peel
- 1 cup orange juice
- 1/2 cup milk
- 3 tablespoons sugar
- 1 teaspoon cinnamon
- 1 teaspoon vanilla extract
- 4 large eggs
- 1 loaf French bread, sliced 1" thick

Instructions

At Home Preparation: Chop the pecans and place in a container. Grate the orange rind and place in a container. Cut the French bread and place in a container.

On Board Preparation: Coat a 13x9 baking pan with cooking spray. Combine the brown sugar, melted butter and corn syrup and pour into the baking pan. Sprinkle the chopped pecans evenly over the sugar mixture. Combine the orange rind, orange juice, milk, sugar, cinnamon, vanilla and eggs in a bowl, stirring with a whisk. Arrange the bread slices in the baking pan and pour the egg mixture over. Cover and refrigerate 1 hour or overnight. Preheat the oven to 350°. Turn the bread slices to absorb any excess egg mixture. Let stand at room temperature 20 minutes. Bake for 35 minutes or until lightly browned. When serving, turn upside down so that the pecan and sugar mixture is on top.
Serves: 12.

Banana and Spice Muffins

- 3 whole ripe bananas
- 1/4 cup orange juice
- 1/2 cup Irish butter
- 1/2 cup raisins
- 1/2 cup chopped pecans
- 1/2 cup brown sugar
- 2 cups unbleached flour
- 1/2 teaspoon salt
- 1/2 teaspoon baking powder
- 1/2 teaspoon baking soda
- 4 teaspoons pumpkin pie spice
- 2 whole bananas (optional)

Instructions

At Home Preparation: Mix the flour, salt, baking powder, baking soda, raisins, nuts and pumpkin pie spice together with a whisk. Place in a container.

On Board Preparation: Preheat the oven to 375°. Bring the butter to room temperature. In a large bowl, mash the ripe bananas and mix with the orange juice, butter, and brown sugar. Add the dry ingredients to the wet and mix well. Slice the optional bananas. Spoon the batter evenly into a 12 non-stick muffin pan or line with paper muffin cups. Add the optional banana slices, if desired. Bake for 30 minutes.
Serves: 6.

Recipe Notes
Irish butter is a richer, creamier butter that is especially great for baking. It's a little more expensive but well worth it!

Blue Cheese and Walnut Omelet

    8 whole eggs
    4 tablespoons milk
    4 tablespoons butter
    4 tablespoons chopped walnuts
    4 tablespoons crumbled blue cheese

Instructions

At Home Preparation: Chop the walnuts and place in a container. Crumble the blue cheese and place in a container.

On Board Preparation: Beat eggs with milk. Set aside. Melt the butter in a large omelet pan. Add the egg mixture. Cook over medium heat, shaking pan to cook egg evenly. When cooked add the walnuts and the cheese to center of omelet; fold edges over filling. Heat through. Cut into four servings and serve immediately.
Serves: 4.

GALLEY TIP
To test an egg for freshness, place in a little water. If it's fresh, it will sink. If it's stale, it will float.

Breakfast Bread Pudding

    1   large baguette
  1/2   stick unsalted butter, melted
    2   medium onions, chopped
    2   tablespoons olive oil
    1   pound cooked ham
    4   large eggs
    1   quart milk
    1   teaspoon salt
  1/4   teaspoon grated nutmeg
    5   cups coarsely chopped spinach
  3/4   pound grated fontina cheese

Instructions

At Home Preparation: Preheat the broiler. Cut the baguette crosswise into 3/4-inch slices. Brush both sides with melted butter. Toast on a baking sheet in the broiler until golden, about 30 seconds each side. Cool and place in a container. Chop the onions and place in a container. Cut the ham into 1/2-inch cubes and place in a container. Wash the spinach, remove stems, dry completely, chop coarsely and place in a container. Grate the cheese and place in a container. Sauté the onions in the olive oil over medium-high heat, stirring, until golden. Add the ham and sauté, until ham is lightly browned. Cool completely and place in a container.

On Board Preparation: Preheat oven to 350°. Whisk eggs in a large bowl, then whisk in the milk, salt, nutmeg and pepper to taste. Add the toasted bread and toss gently. Let the bread saturate then transfer to a shallow 3-quart casserole, arranging in slightly overlapping design. Add any remaining egg mixture. Tuck the spinach and ham between slices, reserving a little ham to sprinkle on top. Sprinkle cheese over the top. Sprinkle reserved ham on top and bake 45-60 minutes or until puffed, edges of the bread are browned and custard is set in the middle.   *Serves: 6.*

Breakfast Empanada

     6   ounces cream cheese, softened
 1 1/2   tablespoons minced fresh parsley
   3/4   teaspoon seasoned salt
   1/4   teaspoon freshly ground pepper
   2/3   cup shredded sharp Cheddar cheese
     2   tablespoons butter
     5   large eggs, beaten
17 1/3   ounces refrigerated jumbo flaky biscuit dough
     8   slices bacon
          cooking spray
     1   whole egg white, lightly beaten
     2   teaspoons sesame seeds

Instructions
At Home Preparation: Mince the parsley, mix with the cream cheese, salt, pepper and cheese and place in a container. Cook the bacon, cool, and place in a container.

On Board Preparation: Preheat the oven to 375°. Melt the butter in a skillet over medium heat. Add the eggs and cook without stirring until the eggs begin to set on bottom. Draw a spatula along the bottom of the skillet to form large curds. Continue cooking until eggs are slightly thickened but still moist. (Do not stir.) Remove from heat and let cool. Flatten each biscuit into a 5 inch circle. Spread cream cheese mixture over tops of dough circles, leaving 1/2-inch border around edge. Top evenly with eggs and bacon. Fold circles in half over mixture, pinching edges to seal. Place, 2 inches apart on a baking sheet coated with cooking spray. Brush tops evenly with egg white and press the sealed edges with tines of a fork. Sprinkle with sesame seeds. Bake for about 15 minutes or until golden brown. Remove to a wire rack and cool slightly before serving. Store leftovers in plastic wrap and reheat by wrapping in paper towels and microwave at 50% power for 1-2 minutes.
Serves: 4.

Breakfast Pockets

1	pound hot bulk pork sausage
1	medium onion, finely chopped
4	tablespoons butter
12	whole eggs, beaten
2	sheets frozen puff pastry, thawed
1 1/2	cups shredded Cheddar cheese

Instructions
At Home Preparation: Brown the sausage, drain, cool and place in a container. Chop the onion, sauté just until tender, cool and place in a container. Shred the cheese and place in a container.

On Board Preparation: Combine the sausage and onion in a bowl. Melt the butter in a skillet and add the eggs. Scramble until cooked through and add to the bowl with the sausage mixture. Mix well and let cool. (Note: you can prepare this 1 day ahead, cover and refrigerate.) Preheat the oven to 400°. Roll the thawed pastry out on 2 parchment lined baking sheets. Add the Cheddar cheese to the cooled egg mixture and mix well. Spoon the egg mixture lengthwise down the center of each pastry sheet. Fold in the sides to cover the filling and seal the ends with a seam up the middle. Bake for 30 minutes or until puffed and golden brown. Cut into slices to serve.
Serves: 8.

Breakfast Sandwich

  4 large potatoes, peeled & quartered
  4 slices bacon
  1 cup shredded Cheddar cheese
  4 whole eggs, beaten
      cooking spray
  2 tablespoons vegetable oil
1/4 teaspoon salt
1/8 teaspoon pepper

Instructions

At Home Preparation: Place the potatoes in a large saucepan with water to cover. Bring to a boil and cook until tender, about 5 minutes. Drain and run the potatoes under cool water. Drain and pat dry. Using a shredder or grater, grate the potatoes and separate into two sections, placing each on a piece of waxed paper. Pat each section into a 6" circle. Place in a container. Freeze. Cook the bacon until crisp. Drain on paper towel, cool and place in a container.

On Board Preparation: Thaw the potatoes. Scramble the eggs in a non-stick skillet sprayed with cooking spray. Remove to a plate and keep hot. Add the oil to the skillet and reduce heat to medium. Place one potato patty in the skillet. Top with the scrambled eggs, cheese and bacon slices. Top with the other potato patty. Cook until the potato is golden brown. Using a large spatula, flip the sandwich and cook until the other potato patty is browned. Cut into 4 wedges and serve.
Serves: 4.

Breakfast Scramble

  2 cups potatoes, peeled & sliced
  2 tablespoons olive oil
  1 medium onion, coarsely chopped
1/4 teaspoon cayenne pepper
  4 whole eggs, beaten
  1 teaspoon Italian seasoning
1/2 cup shredded sharp Cheddar cheese
  1 dash sea salt
  1 dash pepper

Instructions

At Home Preparation: In a large saucepan, cook the potatoes in the olive oil until tender (about 10 minutes) over medium heat. Add the onion and cayenne pepper and cook another 3-5 minutes, until the onions are lightly browned. Cool completely and place in a container.

On Board Preparation: Place the potato mixture in a large saucepan over medium heat until heated through. Turn heat to low. Add the beaten eggs and Italian seasoning and stir until well blended. Cover with a lid and heat on low for 4 minutes; add the cheese and stir. Cover and cook about another minute or until the cheese is melted. Remove the lid and sprinkle with salt and pepper.
Serves: 2.

Brie and Sausage Casserole

8 ounces brie
1 pound hot bulk pork sausage, ground
6 slices white bread
1 cup grated Parmesan cheese
7 large eggs
3 cups whipping cream
2 cups milk
1 tablespoon chopped fresh sage
1 teaspoon seasoned salt
1 teaspoon mustard powder
2 pieces green onions, chopped
3/4 cup shaved Parmesan cheese

Instructions

At Home Preparation: Trim the rind from the Brie and discard. Cut into cubes and place in a container. Cut the crusts from the bread slices and place both the crusts and the slices in a container. Grate the Parmesan and place in a container. Chop the sage and place in a container. Chop the green onions and place in a container. Shave 3/4 cup Parmesan for garnish and place in a container. Cook the sausage in a skillet until it crumbles and is no longer pink. Drain well, cool and place in a container.

On Board Preparation: Place the bread crusts evenly in the bottom of a lightly greased 13x9 baking pan. Layer evenly with bread slices, sausage, brie, and Parmesan. Whisk together 5 eggs, 2 cups whipping cream, milk, sage, seasoned salt and dry mustard. Pour evenly over the cheese. Cover and chill for 8 hours. Preheat oven to 350°. Whisk together the remaining 2 eggs and remaining 1 cup whipping cream and pour evenly over the chilled mixture. Bake for 1 hour or until casserole is set. Garnish with chopped green onion and shaved Parmesan.
Serves: 8.

Broccoli and Cheese Breakfast Casserole

- 4 slices bacon
- 1 cup chopped broccoli
- 4 slices white bread
- 1 tablespoon butter, softened
- 1/2 cup shredded Cheddar cheese
- 1 cup milk
- 6 whole eggs
- 1/4 teaspoon mustard powder
- 1/4 teaspoon salt
- 1/8 teaspoon pepper

Instructions

At Home Preparation: Cook the bacon, cool and crumble. Place in a container. In a medium pot of boiling water, cook the chopped broccoli until just tender but firm, about 10 minutes. Drain and cool completely. Place in a container.

On Board Preparation: Preheat the oven to 325°. Lightly grease a 9" square baking dish. Spread butter over each slice of bread and line the bottom of the baking dish with the buttered bread. Cover the bread with the cheese, crumbled bacon and cooked broccoli. In a large bowl, whisk the eggs, milk dry mustard and salt and pepper. Pour into the baking dish. Bake for 20 minutes, until eggs are completely cooked, about 1 hour.
Serves: 4.

Brunch Soufflé Pancake

- 6 whole egg whites
- 5 tablespoons powdered sugar
- 3 whole egg yolks, beaten
- 1 teaspoon flour
- 1 teaspoon grated lemon peel
- 3 tablespoons unsalted butter
- 2 tablespoons milk
- 1 tablespoon sugar
- 1/4 cup powdered sugar, optional

Instructions

At Home Preparation: Separate 6 eggs, placing all 6 whites in a plastic container. Place 3 of the yolks in a plastic container and reserve the other 3 for another use. Grate the lemon rind and place in a container.

On Board Preparation: Preheat the oven to 450°. Beat the egg whites until stiff. Add the powdered sugar and continue to beat until very thick. Fold in the yolks, flour and lemon rind. In a 10-inch, deep pie plate, combine the butter, milk and sugar.

Heat until the butter melts. Scoop 4 large mounds of egg mixture onto the butter mixture. Bake for about 6 minutes or until peaks are golden brown. Sprinkle with additional powdered sugar (optional).
Serves: 4.

Caribbean French Toast

  1 large baguette
  3 large eggs
 1/2 cup coconut cream
 1/2 teaspoon sugar
  2 tablespoons lemon juice
  2 tablespoons butter
  4 servings maple syrup

Instructions

At Home Preparation: Cut the baguette into 12 slices about 1-1/2 inches thick. Place in a container.

On Board Preparation: Beat the eggs, coconut cream, sugar and lemon juice together with a wire whisk. Dip the bread slices into the mixture and soak well. Melt the butter in a skillet and cook the bread slices slowly until golden brown and eggs are set. Serve with warm syrup.
Serves: 4.

GALLEY TIP
Unsalted butter is always better. Salt masks imperfections in the cream.

Carmelized Onion, Canadian Bacon And Egg Sandwich

          2   teaspoons canola oil
      2 1/2   cups thinly sliced onions
        1/2   teaspoon sugar
        1/2   teaspoon tarragon vinegar
        1/4   teaspoon salt
        1/4   teaspoon ground pepper
          4   slices Canadian bacon
               cooking spray
          4   large eggs
          8   slices hearty white bread, toasted

Instructions

At Home Preparation: Slice the onions vertically. Heat canola oil in a large non-stick skillet over medium-high heat. Add onion, sugar, vinegar, salt, and pepper; sauté 6-7 minutes or until just beginning to turn golden. Remove from pan and cool. Place in a container.

On Board Preparation: Reheat the onions by sautéing about 1 minute in a non-stick skillet over medium-high heat. Remove from the pan and cover to keep warm. Add the Canadian bacon to the pan and cook 1 minute on each side or until lightly browned. Remove from the pan and keep warm. Wipe the pan clean with a paper towel. Coat the pan with cooking spray. Reduce the heat to medium. Add the eggs and cook 2 minutes on each side or until desired degree of doneness. Layer 1 bacon slice, 1/4 cup onion mixture, and 1 egg on each of 4 bread slices. Top with remaining bread slices.
Serves: 4.

Recipe Notes
Use yellow onions for a very sweet taste.

Cheddar Pancakes with Sautéed Apples and Bacon

      1 1/3   cups all-purpose flour
          1   tablespoon sugar
      1 1/4   teaspoons baking powder
        1/4   teaspoon salt
        1/4   teaspoon baking soda
        1/4   teaspoon ground nutmeg
      1 1/3   cups plain yogurt
      1 1/4   cups shredded extra sharp Cheddar cheese
          2   tablespoons water
          2   tablespoons Dijon mustard

2   teaspoons vegetable oil
2   large eggs
2   slices bacon
8   cups sliced Granny Smith apples
2   tablespoons sugar

Instructions

At Home Preparation: Shred the Cheddar and place in a container. For the sautéed apples, cook the bacon in a skillet over medium heat until crisp. Remove, reserving the drippings in the pan. Add the apples and sugar and sauté about 8 minutes or until apples are golden. Crumble the bacon into the apple mixture. Let cool completely and place in a container. Combine the flour, and next 5 ingredients and place in a container.

On Board Preparation: Combine the yogurt and the next 5 ingredients and add the flour mixture, stirring until smooth. Spoon about 1/4 cup batter onto a hot nonstick griddle or skillet. Turn pancakes when tops are covered with bubbles and edges look cooked. Reheat the sautéed apples just enough to heat through. Serve the pancakes topped with sautéed apples.
Serves: 4.

Cheesy Corn Bread

1/2 cup vegetable oil
  3 large eggs
  1 cup buttermilk
 16 ounces cream-style corn
  2 cups yellow cornmeal
  2 teaspoons baking powder
  1 teaspoon salt
  1 cup grated sharp Cheddar cheese
1/4 cup diced jalapeno pepper

Instructions

At Home Preparation: Grate the cheese and place in a container. Dice the jalapenos and place in a container. Mix together the cornmeal, baking powder, and salt and place in a container.

On Board Preparation: Preheat the oven to 350°. Brush 1 tablespoon oil into a 9-inch square or round baking dish. Or, heat a 10-inch cast iron skillet in the oven for about 10 minutes, then brush with the oil. (Using the cast iron skillet will give the bread a crisper crust.) Whisk the remaining oil and eggs in a mixing bowl with a wire whisk. Stir in the buttermilk and corn. Add the cornmeal mixture to the egg mixture and stir just until the dry ingredients are moistened. Fold in the 1/2 cup of the cheese and jalapenos. Sprinkle the remaining cheese on top. Bake about 40 minutes until the firm to the touch and lightly browned. Cool 10 minutes.
Serves: 8.

Cinnamon Breakfast Rounds

- 1/2 cup peanut butter
- 4 whole English muffins, split
- 1 large apple, cored & sliced
- 1/4 cup brown sugar
- 2 tablespoons butter
- 1/2 teaspoon cinnamon

Instructions
Lightly toast the English muffin halves. Spread each with 1 tablespoon peanut butter and top with the apple slices. In a small microwave safe bowl, combine the brown sugar butter and cinnamon. Heat in the microwave until melted. Stir the mixture and drizzle lightly over each serving.
Serves: 4.

Cream Cheese Eggs

- 8 tablespoons butter
- 8 large eggs
- 3 tablespoons cubed cream cheese
- 2 tablespoons chopped chives
- 1/2 teaspoon salt
- 1/4 teaspoon pepper

Instructions
At Home Preparation: Chop the chives and place in a container. Cut the cream cheese into small pieces and place in a container.

On Board Preparation: Melt the butter in a 10-inch skillet over medium heat. Carefully add eggs without breaking the yolks. Carefully add the cream cheese, one piece at a time, at the edge of the skillet. Sprinkle with chopped chives, salt and pepper to taste. As the cheese melts into the butter, and egg whites begin to cook, gently spoon cheese mixture over yolks, being careful not to break the yolks, until whites are cooked but yolks are still soft.
Serves: 4.

Eggs Magnifique

- 8 large eggs
- 4 large egg yolks
- 2 tablespoons orange juice
- 1/4 teaspoon salt
- 1 cup butter
- 24 whole asparagus spears
- 4 whole English muffins

Instructions

At Home Preparation: Rinse the asparagus spears and snap off the woody stems. Cook the asparagus spears until crisp-tender. Cool completely and place in a container.

On Board Preparation: Split the English muffins; toast and butter. Keep warm. In a saucepan, over low heat, blend the 4 egg yolks with the orange juice and salt. Add the butter, 1/2 stick at a time, and mix after each addition with a wire whisk until blended. When all the butter has been added, cook stirring constantly until thickened. Meanwhile, poach the 8 eggs in an egg poacher until whites are cooked and yolks are still soft. Place 3 asparagus spears on each English muffin half, top with a poached egg and spoon orange sauce over all.
Serves: 4.

Gruyere Onion and Proscuitto Strata

    4   cups chopped sweet onion
    1   cup chopped prosciutto
  1/3   cup water
2 1/2   cups milk
  1/4   teaspoon mustard powder
  1/8   teaspoon pepper
    8   ounces egg (or liquid substitute)
    8   cups cubed French bread
    1   cup shredded gruyere

Instructions

At Home Preparation: Chop the onion and place in a container. Chop the prosciutto and place in a container. Cut the French bread into cubes and place in a container. Shred the Gruyere and place in a container.

On Board Preparation: In a non-stick skillet over medium heat, sauté the onion and prosciutto for 5 minutes or until the onion begins to brown. Add the water, cover, reduce heat to low and simmer 30 minutes. Uncover and simmer 30 minutes or until liquid almost evaporates. Cool. Combine the milk, mustard, pepper, and eggs (or egg substitute) in a large bowl and whisk until well blended. Stir in the onion mixture. Add the bread cubes and toss gently to coat. Arrange half of the bread mixture in a single layer in 7x11 baking dish. Sprinkle with 1/2 cup cheese and top with the remaining bread mixture. Cover and chill 8 hours or overnight. Preheat oven to 350°. Uncover the strata and bake for 25 minutes. Sprinkle with 1/3 cup cheese and bake an additional 20 minutes or until set.
Serves: 8.

Ham and Swiss Bread Pudding

　1 1/4　cups chopped green onions
　　3/4　cup chopped ham
　　　2　cloves garlic, chopped
　　　7　Hawaiian bread rolls
　1 3/4　cups milk
　　3/4　cup egg (or liquid substitute)
　　　2　tablespoons Dijon mustard
　　1/4　teaspoon salt
　　1/4　teaspoon freshly ground black pepper
　　3/4　cup shredded Swiss cheese

Instructions

At Home Preparation: Chop the green onions and place in a container. Chop the ham and place in a container. Chop the garlic and place in a container. Cut the rolls into 1/2-inch cubes and place in a container. Shred the Swiss cheese and place in a container. Preheat the oven to 350°. Arrange the bread cubes on a baking sheet and bake for about 15 minutes or until lightly browned, turning occasionally. Cool completely and place in a container.

On Board Preparation: Whisk together the milk, egg (or egg substitute), Dijon mustard, salt, pepper and nutmeg. Stir in the ham mixture. Add the toasted bread, tossing gently to coat. Arrange half the bread mixture in an 8-inch baking dish coated with cooking spray. Sprinkle with half the cheese, and top with the remaining bread mixture. Bake for 25 minutes; sprinkle with the remaining cheese and bake an additional 20 minutes or until set.
Serves: 4.

Ham, Gruyere and Spaetzle Bake

　1 2/3　cups all-purpose flour
　　　1　teaspoon salt
　　1/4　teaspoon baking powder
　2 1/4　cups milk, divided
　　　4　large eggs, divided
　　　2　quarts water
　　　1　cup finely chopped onion
　　3/4　cup ham, diced fine
　　　2　tablespoons all-purpose flour
　　1/4　teaspoon freshly ground black pepper
　　3/4　cup shredded Gruyere cheese

Instructions

At Home Preparation: Chop the onion and place in a container. Chop the ham and place in a container. Shred the cheese and place in a container. Sift together the flour , 1/2 teaspoon salt and baking powder. Combine 3/4 cup milk and 2 eggs, stirring with a whisk. Add the milk mixture to the flour mixture, stirring with a whisk until combined. Let stand 10 minutes. Bring 2 quarts water to a boil. Hold a colander over the boiling water, spoon about 1/2 cup dough into the colander. Press the dough through holes with a rubber spatula to form spaetzle. Cook 3 minutes or until spaetzle rises to the surface. Remove with a slotted spoon and drain in a strainer. Repeat procedure with remaining dough. Let cool completely and place in a container. Heat a medium nonstick skillet coated with cooking spray over medium heat. Add the onion, cook 5 minutes or until lightly browned, stirring frequently. Remove from heat and stir in the ham. Cool completely and place in a container.

On Board Preparation: Preheat the oven to 375°. Combine the spaetzle and onion mixture in a 2-quart baking dish coated with cooking spray, tossing gently. Combine remaining 1/2 teaspoon salt 1-1/2 cups milk, 2 eggs, 2 tablespoons flour and pepper, stirring with a whisk. Pour milk mixture over spaetzle mixture. Sprinkle evenly with cheese. Bake for 35 minutes or until cheese is lightly browned.
Serves: 6.

Hearty Frittata

1	cup baking potato, peeled & diced
1/2	cup shredded Cheddar cheese
4	large eggs, slightly beaten
2	teaspoons butter
1/2	cup diced red onion
1/2	cup diced red bell pepper
1/2	cup diced Canadian bacon
2	cloves garlic, minced
1/4	cup sour cream

Instructions

At Home Preparation: Place the diced potato in a saucepan, cover with water and bring to a boil. Cook 10 minutes or until tender; drain. Cool completely and place in a container. Dice the red onion and bell pepper and place in a container. Dice the Canadian bacon and place in a container. Mince the garlic and place in a container.

On Board Preparation: Preheat the oven to 450°. Lightly beat the eggs. Combine 1/4 cup cheese and the eggs in a bowl and stir. Set aside. Melt the butter in a 10-inch nonstick skillet over medium heat. Add the potato, onion, bell pepper, bacon and garlic; sauté 5 minutes. Stir in the egg mixture, spreading evenly in the pan. Cook over medium-low heat 5 minutes or until almost set. Wrap the handle of the skillet with foil and place in the oven to bake for 5 minutes or until set. Sprinkle with the remaining cheese and bake an additional minute or until the cheese melts. Top each serving with sour cream.
Serves: 2.

Italian Brunch Casserole

   8 ounces sweet Italian sausage
   8 medium green onions, sliced
   3 cups diced zucchini
   1 teaspoon salt
 1/2 teaspoon pepper
   7 ounces roasted red peppers, drained and chopped
 16 ounces Italian bread, cut into 1" cubes
   2 cups shredded sharp Cheddar cheese
   6 large eggs
1 1/2 cups milk

Instructions

At Home Preparation: Remove the sausage from the casing. Cook the sausage in a large skillet until it just begins to crumble and is no longer pink. Drain. Add the green onions, zucchini, salt and pepper and sauté 4 minutes or until vegetables are tender. Cool and place in a container. Slice the green onions and place in a container. Dice the zucchini and place in a container. Drain and chop the roasted bell peppers and place in a container. Cube the loaf of bread and place in a container. Shred the Cheddar and place in a container.

On Board Preparation: Stir the roasted peppers into the sausage mixture. Spread 4 cups of bread cubes in a lightly greased 13x9 baking dish. Top with half each of the sausage mixture and cheese. Repeat with remaining bread, sausage and cheese. Whisk together eggs and milk. Pour egg mixture over the bread, cover and chill 8 hours or overnight. Preheat oven to 325°. Bake for 1 hour or until bubbly and hot.
Serves: 4.

John Wayne Casserole

   1 pound Monterey Jack cheese, grated
 12 ounces canned green chiles, diced
   1 pound Cheddar cheese, grated
   4 large eggs, separated
   1 tablespoon flour
 1/2 teaspoon salt
 1/4 teaspoon pepper
1 1/3 cups half & half
   2 medium tomatoes, halved and sliced

Instructions

At Home Preparation: Grate the Monterrey Jack cheese and place in a container. Drain the chiles, dice and place in a container. Grate the Cheddar and place in a container. Cut the tomatoes and place in a container.

On Board Preparation: Preheat the oven to 300°. Combine the cheese and chiles and place in a buttered 13x9 casserole dish. Separate the eggs. Beat the whites to stiff peaks. Mix the egg yolks, flour, salt, pepper and cream. Fold in the stiffly beaten whites. Pour over the cheese and let the mixture soak through, helping it with a fork if necessary. Bake 1 hour. Remove from the oven and arrange the tomatoes attractively on top. Return to the oven and bake an additional 20-30 minutes more or until a knife inserted in the center comes out clean. Cut into 8 squares.
Serves: 8.

Leek and Bacon Tart

1	cup all-purpose flour
1/4	teaspoon salt
2	tablespoons butter, cut in small pieces
2	tablespoons shortening
1/4	teaspoon cider vinegar
4	tablespoons ice water
3	slices bacon, cut crosswise
7	cups chopped leeks
1/2	teaspoon salt
1/4	teaspoon freshly-ground black pepper
1 1/4	cups egg (or liquid substitute)
2/3	cup milk

Instructions

At Home Preparation: Combine the flour and 1/4 teaspoon salt in a bowl, cut in butter and shortening with a pastry blender or 2 knives until mixture resembles coarse meal. Add the vinegar, and ice water, 1 tablespoon at a time, toss with a fork until moist. (Add an additional tablespoon or two of ice water if necessary.) Gently press into a 4-inch circle on heavy-duty plastic wrap. Cover with additional plastic wrap. Roll the dough into a 12-inch circle; chill 10 minutes. Preheat the oven to 425°. Remove 1 sheet of plastic wrap and let the dough stand 1 minute or until pliable. Fit the dough, plastic-wrap side up, into a 10-inch round tart pan with a removable bottom. Remove the remaining plastic wrap. Press the dough into the bottom and sides of the pan. Fold edges under. Line the dough with a piece of foil, arrange pie weights on the foil. Bake for 10 minutes or until edge is lightly browned. Remove pie weights and foil before cooling on a wire rack, and place in container. Chop the leeks and place in a container.

On Board Preparation: Preheat the oven to 425°. Cook the bacon for 4 minutes, remove from the pan and reserve 2 teaspoons drippings. Add the leeks to the drippings and cover and cook for 20 minutes, stirring occasionally over medium heat. Season with 1/4 teaspoon salt and 1/8 teaspoon pepper. Remove from the heat and arrange the leek mixture and bacon in the prepared crust. Whisk the egg (or egg substitute), milk, and the remaining salt and pepper together. Pour over the leeks and bacon. Bake for 25 minutes or until a knife inserted in the center comes out clean. Let stand 10 minutes before serving.
Serves: 8.

Lemon Pancakes

       2 cups flour
   2 1/2 tablespoons sugar
   1 1/2 tablespoons baking powder
     1/2 teaspoon salt
       2 large eggs, separated
   2 1/2 cups milk
       2 tablespoons butter, melted
       1 medium lemon peel, grated
       2 tablespoons lemon juice
       4 tablespoons butter
     1/2 cup honey, warm

Instructions

At Home Preparation: Grate the lemon rind and place in a container. In a bowl, sift flour, sugar, baking powder and salt. Place in a container.

On Board Preparation: In a bowl, beat the egg yolks and stir in the milk, melted butter, lemon rind and lemon juice. Place the flour mixture in a large bowl. Stir liquid into flour mixture until just moistened. (Batter will be lumpy.) Beat the egg whites to stiff peaks and fold into the batter. Drop the batter by tablespoons onto hot oiled skillet and cook until they are bubbling on the surface. Turn and brown on the other side. Serve with butter and warm honey.
Serves: 4.

Mariners' Scrambled Eggs

       8 large eggs
       3 tablespoons milk
     1/2 cup cottage cheese
       3 tablespoons chopped chives
       1 small tomato, peeled, seeded and chopped
       3 tablespoons butter

Instructions

At Home Preparation: Chop the fresh chives and place in a container. Peel, seed and chop the tomato. Place in a container.

On Board Preparation: Beat the eggs and milk with a wire whisk. Add the cottage cheese, chives and tomato and stir. Melt the butter in a skillet. Add the egg mixture. Cook over medium heat stirring frequently until cooked but still slightly soft.
Serves: 4.

Monkey Bread Bites

      1/2 cup sugar
        1 tablespoon cinnamon
       18 ounces refrigerated buttermilk biscuit dough
      1/2 cup butter
        2 tablespoons butter
      1/4 cup firmly packed light brown sugar
        1 teaspoon vanilla extract
      1/2 cup pecans, chopped and toasted
       12 large foil muffin cups

Instructions

At Home Preparation: Combine the sugar and cinnamon and place in a container. Chop and toast the pecans, cool, and place in a container. Cut the biscuits into fourths, add to sugar mixture and toss to coat. Place in a container.

On Board Preparation: Preheat the oven to 400°. Melt the butter over medium heat. Add the brown sugar, stirring until sugar dissolves. Remove from heat; stir in vanilla and pecans. Arrange 5 coated biscuit pieces in a lightly greased foil muffin cup; place in a muffin pan. Repeat using all pieces. Drizzle evenly with the pecan mixture. Bake for 18 minutes or until golden brown.
Serves: 6.

Oatmeal Banana Muffins

      1/2 cup sugar
      1/2 cup butter
        2 large eggs
        3 medium bananas, mashed
      3/4 cup honey
    1 1/2 cups all-purpose flour
        1 teaspoon baking powder
        1 teaspoon baking soda
      3/4 teaspoon salt
        1 cup quick cooking oats

Instructions

Preheat the oven to 375°. In a large mixer bowl, cream together sugar and butter. Beat in eggs, bananas and honey. In another bowl, sift together flour, baking powder, soda and salt. Add to creamed mixture, beating until just blended. Stir in the oats. Line muffin pans with 24 paper baking cups and fill to 2/3 with batter. Bake for 18-20 minutes. Remove muffins from the pan and cool on a wire rack. Store in an airtight plastic container.
Serves: 12.

Peanut Butter Coffee Cake

1/2 cup packed brown sugar
1/2 cup all-purpose flour
1/4 cup creamy peanut butter
  2 tablespoons butter, melted
1/4 cup shortening
1/2 cup creamy peanut butter
  1 cup packed brown sugar
  2 large eggs
  2 cups flour
  2 teaspoons baking powder
  2 teaspoons cinnamon
1/2 teaspoon salt
1/2 teaspoon baking soda
  1 cup milk

Instructions

At Home Preparation: Prepare the topping by combining the 1/2 cup brown sugar, 1/2 cup flour, 1/4 cup peanut butter and 2 tablespoons melted butter until crumbly. Place in a container. Whisk together the 2 cups flour, baking powder, cinnamon, salt and baking soda. Place in a container.

On Board Preparation: Preheat the oven to 375°. Butter a 13x9 baking dish. Set aside. Cream 1/2 cup peanut butter and shortening in an electric mixer. Slowly add 1 cup brown sugar and the eggs one at a time and beat until light. Add the dry ingredient mixture alternately with the milk to the creamed mixture, beating after each addition. Spread the batter into the baking dish. Top with the topping mixture and bake for 30-35 minutes or until a toothpick inserted in the center comes out clean.

Serves: 12.

Potato-Crusted Texas Toast

  3 large eggs
1/2 cup buttermilk
1/2 teaspoon dried thyme
1/2 teaspoon salt
1/3 teaspoon pepper
  3 green onions, finely chopped
  1 dash hot sauce
  6 slices white bread, cut in half diagonally
  2 cups instant potato flakes
  5 tablespoons butter

Instructions

At Home Preparation: Chop the green onions and place in a container. Cut the bread slices and place in a container.

On Board Preparation: Combine first 7 ingredients; dip the bread triangles in the mixture and dredge in potato flakes. Melt 2 tablespoons butter in a large skillet; add 4 bread triangles and cook over medium-low heat until golden brown. Remove from pan; keep warm. Repeat procedure twice.
Serves: 4.

Recipe Notes
Use thick sliced bread, 1-inch thick slices.

Scrambled Eggs on Bread Rounds

      8 large eggs
    1/4 cup sour cream
      6 tablespoons butter
      8 slices white bread
      1 teaspoon grated orange peel
      1 orange

Instructions

At Home Preparation: With a 3-inch round biscuit cutter, cut circles from bread slices. Place in a container. Grate the orange rind and place in a container. Peel and section the orange and place in a container.

On Board Preparation: Beat the eggs and sour cream together. Set aside. Melt 4 tablespoons butter in a skillet. Sprinkle the grated orange rind over the melted butter. Add the bread slices and lightly brown on both sides. Remove and keep warm. Melt 2 tablespoons butter in the skillet. Add egg mixture. Cook, stirring until done. Place 2 bread rounds on each of 4 plates. Top with equal portions of eggs and garnish with orange sections.
Serves: 4.

GALLEY TIP
Adding baking soda to boiling vegetables will brighten the color but diminish the nutrients.

Southwest Breakfast

    4   6-inch tortillas, cut into 8 wedges
    1   cup seasoned black beans, drained
  2/3   cup chopped tomato
    1   tablespoon sliced green onion
    1   teaspoon chili powder
1 1/2   cups water
    2   large eggs
    2   tablespoons mild salsa
    2   tablespoons sour cream
    2   teaspoons finely chopped fresh cilantro

Instructions

At Home Preparation: Preheat the oven to 350°. Cut the tortillas into wedges. Place the tortilla wedges in a single layer on a baking sheet and bake for 6 minutes or until crisp. Cool and place in a container. Chop the tomatoes (do not peel) and place in a container. Slice the green onions and place in a container. Chop the cilantro and place in a container.

On Board Preparation: Combine the beans, tomatoes, green onions and chili powder in a medium saucepan. Cook over medium heat 5 minutes or until thoroughly heated. Remove from heat and keep warm. In a skillet, bring water to a boil. Break eggs into 2 custard cups and slip gently into the water. Cover, reduce heat and simmer 5 minutes. Remove with a slotted spoon. Place 16 tortilla wedges around the edge of each of two plates. Top each with 3/4 cup bean mixture, 1 egg, 1 tablespoons salsa, 1 tablespoon sour cream and 1 teaspoon cilantro.
Serves: 2.

Spanish Tortilla Omelet

    1   tablespoon olive oil
1 1/2   pounds potatoes, peeled and cut 1/8 inch slices
    2   cubanelle peppers, cored, seeded and thinly slice
    1   medium onion, thinly sliced
  1/4   teaspoon salt
  1/8   teaspoon pepper
    6   large eggs

Instructions

At Home Preparation: Using protective latex gloves, core and seed the peppers and thinly slice. Place in a container. Slice the onion and place in a container. Peel the potatoes, slice and place in a container.

On Board Preparation: In a large nonstick skillet over medium-low heat, heat 1-1/2 teaspoons oil. Add the potatoes, peppers and onions. Season with salt and pepper. Cover and cook for 15 minutes, turning the vegetables occasionally, until the potatoes are tender and lightly browned. Set aside to cool slightly. In a large bowl, beat the eggs, 1/4 teaspoon salt and fresh ground pepper to taste with a whisk. Add the cooled potato mixture and stir gently to thoroughly coat. Wipe the skillet clean with a paper towel. Pour the remaining oil into the skillet and heat over medium heat. Add the egg mixture, spreading the vegetables evenly. Cook for 4 to 5 minutes until the underside is browned but still slightly soft in the center. Invert a plate over the skillet and turn out onto the plate. Slide back into the skillet and cook for 2-3 more minutes until the underside is brown. The omelet will be firm but still moist. Transfer to the serving plate and let stand a minute or two before cutting into wedges. Serve hot or at room temperature.
Serves: 6.

Strawberry Omelet

4	large eggs
2 1/2	teaspoons powdered sugar
2	drops vanilla extract
2	teaspoons butter
4	tablespoons sour cream
1	cup sliced strawberries
1/2	teaspoon grated orange peel
1/8	cup powdered sugar

Instructions
At Home Preparation: Slice the strawberries and place in a container. Grate the orange peel and place in a container.

On Board Preparation: Beat the eggs with an electric mixer until light and fluffy. Stir in 2 teaspoons powdered sugar and the vanilla. In an omelet pan, melt the butter over medium-low heat. Pour the egg mixture in the pan, cover and cook about 4 minutes. (Top will be a little soft.) Combine the sour cream, 1/2 teaspoon powdered sugar and the orange peel. Spread over the omelet; remove to a plate and fold in half. Top with the sliced strawberries and sprinkle with the 1/8 cup powdered sugar to garnish. Cut in half to serve.
Serves: 2.

GALLEY TIP
White pepper has twice as strong a taste as black pepper.

Tropical Coconut French Toast

1 1/2 cups chopped fresh pineapple
1 cup peeled & chopped mango
1 cup peeled & chopped papaya
1 cup peeled & chopped kiwi fruit
3 tablespoons sugar
3 tablespoons lime juice
16 slices French bread, diagonally cut
1 1/4 cups coconut milk
2 large eggs
1/2 cup sugar
1 tablespoon vanilla extract
1/2 cup shredded coconut

Instructions
At Home Preparation: Combine the fruits with the sugar and lime juice to make a compote. Cover and refrigerate for 8 hours or overnight. Cut the French bread and place in a container.

On Board Preparation: Arrange the bread slices in a 13x9 baking dish coated with cooking spray. Combine the coconut milk, eggs, 1/2 cup sugar and 1 tablespoons vanilla, stirring with a whisk and pour evenly over the bread. Turn the bread slices to coat. Cover and refrigerate for 8 hours or overnight. Preheat the oven to 350°. Uncover the baking pan containing the bread. Turn the slices and sprinkle evenly with coconut. Let stand at room temperature for 15 minutes. Bake, uncovered for 30 minutes or until coconut is golden. Serve with the compote spooned over.
Serves: 8.

Ultimate French Toast

1 loaf French bread
3 large eggs
1 cup heavy cream
1/8 teaspoon salt
1 teaspoon cinnamon
4 tablespoons butter
1/4 cup powdered sugar
4 servings maple syrup

Instructions
At Home Preparation: Cut the French bread into 16 thick slices at least 1-1/2 to 2" thick. Place in a container.

On Board Preparation: Beat the eggs, cream, salt and cinnamon together in a bowl with a whisk. Melt the butter in a skillet at medium-high heat. Dip the bread in the egg mixture to coat both sides. Place slices in the pan in batches and cook until golden brown on both sides. Repeat until all slices are cooked. Sprinkle with confectioner's sugar and serve with warm maple syrup.
Serves: 4.

Meat Main Dishes

BBQ Pork

    2   tablespoons butter
  1/2   cup minced celery
    3   tablespoons minced onions
    1   cup ketchup
    3   tablespoons lemon juice
    2   tablespoons brown sugar
    2   tablespoons cider vinegar
    1   tablespoon Worcestershire sauce
    1   teaspoon mustard powder
  1/4   teaspoon ground pepper
    2   pounds pork ribs

Instructions

At Home Preparation: In a small saucepan, melt the butter and cook the celery and onion until soft, stirring regularly, about 5 minutes. Add the next 6 ingredients and season to taste with the pepper. Bring to a boil. Turn down the heat and simmer for 15 minutes. Remove from the heat and cool completely. Divide in two equal portions and place each in a container. Freeze one container for future use.

On Board Preparation: Prepare the grill and cook the meat to desired doneness, basting with some of the sauce during the last part of the cooking. Heat the remaining sauce for dipping.
Serves: 4.

Recipe Notes
This is also great for pork chops or pork loin.

Chorizo Carbonara

  1/2   pound chorizo sausage, crumbled
    1   cup half & half
    2   cups shredded Monterey Jack cheese with peppers
4 1/2   ounces canned green chiles, chopped
  1/2   teaspoon cumin
   16   ounces spaghetti, cooked

Instructions

At Home Preparation: Shred the cheese and place in a container. Cook the spaghetti according to package directions, drain, cool and place in a container. Brown the chorizo over medium heat, drain well on paper towels, cool, and place in a container.

On Board Preparation: Heat the half-and-half in a saucepan. Add the sausage, cheese, green chiles, cumin and spaghetti tossing lightly until the cheese melts. Remove from heat and serve. ***Serves: 8.***

Fiesta Pie with Corn Bread

- 1/3 cup milk
- 1 large egg
- 1/2 cup sour cream
- 1/4 cup butter, melted
- 3 whole chipotle peppers, seeded & chopped
- 1 package corn muffin mix
- 1 pound lean ground beef
- 1/3 cup chopped green peppers
- 1/3 cup chopped onion
- 1 whole garlic clove, minced
- 1 cup salsa
- 1 cup frozen white corn
- 1 envelope taco seasoning
- 1/2 cup shredded sharp Cheddar cheese

Instructions

At Home Preparation: Using rubber gloves, seed and chop the chiles and place in a container. Chop the green pepper and onion and place each in a container. Mince the garlic and place in a container. Shred the Cheddar and place in a container. Partially brown the ground beef, drain, cool and place in a container.

On Board Preparation: Preheat the oven to 375°. For the corn bread, mix the milk, egg, sour cream, melted butter and chiles together in a bowl. Add the corn muffin mix and stir just until incorporated. Set aside. For the pie, place the partially browned ground beef in a skillet and add the bell pepper, onion and garlic and cook until tender. Stir in the salsa, corn and seasoning mix. Pour into a 9" pie plate and spoon the cornbread batter over the top. Bake for 30-40 minutes or until a wooden toothpick inserted in the corn bread comes out clean. Sprinkle the Cheddar over the top and bake until the cheese is melted and bubbly.

Serves: 4.

GALLEY TIP

Us a potato peeler to make elegant cheese curls or chocolate curls for garnishing.

Filets in Mushroom Sauce

   2 cups sour cream
   1 cup finely chopped chives
   2 cups mayonnaise
1/4 cup red wine
3/4 cup buttermilk
1/2 pound Roquefort cheese, crumbled
   1 tablespoon Worcestershire sauce
   1 teaspoon pepper, coarsely ground
   1 tablespoon lemon juice
   1 teaspoon white vinegar
1/2 teaspoon celery seed
1/2 teaspoon garlic salt
   1 cup finely chopped onion
   2 dashes Tabasco sauce
 10 8 oz. beef filets
   1 pound mushrooms, sliced
1/2 cup chopped green onion
   3 cloves garlic
1/4 cup minced parsley
1/2 cup butter

Instructions

At Home Preparation: Chop the onion and place in a container. Wash and thickly slice the mushrooms, sprinkle with a little lemon juice, and place in a container. Mince the garlic and parsley and place each in a container.

On Board Preparation: Mix buttermilk, Roquefort, Worcestershire, pepper, lemon juice, white vinegar, celery seed, garlic salt, chopped onion and Tabasco in a large bowl to make the marinade. Place the steaks in a 13x9 pan and pour the marinade over. Cover, and refrigerate overnight or up to 72 hours. Sauté the mushrooms, onions, garlic and parsley in the butter until tender. Keep warm. Prepare the grill. Gently remove the steaks from the marinade, leaving as much on as possible. Grill the steaks to desired doneness, brushing with a little more marinade if desired. Place on the serving plates. Pour the sauce over the steaks and serve.
Serves: 10.

Filets with Madeira Sauce

    4 8 oz. beef filets
    2 tablespoons butter
    2 tablespoons minced shallots
1 1/2 cups brown sauce
    2 tablespoons lemon juice
 1/4 cup Madeira

Instructions

At Home Preparation: Melt the butter in a saucepan and sauté the shallots for about 5 minutes over low heat, being careful not to let the butter brown. Add the brown sauce, and lemon juice. When the liquid comes to a boil, add the wine and simmer gently for 5 minutes. Cool completely and place in a container.

On Board Preparation: Place the Madeira sauce in a saucepan and slowly reheat over low heat. Prepare the grill and grill the filets to desired doneness. Serve with the warmed Madeira sauce.
Serves: 4.

Recipe Notes
Look for brown sauce in the gourmet section of the grocery store.

Filets with Peppercorn Sauce

2	small shallots
1	ounce green pepper corns in brine
1 1/2	ounces butter
7	ounces beef stock
3	ounces heavy cream
1/2	teaspoon salt
1/4	teaspoon pepper
2	8 oz. beef filets
2	teaspoons sunflower oil
2	tablespoons brandy

Instructions

At Home Preparation: Finely chop the shallots and place in a container. Drain the peppercorns well and crush with a fork. Melt the butter in a saucepan and cook the shallots over low heat for 2-3 minutes; do not brown. Add the peppercorns and cook 2 minutes. Add the stock and bring to a boil for 5-10 minutes, or until reduced by one-half. Cool completely and place in a container.

On Board Preparation: Put the stock mixture in a saucepan and slowly heat to just boiling. Add the cream and simmer gently for 5 minutes. Salt and pepper to taste and set aside but keep warm. Heat a skillet over medium heat. Season the filets with salt and pepper. Add the remaining butter and the oil to the pan and heat until the butter is foaming. Add the steaks and cook 2-4 minutes on each side or to desired doneness. Remove and keep warm. Pour off the fat from the pan and return to the heat. Add the steaks, brandy and the sauce and cook for 30 seconds on each side. To serve, pour the sauce over the steaks.
Serves: 2.

Flank Steak with Oriental Marinade

  1 1/2 cups unsweetened orange juice
    1/3 cup dry sherry
    1/3 cup low sodium soy sauce
      3 tablespoons dark brown sugar
      2 tablespoons peeled & chopped ginger root
      1 tablespoon grated orange peel
      2 cloves minced garlic
  1 1/2 teaspoons crushed coriander seed
  1 1/2 teaspoons ground pepper
    1/4 teaspoon salt
      2 pounds flank steak

Instructions
At Home Preparation: To make the marinade combine all ingredients except the flank steak and place in a container.

On Board Preparation: Pour the marinade over the flank steak and refrigerate 8 hours. Prepare grill and grill until desired doneness brushing with the marinade during cooking if desired.
Serves: 4.

Grilled Filet with Mushroom Sauce

      4 pounds beef filets
    1/4 cup olive oil
    1/4 teaspoon salt
    1/8 teaspoon freshly ground black pepper
      2 tablespoons unsalted butter
      1 tablespoon olive oil
      1 clove garlic, finely chopped
    1/2 teaspoon dried marjoram
      1 pound fresh shiitake mushrooms
      1 tablespoon lemon juice
    1/2 teaspoon salt
    1/4 teaspoon freshly ground black pepper
    1/2 cup beef broth
      1 cup dry red wine

Instructions
At Home Preparation: Trim the excess fat from the filet, roll it securing with string at 1-1/2 -inch intervals and place in a container. Wash the mushrooms, remove the stems and slice. Sprinkle lightly with lemon juice and place in a container.

On Board Preparation: Prepare the grill. Rub the filet with the olive oil and season with salt and pepper to taste. Grill, turning frequently for about 30 minutes or until desired doneness. While the filet is grilling, prepare the mushroom sauce by heating the butter and oil in a large skillet over medium-high heat. When the butter is foaming, add the garlic and herbs. Stir until the garlic is fragrant, about 1 minute. Add the mushrooms and toss to coat. Reduce the heat to medium and cook, covered, stirring occasionally, until the mushrooms have softened and are beginning to brown, about 5 minutes. Season with salt and pepper, and add the broth and wine. Bring to a boil and cook, stirring occasionally, about 5 minutes, or until the liquid is reduced by half and the sauce is slightly thickened. Serve with the filet, sliced into 8 servings. *Serves: 8.*

Recipe Notes
This is best done with one large filet.

Grilled Flank Steak with Bourbon Sauce

1 1/2	pounds flank steak, trimmed
1	tablespoon chopped fresh rosemary
1/2	teaspoon freshly ground black pepper
1/4	teaspoon kosher salt
	cooking spray
1	teaspoon olive oil
2	tablespoons finely chopped shallots
2	tablespoons tomato paste
1/4	cup beef broth
2	teaspoons brown sugar
1	tablespoon bourbon
2	teaspoons balsamic vinegar
1/8	teaspoon salt

Instructions
At Home Preparation: Heat the oil in a small saucepan over medium-high heat. Add the shallots and sauté 1 minute. Add the tomato paste and cook 1 minute. Stir in broth and sugar. Bring to a boil and cook 3 minutes or until thickened. Cool completely and place in a container.

On Board Preparation: Coat grill rack with cooking spray. Prepare grill. Sprinkle the steak with rosemary, pepper, and kosher salt. Grill 7 minutes over medium-high heat on each side or until desired degree of doneness. Remove from grill and let stand for 10 minutes, covered to keep warm. Place the pre-prepared sauce mixture in a pan and heat to just below boiling. Remove from heat; stir in bourbon, vinegar, and 1/8 teaspoon salt. Cut the steak diagonally across the grain into thin slices. Serve with the sauce.
Serves: 4.

Grilled Flank Steak with Cinnamon-Soy Marinade

    2 tablespoons soy sauce
    2 tablespoons dry sherry
    2 tablespoons sugar
  1/2 teaspoon cinnamon
1 1/2 pounds flank steak

Instructions

At Home Preparation: Combine all ingredients except flank steak, stirring until sugar dissolves. Place in a container.

On Board Preparation: Pour the marinade over the flank steak and refrigerate 8 hours. Prepare the grill and grill the flank steak to desired doneness. Slice and serve. *Serves: 4.*

Grilled Lamb

    5 pounds leg of lamb
       cooking spray
       For Marinade:
  1/2 cup olive oil
  1/3 cup orange juice
    1 teaspoon grated orange peel
    2 large garlic cloves, minced
1 1/2 teaspoons minced fresh thyme
    1 large bay leaf, crumbled
    1 tablespoon minced fresh parsley
  1/2 teaspoon freshly ground black pepper
  1/2 teaspoon salt
       For Sauce:
    3 tablespoons water
  1/3 cup sugar
  1/4 teaspoon unflavored gelatin
    1 teaspoon hot water
  1/4 cup shredded fresh mint leaf
    2 large jalapeno peppers, seeded
  1/4 teaspoon crushed red pepper flakes
    2 drops vanilla extract

Instructions

At Home Preparation: Trim any excess fat from the lamb and divide into two pieces, separating the thicker piece from the thin one. Place in a container. Grate the orange peel and place in a container. Mince the garlic, thyme and parsley and place each in a container. Shred the mint leaves and place in a container. Wearing rubber gloves, seed and mince the jalapeno peppers and place in a container.

On Board Preparation: Combine the marinade ingredients. Place the lamb in the marinade and turn to coat. Cover and refrigerate overnight. Remove the lamb from the refrigerator and allow to come to room temperature. In a saucepan, combine 3 tablespoons water and sugar. Stir over low heat until sugar dissolves. Soften the gelatin in 1 teaspoon water and add to the sugar mixture, increasing the heat to bring to a boil. Combine the mint, jalapenos and red pepper; add to boiling syrup. Let stand until cool, stirring occasionally. Add the vanilla and refrigerate 15 minutes or until chilled. Prepare the grill. Coat the grill with cooking spray. Brush each piece of lamb with the marinade. Sear on the hot grill for 1 minutes each side. Move the thinner piece away from the direct heat to prevent charring. Grill, basting frequently with marinade until the internal temperature reaches 140 degrees for medium rare, about 20-25 minutes, or to desired doneness. Slice on diagonal and serve with sauce.
Serves: 6.

GALLEY TIP
Muffins will lift out of the pan easily if you place a wet towel underneath for a minute before removing.

Grilled Lamb with Mustard Vinaigrette

          7 pounds boned leg of lamb
          3 cloves garlic, minced
          2 teaspoons crumbled rosemary
          4 tablespoons Dijon mustard
        1/4 teaspoon freshly ground black pepper
             For Vinaigrette:
          3 tablespoons fresh lemon juice
          2 tablespoons dry sherry
          2 tablespoons soy sauce
          4 tablespoons olive oil
          2 tablespoons Dijon mustard
          2 tablespoons finely chopped shallots
          1 clove garlic, finely chopped
        1/4 cup fresh lemon juice
        1/2 teaspoon salt
        3/4 cup olive oil
          3 tablespoons finely chopped fresh mint leaves

Instructions

At Home Preparation: Trim excess fat from the lamb, bone and butterfly. Place in a container. Crush the garlic cloves and place in a container. Combine all the vinaigrette ingredients except the mint in a bowl with a whisk. Add the mint to taste, stir and place in a container.

On Board Preparation: Rub the lamb with garlic, rosemary, mustard and pepper. Place in a heavy zip top plastic bag with the remaining ingredients. Expel the air and close tightly. Distribute the marinade evenly and marinate for 1-3 hours at room temperature, turning occasionally to distribute the marinade. (Can also be refrigerated for up to 2 days and allow to come to room temperature before cooking.) Prepare the grill. Grill the lamb about 15 minutes per side for medium-rare or longer to desired doneness. Remove to a carving board and let rest for 10 minutes before carving. Serve the carved lamb with the Vinaigrette.
Serves: 4.

Grilled Pork Tenderloin

          2 pounds pork tenderloin
        1/2 cup red wine
        1/2 cup vegetable oil
          3 cloves garlic, split

1   teaspoon dried thyme
2   tablespoons finely chopped fresh parsley
1/4   cup chopped onion
1/4   teaspoon freshly ground black pepper

Instructions
At Home Preparation: Mix together all ingredients except the pork tenderloin. Place in a container.

On Board Preparation: Place the pork tenderloin in the marinade and marinate for 4 hours, or overnight. Prepare the grill and cook the pork tenderloin over medium-high heat until it reaches desired doneness, basting with the marinade occasionally throughout cooking.
Serves: 4.

Recipe Notes
Substitute rosemary or marjoram for the thyme or combine them for a different flavor.

GALLEY TIP
Slicing or chopping onions and potatoes in varying sizes will result in a subtle variety of flavors and add an additional dimension to your dish.

Grilled Pork Tenderloin with Rosemary Apple Marinade

1/4 cup frozen apple juice concentrate, thawed
2 tablespoons Dijon mustard
1 1/2 teaspoons Dijon mustard
2 tablespoons olive oil
2 tablespoons chopped fresh rosemary
4 cloves garlic, minced
1 teaspoon crushed peppercorns
1 1/2 pounds pork tenderloin, trimmed
1 tablespoon minced shallot
3 tablespoons port
2 tablespoons balsamic vinegar
1/2 teaspoon salt
1/4 teaspoon pepper
10 sprigs rosemary

Instructions

At Home Preparation: In a small bowl, whisk together apple juice concentrate, 2 tablespoons Dijon mustard, 1 tablespoon olive oil, the rosemary, garlic and crushed peppercorns. Place in a container. In a small bowl, combine the shallots, port, vinegar, salt, pepper and the remaining 1 1/2 teaspoons mustard and 1 tablespoon olive oil; whisk until blended. Place in a container.

On Board Preparation: Measure 3 tablespoons of the apple juice mixture and reserve for basting. Place the tenderloins in a shallow dish and pour the remaining marinade over, turning to coat. Cover and marinate in the refrigerator for at least 20 minutes, or up to 2 hours, turning several times. Prepare the grill. Grill the tenderloins, covered, turning several times and basting browned sides with the reserved marinade, until the outside is browned and the inside has just a trace of pink, 12-16 minutes. (An instant read thermometer inserted in the center should register 150°F.) Transfer the tenderloins to a clean cutting board and let rest for about 5 minutes. Carve into 1/2 inch slices. Pour any juices that have accumulated on the cutting board into the port vinaigrette. Drizzle over the slices and garnish with the rosemary sprigs.
Serves: 6.

Marinated Beef Tenderloin

2	medium carrots, sliced
2	medium onions, sliced
10	whole peppercorns
1	whole clove
2	large bay leaves
1/2	teaspoon parsley
1/4	teaspoon thyme
4	whole garlic cloves
1/2	cup red wine vinegar
2	tablespoons olive oil
2	medium shallots, chopped
2	tablespoons lemon juice
2	cups sherry
1	tablespoon Worcestershire sauce
5	pounds beef tenderloin
1	stick butter

Instructions

At Home Preparation: Peel and slice the carrots and place in a container. Slice the onion in thin slices and place in a container. Chop the shallots and place in a container.

On Board Preparation: In a large Dutch oven, place all ingredients except the beef tenderloin and butter. Mix thoroughly. Puncture the beef tenderloin with a fork and place in the marinade. Refrigerate at least 24 hours. Preheat the oven to 450°. Drain the meat, discarding the marinade. Dot the meat with butter. Roast for 30 to 45 minutes to desired doneness.
Serves: 8.

GALLEY TIP
Slice or cube meat when half frozen for thinner and neater pieces.

Marinated Flank Steak with Horseradish Riata

- 1/2 teaspoon finely grated fresh ginger
- 1/4 teaspoon salt
- 1/4 teaspoon sugar
- 8 ounces plain yogurt
- 1 1/2 teaspoons finely grated horseradish
- 1 tablespoon mustard seed
- 2 teaspoons Szechwan peppercorns
- 1 1/2 teaspoons whole allspice
- 1 1/2 teaspoons coriander seed
- 1 teaspoon cumin seed
- 1/2 teaspoon kosher salt
- 1 pound flank steak, trimmed
- 8 sprigs parsley

Instructions

At Home Preparation: To make the riata, combine the ginger, salt sugar, yogurt and horseradish and place in a container. Combine the mustard seeds, peppercorns, allspice, coriander and cumin in a spice grinder and pulse until coarsely ground. Stir in the kosher salt and place in a container.

On Board Preparation: Rub the spice mixture over both sides of the steak, cover and chill 4 hours. Coat the grill rack with cooking spray. Prepare the grill. Grill the steak over medium-high heat for 3 minutes on each side or until desired degree of doneness. Place on a platter or cutting board and let stand for 5 minutes. Cut diagonally across the grain into thin slices. Serve with riata.
Serves: 4.

Marinated Grilled Flank Steak

- 1/4 cup soy sauce
- 3 tablespoons lemon juice
- 2 tablespoons honey
- 3 tablespoons dry sherry
- 1 clove garlic, minced fine
- 1 teaspoon minced fresh ginger
- 2 tablespoons vegetable oil
- 2 teaspoons sesame seeds, toasted
- 2 medium green onions, chopped, both white and green parts
- 1 1/2 pounds flank steak

Instructions

At Home Preparation: Mince the garlic and ginger and place each in a container. Toast the sesame seeds, cool and place in a container. Chop the green onion and place in a container.

On Board Preparation: Prepare the grill. Mix the soy sauce, lemon juice, honey, sherry, garlic, ginger, oil, sesame seed and green onion together and pour over the flank steak. Let marinate for at least 4 hours, refrigerated, turning occasionally. Grill for 7-10 minutes and slice across the grain to serve.
Serves: 4.

Marinated Pork Tenderloin

- 1/2 cup peanut oil
- 1/4 cup hoisin sauce
- 1/4 cup soy sauce
- 1/2 cup rice wine vinegar
- 1/4 cup dry sherry
- 1/2 teaspoon hot chili oil
- 1 tablespoon dark sesame oil
- 4 whole green onions, finely chopped
- 4 cloves garlic, minced
- 2 tablespoons minced fresh ginger
- 3 pounds pork tenderloin

Instructions

At Home Preparation: Chop the green onions, including the green tops and place in a container. Mince the garlic and place in a container. Peel the ginger root (do not mince until ready to use) and place in a container.

On Board Preparation: Mince the ginger root and combine with the rest of the ingredients, except the pork. Pour over the pork tenderloins in a flat dish, cover and marinate at room temperature 4 hours or overnight in the refrigerator. Prepare the grill and coat the rack with cooking spray. Grill the tenderloins over medium-high heat or coals about 10 minutes per side, basting frequently with the marinade.
Serves: 4.

Pork Tenderloin with Bourbon Sauce

1/4 cup bourbon
1/4 cup soy sauce
1/4 cup firmly packed brown sugar
3 cloves garlic, minced
1/4 cup Dijon mustard
1 teaspoon minced fresh ginger
1 teaspoon Worcestershire sauce
1/4 cup vegetable oil
2 pounds pork loin

Instructions

At Home Preparation: Mince the garlic and ginger and place each in a container. Combine all ingredients except the pork with a whisk and place in a container.

On Board Preparation: Place the tenderloin in the marinade and refrigerate overnight. Prepare the grill. Place the pork tenderloins on the grill and cook until the internal temperature reaches 165°, basting frequently with the marinade while cooking, about 15-25 minutes. Cut into 1/2-inch slices.
Serves: 6.

Saltimbocca

1/8 teaspoon pepper
1 bunch fresh sage
3 1/2 ounces prosciutto
4 tablespoons olive oil
8 ounces dry white wine
1/4 teaspoon salt
1/8 teaspoon pepper
20 ounces veal, sliced into 4 slices

Instructions

At Home Preparation: Put the veal between pieces of plastic wrap and pound thin. Cut each piece into small squares, making about 30 pieces in all. Cut the prosciutto into small pieces. Grind pepper to taste over the veal pieces then place 1 or 2 small sage leaves on top of each. Divide the prosciutto evenly over the pieces of veal and roll up each piece and secure with a toothpick. Place in a container.

On Board Preparation: Heat the oil in a large skillet over medium-high heat. Cook the veal in batches for no longer than 2-3 minutes, until browned on all sides. Remove and keep warm. Add the wine to the skillet and boil until reduced, stirring to deglaze the pan. Season with salt to taste. Remove the toothpicks from the veal and divide among 4 plates. Top with the sauce and garnish with sprigs of fresh sage.
Serves: 4.

Sausage and Pasta in Cream Sauce

1/4	cup butter
1 1/2	pounds Italian sausage
2	cups heavy cream
1	cup dry white wine
1	tablespoon minced fresh parsley
1/2	teaspoon nutmeg
1/2	cup grated Parmesan cheese
12	ounces bow tie pasta
1/2	cup grated Parmesan cheese
1	tablespoon minced fresh parsley

Instructions

At Home Preparation: Cook the pasta according to package directions until al dente, drain, cool completely and place in a container. Grate the Parmesan and place in a container. Mince the parsley and place in a container. Remove the sausage from it's casing. In a skillet, brown the sausage in the butter. Drain, cool completely and place in a container.

On Board Preparation: Place the browned sausage in a skillet, reheat slightly and stir in cream, wine, 1 tablespoon parsley, nutmeg and 1/2 cup Parmesan. Simmer for 3-4 minutes over medium-low heat stirring occasionally and being careful not to burn. Reheat the pasta by placing in the microwave with about a tablespoon of water and heating on high for about 1 minute or until heated through. Place the pasta in a heated serving dish and stir in 2 tablespoons of the sausage mixture and the remaining 1/2 cup Parmesan. Pour the remaining sausage mixture over the pasta and sprinkle with 1 tablespoons minced parsley.
Serves: 6.

GALLEY TIP
If you substitute dried herbs for fresh, use one-third of the amount called for in your recipe.

Veal Scallops with Hazelnut Sauce

    1 1/2 pounds veal scallops
      1/4 cup flour, seasoned with salt and pepper
        3 tablespoons olive oil
        4 tablespoons unsalted butter
      1/3 cup white wine
        1 clove garlic, crushed
        1 sprig fresh sage
      1/2 cup finely chopped hazelnuts

Instructions
At Home Preparation: Pound the veal thin with a meat mallet and place in a container. Chop the hazelnuts and place in a container.

On Board Preparation: Dredge the veal through the seasoned flour, patting in the flour then shaking off excess. In a heavy skillet, heat the oil and 1 tablespoon butter. Sauté the veal in batches over medium high heat until golden brown about 2 minutes on each side. Transfer to a serving dish and keep warm. Deglaze the pan with the white wine, scraping up the browned bits. Add the crushed garlic clove, sage, hazelnuts and remaining butter. Stir frequently and cook until nuts are a light golden brown. Discard the garlic and sage. Pour over the veal and serve.
Serves: 6.

Vermicelli with Sweet-Hot Beef

        7 ounces vermicelli, cooked
        1 pound lean ground beef
      1/4 cup raisins
    1 1/4 teaspoons pepper
    1 1/4 teaspoons ground cumin
      1/2 teaspoon salt
      1/4 teaspoon ground cinnamon
      1/8 teaspoon ground red pepper
      1/2 cup water
        8 ounces tomato sauce
        2 teaspoons lemon juice
      1/4 cup chopped fresh parsley

Instructions
At Home Preparation: Cook vermicelli according to package directions. Place in a container. Cook the ground chuck in a large skillet until browned. Drain and pat dry with a paper towel. Cool; place in a container.

On Board Preparation: Place the browned meat in a skillet and add the raisins and next 7 ingredients, stirring well. Cook over low heat 15 minutes, stirring occasionally. Stir in lemon juice. Place a few drops of water on the vermicelli and reheat in the microwave about 60 seconds or until hot. Serve the meat over the vermicelli.
Serves: 4.

Poultry Main Dishes

Beer and Lemon Grilled Chicken

       1   cup beer, lager style
     1/4   cup lemon juice
       3   tablespoons low sodium soy sauce
   1 1/2   tablespoons olive oil
       2   teaspoons chopped fresh oregano
       1   teaspoon chopped fresh thyme
       1   teaspoon ground black pepper
       2   teaspoons honey
     1/4   teaspoon Worcestershire sauce
       3   cloves garlic, minced
           cooking spray
       4   boneless skinless chicken breast halves

Instructions
At Home Preparation: Combine the first 10 ingredients. Place in a container.

On Board Preparation: Combine the marinade and the chicken in a large zip-top plastic bag, seal and refrigerate for 3 hours, turning the bag occasionally. Remove the chicken and discard the marinade.   Coat the grill rack with cooking spray. Prepare the grill. Place the chicken on the grill rack and grill 5 minutes on each side or until done.
Serves: 4.

Recipe Notes
Make extra and chill the leftovers then slice and place on top of salad greens, as a base for chicken salad, or for sandwiches.

Boston Beach Jerk Chicken

   3 1/2   pounds frying chicken
           cooking spray
       4   cups sliced green onions
     1/4   cup fresh thyme
       2   tablespoons vegetable oil
       1   tablespoon ground pepper
       1   tablespoon ground coriander seed
       3   tablespoons grated ginger root
       2   tablespoons lime juice
       2   teaspoons freshly ground allspice
       1   teaspoon freshly ground nutmeg
       1   teaspoon cinnamon
       5   cloves garlic, halved
       3   whole bay leaves
       2   whole habanera peppers, seeded

Instructions

At Home Preparation: Peel the ginger root. Cut the peppers in half and seed. Peel the garlic cloves and cut in half. To make the Wet Jerk Rub, place all ingredients except the chicken and cooking spray in a food processor and process until a thick paste forms, scraping the sides of the bowl once. Place in a container. Remove the giblets from the chicken, rinse under cold water and pat dry. Split in half lengthwise. Remove skin and excess fat. Place in a container.

On Board Preparation: Place the chicken in a shallow dish. Put on gloves and spread 1-1/4 cups of the Wet Jerk Rub over both sides of chicken. Cover and marinate in refrigerator 1-4 hours. Coat the grill rack with cooking spray. Place chicken on the grill over medium-high heat. For a more authentic taste, add oak, pecan or hickory wood to the charcoal. (For gas grills, follow the manufacturer instructions for adding wood flavoring.) Place the chicken on the rack and cook 45 minutes or until done, turning occasionally and basting with remaining Wet Jerk Rub.

Serves: 6.

Recipe Notes

You can use Scotch bonnets or Serrano chilies in place of the habanera peppers if you prefer. Always wear gloves when working with any hot peppers.

Brandied Chicken

4	whole chicken breasts, halved
1/4	cup flour
2	tablespoons olive oil
6	ounces frozen orange juice, thawed
3/4	teaspoon garlic powder
1	teaspoon onion powder
1	teaspoon ground ginger
1/4	cup brandy
4	cups cooked rice

Instructions

At Home Preparation: Cook the rice, cool and place in a container. Combine the thawed orange juice and the spices, mixing thoroughly and place in a container.

On Board Preparation: Lightly dust the chicken in the flour and brown slowly in a skillet with the olive oil. Pour the orange juice mixture over the chicken in the skillet; add the brandy and simmer slowly until the chicken is tender. (Add a little water if needed while cooking.) Reheat the rice by placing a few drops of water on it and cook, covered in the microwave for about 60-90 seconds or until heated through. Serve the chicken over the rice with a little of the sauce poured over.

Serves: 4.

Cashew Chicken

2 tablespoons olive oil
1 cup thinly sliced carrots
2 cups chopped broccoli
1 pound boneless & skinless chicken breast, sliced thin
1 cup water
2 tablespoons soy sauce
1 tablespoon sesame oil
1 tablespoon minced garlic
1/4 cup chopped cilantro (optional)
1 cup cashews, roasted
2 tablespoons sesame seeds, toasted
1 cup cooked rice

Instructions

At Home Preparation: Wash, peel and slice the carrots. Place in a container. Wash and chop the broccoli and place in a container. Wash and slice the chicken and place in a container. Combine the water, soy sauce and sesame oil and place in a container. Chop the cilantro and toast the sesame seeds and place each in a container. Cook the rice, cool and place in a container.

On Board Preparation: In a large skillet or saucepan, heat the olive oil. Add the carrots and broccoli and cook over medium heat for 2 minutes. Add the chicken and stir well. Pour the soy sauce mixture over the chicken and vegetables. Add the garlic and stir well. Cover and heat over medium heat, stirring occasionally. Reheat the rice by adding a few drops of water and heating in the microwave for about a minute. If desired, add the cilantro to the chicken and vegetables in the last minute of cooking. Remove from the heat and add the cashews. Serve over rice.
Serves: 2.

Champagne Chicken and Shrimp

2 pounds shrimp
2 green onions
3 tablespoons lemon juice
1 1/2 teaspoons salt
3 tablespoons butter
3 whole chicken breasts, boneless & skinless
3/4 pound mushrooms, sliced
1 1/3 cups water
1/3 cup flour
1 chicken bouillon cube
1 1/2 cups half & half
3/4 cup Champagne

Instructions

At Home Preparation: Shell and devein the shrimp and place in a container. Cut the green onions into 1-inch pieces and place in a container. Cut the chicken breasts in half and place in a container. Slice the mushrooms (if not purchased already sliced), sprinkle with a little lemon juice and place in a container.

On Board Preparation: In a bowl, combine the shrimp, green onions, lemon juice and salt and set aside. In a skillet over medium to high heat, cook the chicken breasts in butter until well browned and fork tender, about 10 minutes. Remove to a heated platter and keep warm. In the same skillet, cook mushrooms until tender, about 5 minutes. With a slotted spoon, remove to a small bowl and keep warm. Add the shrimp mixture to the skillet over high heat and cook just until they turn pink, about 5 minutes. With a slotted spoon, remove to the heated platter with the chicken. In a small bowl, combine water, flour and bouillon. Stir into the hot liquid in the skillet until blended. Gradually add the half and half and champagne. Cook, stirring constantly, until it boils and thickens. Stir in the mushrooms and heat thoroughly. Pour over the chicken and shrimp to serve.
Serves: 6.

Chicken and Asparagus Casserole

6	ounces egg noodles
1 1/3	tablespoons vegetable oil
1	medium onion, chopped
1	chicken breast half, boneless & skinless
1	medium red bell pepper, chopped
2	stalks celery, chopped
1	cup chicken broth
1 1/2	cups sour cream
1/2	teaspoon oregano
1	pound fresh asparagus
1/2	cup grated Parmesan cheese

Instructions

At Home Preparation: Chop the onion, bell pepper and celery and place each in a container. Clean and trim the asparagus. Cook until just tender, about 1 to 2 minutes. Run under cold water, drain and pat dry. Cool and place in a container. Cut the chicken breast into bite size pieces and place in a container. Cook the egg noodles according to package direction, until al dente, rinse and cool completely. Place in a container.

On Board Preparation: Preheat the oven to 350°. In a large skillet over medium heat, cook the chopped onion in the vegetable oil until just tender. Add the chicken breast and heat until cooked through. Add the red bell pepper, celery and chicken broth. Bring to a boil, reduce heat and simmer for 5 minutes. Stir in the sour cream and oregano. Spread half the chicken mixture in a 13x9 baking dish. Arrange the asparagus and noodles over the chicken mixture. Top with the remaining chicken mixture and sprinkle with the grated Parmesan. Bake in the oven for 30 minutes, until cheese is lightly browned.   *Serves: 4.*

Chicken Blue

2 tablespoons butter
4 boneless chicken breast halves
1 medium white onion
1/3 cup chopped green pepper
3 ounces dry vermouth
1 cup sour cream
1/4 cup crumbled blue cheese
1 tablespoon lemon juice
1/2 teaspoon salt
1 dash garlic salt
1 dash pepper
1 dash tarragon
1 dash paprika
4 tablespoons chopped fresh parsley

Instructions

At Home Preparation: Cut each of the chicken breasts in half. Melt the butter in a skillet over medium-high heat. Sauté the chicken, turning several times, until lightly browned. Retain the pan juices. Cool and place the chicken in a container. Peel and quarter the onion. Chop the parsley and place in a container. In a blender, place the pan juices, onion and remaining ingredients except the parsley. Combine well and place in a container.

On Board Preparation: Preheat the oven to 350°. Place the chicken in a 2-quart casserole. Pour the pan juices mixture over the chicken and bake, covered, for 1 hour. Garnish with the parsley before serving.
Serves: 4.

Chicken Breast with Boursin Cheese

4 whole chicken breasts, boned
8 ounces boursin cheese
2 large eggs, lightly beaten
1 cup Panko bread crumbs
4 tablespoons butter
1 large lemon, sliced

Instructions

At Home Preparation: Halve the chicken breast and pound flat between pieces of waxed paper. Spread each with 1 ounce of boursin cheese. Roll tightly and secure with a toothpick. Place in a container. Slice the lemon and place in a container.

On Board Preparation: Dip the chicken in the beaten egg and roll in the Panko. Refrigerate 1 hour. Melt butter in a skillet. Sauté the chicken until lightly browned and cooked through, about 3-4 minutes per side. Garnish with lemon slices.
Serves: 4.

Chicken Breasts with Feta Cheese Sauce

6	boneless chicken breast halves
1	tablespoon butter
1	tablespoon all-purpose flour
1	teaspoon all-purpose flour
12	ounces evaporated skim milk
1	tablespoon dried chives
3/4	cup crumbled feta cheese
	cooking spray

Instructions

Coat a large nonstick skillet with cooking spray; place over medium heat until hot. Add chicken, and cook 7 minutes on each side or until done: set aside, and keep warm. Chicken pieces can also be grilled. Melt butter in a small saucepan over medium heat; add flour. Cook 1 minute, stirring constantly with a wire whisk. Gradually add milk, stirring constantly. Stir in chives. Reduce heat to medium-low and cook 3 minutes or until thickened and bubbly, stirring constantly. Add cheese, and stir until cheese melts. Spoon over chicken.
Serves: 6.

GALLEY TIP

Moisture is an onion's enemy. Store onions away from potatoes as they give off moisture and will spoil the onion faster.

Chicken Stuffed with Crabmeat

    6   whole boneless & skinless chicken breasts
  1/2   cup chopped onion
  1/2   cup chopped celery
    3   tablespoons butter
 7 1/2 ounces crabmeat, drained
  1/2   cup herbed seasoned stuffing mix
    2   tablespoons flour
  1/2   teaspoon paprika
    2   tablespoons butter
10 3/4 ounces canned cream of mushroom soup
  1/4   cup milk
    2   tablespoons dry white wine
  1/2   cup shredded Swiss cheese

Instructions

At Home Preparation: Pound the chicken breasts until flattened and place in a container. Chop the onion and celery and place in a container. Drain the crab meat, flake and place in a container. Shred the Swiss cheese and place in a container.

On Board Preparation: Preheat the oven to 325°. Sprinkle the chicken breasts with salt and pepper. In a skillet, sauté the onion and celery in 3 tablespoons butter just until tender. Remove from heat and add the wine, crab and stuffing mix, tossing to mix. Divide among the six breasts equally. Roll the chicken breasts and secure with toothpicks. Combine the flour and paprika and dust over the chicken. Place the rolled breasts into a greased baking dish and drizzle with 2 tablespoons melted butter. Cover and bake for 1 hour. Uncover and bake an additional 15 minutes. In a saucepan blend the soup and milk cooking until thick, stirring constantly. Add the remaining wine and Swiss cheese and stir until all the cheese melts. Pour some of the sauce over to serve, and pass the remaining sauce.
Serves: 6.

Chicken with Black Bean Sauce

  1/4   cup fresh lime juice
  1/2   cup vegetable oil
  1/2   teaspoon cayenne pepper
    1   clove garlic, crushed
    4   whole chicken breasts, boneless & skinless
    2   tablespoons chopped red onions
    1   medium red bell pepper, diced
    8   sprigs cilantro
        For Sauce:
    2   tablespoons balsamic vinegar
  1/2   cup fresh orange juice
    1   clove garlic, crushed

    1 cup cooked black beans
  1/2 teaspoon salt
  1/4 teaspoon pepper

Instructions

At Home Preparation: Squeeze the lime juice and place in a container. Crush the garlic and place in a container. Cut each chicken breast in half and place in a container. Chop the red onion and dice the bell pepper, parboil, cool, and place in a container. Squeeze the orange juice and place in a container. Crush the garlic clove and place in a container. Cook the black beans, drain, rinse, cool and place in a container.

On Board Preparation: At least 8 hours before cooking, place the lime juice, oil, cayenne 1 clove crushed garlic in a plastic container. Add the chicken breasts and marinate overnight. Prepare the grill. Cook the chicken on the grill until cooked through and juices run clear. Place all sauce ingredients in a blender and process until smooth. Warm in a saucepan or microwave. To serve, place the black bean sauce on the plates. Sprinkle the tops of the chicken breasts with the bell pepper and onion mixture. Place on top of the sauce and garnish with cilantro.
Serves: 4.

Garlic-Lemon Barbecue Chicken

    1 cup olive oil
  3/4 cup lemon juice
    3 teaspoons salt
    1 teaspoon dried oregano
    2 cloves garlic
  1/4 teaspoon pepper
    4 pounds chicken pieces

Instructions

At Home Preparation: In the blender, combine the oil, lemon juice, salt, oregano, garlic and pepper. Blend until smooth and place in a container.

On Board Preparation: Place the chicken pieces in a dish and pour the marinade over. Marinate overnight in the refrigerator. Prepare the grill. Drain the chicken, reserving the marinade. Grill the chicken over medium heat or coals, brushing occasionally with the marinade, until done.
Serves: 6.

Ginger Chicken on the Grill

  5 pounds boneless chicken pieces
  3 cloves garlic, chopped
  2 teaspoons salt
  4 tablespoons fresh lime juice
  2 tablespoons Worcestershire sauce
1/4 cup rum
  1 tablespoon brown sugar
  2 tablespoons finely chopped fresh ginger
1/4 cup vegetable oil

Instructions

At Home Preparation: Wash and dry the chicken pieces and place in a container. Chop the garlic and place in a container. Squeeze the lime juice and place in a container. Chop the ginger root and place in a container.

On Board Preparation: Rub the chicken with garlic and salt and place in a heavy zip top plastic bag. Combine the remaining ingredients and add to the chicken. Marinate for at least one hour or up to 2 days in the refrigerator. Prepare the grill. Grill the chicken turning often and brushing with the marinade until done, about 20-30 minutes.
Serves: 6.

Grand Marnier Chicken

  4 large chicken breasts
1/2 cup flour
  1 teaspoon salt
1/4 cup peanut oil
  6 tablespoons brown sugar
  2 tablespoons butter
  2 large oranges
  4 large peaches
1/2 cup Grand Marnier
3/4 cup almonds, toasted

Instructions

At Home Preparation: Peel and section the oranges and place in a container. Peel and slice the peaches and place in a container. Lightly toast the almonds, cool and place in a container.

On Board Preparation: Lightly salt and flour the chicken breasts. Heat the peanut oil in a skillet and cook the chicken over medium heat until browned and almost cooked through. Remove and set aside. Pour off all of the oil; add the brown sugar and butter, simmering and stirring until smooth. Add the chicken and the orange sections. Place the peaches on top of the chicken pieces. Add the Grand

Marnier and simmer while basting for 5 minutes. Sprinkle with the toasted almonds before serving.
Serves: 4.

Grilled Chicken with Jalapenos

4   whole chicken breasts, skinned & boned
4   pieces bacon
4   ounces cream cheese with pineapple
16 small sweet jalapeno peppers

Instructions
At Home Preparation: Pound the chicken breast to flatten slightly and place in a container. If desired, slit open the jalapenos and remove the seeds and place in a container. (Removing the seeds will lessen the heat of the peppers.)

On Board Preparation: Prepare the grill. Spread each piece of chicken with some cream cheese. Top with 3-4 of the peppers. Roll up and wrap with a bacon slice. Secure with a toothpick and grill until done.
Serves: 4.

Grilled Duck Breast with Apricot Marinade

1/2   cup apricot preserve
2 1/2 tablespoons sherry vinegar
1/4   teaspoon salt
1/4   teaspoon ground cumin
1/8   teaspoon ground red pepper
4   servings duck breast, skinned

Instructions
At Home Preparation: Combine the first 5 ingredients. Place in a container large enough to be able to add the duck.

On Board Preparation: Add the duck to the marinade. Refrigerate for 20 minutes to marinate. Prepare the grill to medium heat. Remove the duck from the marinade, and bring marinade to a boil in a small saucepan over medium-high heat, boiling 1 minute. Remove from heat. Place the duck on the grill rack coated with cooking spray. Grill 5 minutes on each side or until a thermometer inserted into thickest portion registers 170°, basting occasionally with reserved marinade.
Serves: 4.

Herbed Cheese Stuffed Chicken Breast

    6 boneless chicken breast halves
1/2 teaspoon salt
1/4 teaspoon freshly ground black pepper
1/4 cup white wine
1 1/2 cups ricotta cheese
1/2 cup grated fresh Parmesan cheese
   1 large egg
   2 tablespoons chopped fresh parsley
   1 teaspoon dried marjoram

Instructions
At Home Preparation: Wash and thoroughly dry the chicken (do not remove the skin) and place in a container. Grate the Parmesan and place in a container. Chop the parsley and place in a container. Combine the ricotta, Parmesan, egg and herbs in a small bowl. Beat well with a wooden spoon until blended. Season with salt and pepper and place in a container.

On Board Preparation: Preheat the oven to 400°. Season the chicken breast with salt and pepper and sprinkle with a little white wine. Form a pocket in the chicken breast by separating the skin from the chicken with your fingertips, keeping the skin attached along the edges. Stuff generously with the cheese stuffing, patting the skin to distribute evenly. Tuck the edges of the skin under each breast and place in a baking pan about 1/2 inch apart. Bake for 10 minutes then lower the oven to 375° for an additional 30 minutes or until the skin is a nice golden brown.
Serves: 6.

Indian Style Barbecue Chicken

   2 cups orange juice
1/2 cup firmly packed brown sugar
1/2 cup sugar
1/2 teaspoon ground ginger
   1 teaspoon curry powder
   2 tablespoons sherry
   8 whole chicken breasts

Instructions
At Home Preparation: Mix together all ingredients except the chicken and place in a container.

On Board Preparation: Place the sauce mixture in a large saucepan and bring to a boil. Add the chicken and simmer 10 minutes. Prepare the grill. Grill over medium-low heat for about 20 minutes, or until done, basting frequently with the sauce.
Serves: 8.

Marinated Chicken

- 1/2 cup red wine
- 2 tablespoons vegetable oil
- 2 tablespoons brown sugar
- 1 tablespoon soy sauce
- 2 tablespoons tomato paste
- 1 teaspoon minced garlic
- 1/2 teaspoon ground ginger
- 1/2 teaspoon paprika
- 1 pound chicken strips
- 3 tablespoons olive oil

Instructions

At Home Preparation: Combine all the ingredients except the chicken in a bowl and mix well. Place in a container.

On Board Preparation: Place the chicken strips in a shallow pan and pour the marinade over. Refrigerate for at least 4 hours or preferably overnight. Sauté in a skillet in olive oil until cooked through.
Serves: 4.

Raspberry Barbecue Chicken

- 4 chicken breast halves, boneless & skinless
- 1 teaspoon Creole seasoning
  Raspberry Barbecue Sauce:
- 10 ounces seedless raspberry preserves
- 1/3 cup barbecue sauce (KC Masterpiece Original is best)
- 2 tablespoons raspberry vinegar
- 2 tablespoons Dijon mustard
- 1/2 teaspoon hot sauce

Instructions

At Home Preparation: To make the Raspberry Barbecue Sauce, bring the raspberry preserves, barbecue sauce, raspberry vinegar and dijon mustard to a boil in a small saucepan. Reduce the heat to medium and cook 2 minutes or until slightly thickened. Remove from heat and stir in the hot sauce. Let cool and place in a container.

On Board Preparation: Sprinkle the chicken with the Creole seasoning. Spray the grill grate with cooking spray. Prepare grill. Grill the chicken, covered, over medium-high heat for 7 minutes on each side or until done, brushing the Raspberry Barbecue Sauce evenly on 1 side of the chicken during the last 2 minutes of grilling. Heat the remaining sauce for serving.
Serves: 4.

Silver Bullet Chicken

1	teaspoon dried oregano
1/2	teaspoon dried thyme
4	cloves garlic, minced
1	large bay leaf
1/4	teaspoon freshly ground black pepper
1/4	cup wine vinegar
1	cup stuffed green olives, drained
1/4	cup capers, drained
2	chicken bouillon cubes
1/2	cup olive oil
2	sprigs fresh cilantro
5	pounds skinless, boneless chicken breast halves
2	cups rice
1	tablespoon olive oil
2	chorizo sausages, sliced
8	pieces bacon, chopped
2	medium yellow bell peppers, chopped
2	large onions, chopped
56	ounces canned tomatoes
1	cup dry red wine
36	ounces light beers
1	teaspoon salt
1/2	teaspoon pepper
4	ounces pimientos, sliced
10	ounces frozen peas, thawed
10	ounces frozen asparagus, thawed

Instructions

At Home Preparation: To make the marinade, combine the first 11 ingredients and place in a container. (Note: Chicken can be placed in marinade and frozen, if desired.) Slice the chorizo and place in a container. Chop the bacon and place in a container. Chop the bell peppers and place in a container.

On Board Preparation: Place the chicken pieces in the marinade, cover and refrigerate overnight. Wash and rinse the rice well. Cover with water and let sit for 45 minutes. In a large pot, heat the oil and brown the sausage and bacon. Add the peppers and onions and sauté until just starting to soften. Add the chicken and marinade mixture and brown well. Add the tomatoes, including liquid, wine and beer, cooking for 10 minutes. Drain the rice well and add to the pot. Cover and cook for about 25 minutes or until rice is tender. Season to taste with salt and pepper. If too thick, add water to desired consistency. Ten minutes before serving, add the pimientos, peas and asparagus.
Serves: 12.

Recipe Notes
A LOT of ingredients, but well worth it!

Spicy Marinated Chicken

- 4 tablespoons red wine
- 1 tablespoon soy sauce
- 1 tablespoon honey
- 1/2 teaspoon chili powder
- 1 tablespoon chopped fresh coriander
- 1 teaspoon minced garlic
- 2 tablespoons olive oil
- 4 whole chicken breasts

Instructions

At Home Preparation: Combine all ingredients (except chicken) well in a bowl. Place in a container.

On Board Preparation: Pour over the chicken and place in the refrigerator, covered, for at least 4 hours, preferably overnight. Turn several times. Prepare grill. Cook the chicken breast on the grill basting with the sauce until done.
Serves: 4.

Recipe Notes

You can vary the flavor of this dish by using sesame oil or peanut oil in place of the olive oil.

GALLEY TIP
For maximum flavor, add fresh herbs in the final minutes of cooking. If they are added too early, they will lose flavor.

Stuffed Chicken Breast with Tarragon Cream Sauce

- 6 whole chicken breasts, boned & skinned
- 6 ounces seasoned croutons
- 8 ounces walnuts
- 1 cup dry vermouth
- 1/2 cup minced onion
- 1 clove garlic, minced
- 5 tablespoons butter
- 1/4 cup minced fresh parsley
- 1 teaspoon dried tarragon
- 1/4 teaspoon salt
- 1/8 teaspoon pepper
- 3 dashes paprika
- 1 cup dry vermouth
- 2 shallots, minced
- 1 tablespoon tarragon
- 3 tablespoons butter, cut in small pieces
- 3 cups heavy cream

Instructions

At Home Preparation: Roughly crush the croutons. Coarsely chop the walnuts, reserving 12 whole for garnish (optional). Combine the crushed croutons and chopped walnuts and place in a container. Mince the onion, garlic and shallots and place each in a container. Cut the chicken breasts into 12 halves and place in a container.

On Board Preparation: Preheat oven to 350°. Place chicken pieces in a shallow dish just big enough to hold them. Pour the dry vermouth over and set aside. Sauté the onion and garlic in 2 tablespoons of the butter just until onion is translucent. Add crumb mixture; toss well. Add the parsley tarragon, salt and pepper to taste. Add just enough of the vermouth from the chicken so that a handful will hold it's shape when compressed. Make 12 oval mounds of stuffing in a buttered baking pan and shape a chicken breast half over each. Reserve the remaining vermouth for the sauce. Brush each breast generously with butter and sprinkle lightly with paprika. Bake for 20-30 minutes or until done. To make the sauce; in a saucepan, boil the second 1 cup dry vermouth, shallots and 1 tablespoon tarragon until reduced to about 1/3 cup. Lower the heat and whisk in the 3 tablespoons butter a few pieces at a time. Whisk in the 3 cups heavy cream a little at a time. Raise the heat and boil gently until the sauce is reduced to about 2 cups. Serve the chicken garnished with the whole walnuts and the sauce on the side.
Serves: 12.

Recipe Notes
Use French tarragon if you can find it for the best taste. For the seasoned croutons, onion and garlic is my favorite.

<u>Tarragon Chicken Breasts</u>

    4   chicken breast halves, boneless & skinless
  1/4   teaspoon salt
  1/8   teaspoon pepper
    2   tablespoons flour
  1/4   cup butter
    2   tablespoons chopped shallots
  1/3   cup dry white Bordeaux wine
  1/2   teaspoon dried tarragon
  3/4   cup chicken broth
  1/3   cup heavy cream

Instructions

At Home Preparation: Chop the shallots and place in a container. Mix the flour with salt and fresh ground pepper and place in a container.

On Board Preparation: Dredge the chicken pieces in the flour mixture. Reserve remaining flour mixture. In a large skillet heat 3 tablespoons of butter; add the chicken and brown on both sides. Transfer to a heated plate and keep warm. Add the shallots and sauté briefly. Add the wine. Cook over high heat until nearly evaporated, while scraping loose all the brown particles. Add reserved flour and stir to make a paste. Sprinkle with tarragon and stir in chicken broth. Return the chicken to the skillet, cover and cook until tender, about 15-20 minutes. Transfer chicken to a heated platter and keep hot. Add remaining butter and cream to the skillet; heat, stirring. Pour sauce over chicken to serve.
Serves: 4.

Rubs and Marinades

Asian Rub

    2   tablespoons sesame seeds, toasted
    2   teaspoons ground turmeric
    1   teaspoon ground coriander
  1/2   teaspoon salt
  1/2   teaspoon onion powder
  1/4   teaspoon ground cumin
  1/8   teaspoon ground cinnamon

Instructions
Combine all ingredients and store in an airtight plastic container.
Serves: 4.

Beef Marinade

      2   cups olive oil
    1/2   cup tarragon vinegar
      1   clove garlic, chopped
  1 1/2   teaspoons salt
  1 1/2   teaspoons pepper
    1/2   teaspoon curry powder
      2   whole bay leaves
    1/2   teaspoon lemon juice
      3   dashes Tabasco sauce

Instructions
Mix all ingredients in a bowl and place in an airtight plastic container.   Use as a marinade for beef and grill or bake as desired.
Serves: 4.

Creole Rub

      1   tablespoon salt
  1 1/2   teaspoons garlic powder
  1 1/2   teaspoons onion powder
  1 1/2   teaspoons paprika
  1 1/4   teaspoons thyme
      1   teaspoon ground red pepper
    3/4   teaspoon pepper
    1/2   teaspoon ground bay leaf
    1/4   teaspoon chili powder

Instructions
Combine all ingredients and store in an airtight plastic container. Sprinkle on seafood, chicken, or beef before grilling.
Serves: 4.

Herb Rub

1	tablespoon dried thyme
1	tablespoon dried oregano
1 1/2	teaspoons poultry seasoning
1	teaspoon dried rosemary
1	teaspoon dried marjoram
1	teaspoon dried basil
1	teaspoon parsley flakes
1/2	teaspoon salt
1/8	teaspoon pepper

Instructions
Combine all ingredients; store in an airtight plastic container. Sprinkle on your choice of fish, poultry, or pork before grilling.
Serves: 4.

Jalapeno-Lime Marinade

1/2	cup frozen concentrate orange juice, thawed
1	teaspoon grated lime zest
1/4	cup freshly squeezed lime juice
1/4	cup honey
2	teaspoons cumin
1/4	teaspoon salt
3	large garlic cloves, minced
2	medium jalapeno peppers, seeded & chopped

Instructions
Combine all ingredients, stir well and store refrigerated in an airtight plastic container.
Serves: 4.

Jerk Rub

1 1/2 tablespoons sugar
1 tablespoon onion powder
1 tablespoon dried thyme
2 teaspoons ground allspice
2 teaspoons freshly ground black pepper
1 teaspoon salt
3/4 teaspoon ground nutmeg
1/4 teaspoon ground cloves
2 teaspoons ground red pepper flakes

Instructions
Combine all ingredients and store in an airtight plastic container. Sprinkle on chicken or seafood before grilling.
Serves: 4.

Mediterranean Rub

2 tablespoons crushed fennel seeds
1 tablespoon dried chives
1 tablespoon crushed mustard seed
1 teaspoon lemon pepper
1/4 teaspoon garlic powder
1/4 teaspoon salt

Instructions
Combine all ingredients and store in an airtight plastic container.
Serves: 4.

Mexican Rub

1/4 cup chili powder
1 tablespoon onion powder
1 tablespoon ground cumin
2 teaspoons salt
1 1/2 teaspoons dried oregano
1 teaspoon garlic powder
1 teaspoon ground red pepper

Instructions
Combine all ingredients and store in an airtight plastic container. Sprinkle on chicken, ribs, or fish before grilling.
Serves: 4.

Peanut Sauce

        2   medium tomatoes
        1   medium onion
        2   cups water
        2   cloves garlic, crushed
        1   tablespoon soy sauce
        2   dashes chili powder
  1 1/2   cups crunchy peanut butter

Instructions
Blend the tomatoes, onion and water in a blender for 3 minutes. Pour the mixture into a saucepan and heat to warm over medium heat. Add the garlic, soy sauce, chili powder and bring to a boil. Simmer for one minute. Blend in the peanut butter and stir constantly until the sauce boils and thickens. Cool completely and place in an airtight plastic container.
Serves: 4.

GALLEY TIP
For easy grilling, put marinade or barbecue sauce in a squeeze bottle and squeeze directly on the meat.

Roasted Lemon Vinaigrette

8 whole lemons
1/2 cup salt
2 tablespoons sugar
1/4 cup champagne vinegar
1 tablespoon Dijon mustard
1 1/2 cups olive oil
1/4 teaspoon salt
1/8 teaspoon pepper
1 tablespoon fresh tarragon leaves
1/2 teaspoon ground mustard seed
1/3 cup roasted lemon juice

Instructions

At Home Preparation: Prepare the roasted lemon juice; in a casserole dish, toss the 8 whole lemons with salt and sugar. Cover with aluminum foil and bake at 375° until lemons feel soft when squeezed, about 1-1/2 hours. Remove from oven and let cool. Cut lemons in half and juice. Place 1/3 cup in a container. Reserve any remaining for another use.

On Board Preparation: In a medium bowl, combine Roasted Lemon Juice, vinegar and mustard. With a wire whisk, mix in olive oil, pouring in a steady stream. Season with salt and pepper. Add tarragon and mustard seeds if desired.
Serves: 4.

Recipe Notes

This is great on any grilled seafood. You can also use the roasted lemon juice in place of regular lemon juice in other vinaigrettes or sauces for a different taste.

Seafood Seasoning Rub

1 1/2 teaspoons ground bay leaves
1 1/2 teaspoons mustard powder
1 1/2 teaspoons pepper
1 teaspoon salt
3/4 teaspoon ground nutmeg
1/2 teaspoon ground celery seed
1/2 teaspoon ground cloves
1/2 teaspoon ground ginger
1/2 teaspoon paprika
1/2 teaspoon ground red pepper

Instructions

Combine ingredients and store in airtight container. Sprinkle on seafood or chicken before grilling.
Serves: 4.

Spicy Bayou Rub

        2   tablespoons paprika
        2   teaspoons garlic powder
    1 1/2   teaspoons dried thyme
        1   teaspoon ground red pepper
      3/4   teaspoon dried oregano
      1/2   teaspoon salt
      1/2   teaspoon pepper
      1/4   teaspoon ground nutmeg

Instructions
Combine all ingredients and store in an airtight plastic container.
Serves: 4.

Salads

Apple, Pear and Cheddar Salad

- 1 cup apple juice
- 2 tablespoons cider vinegar
- 1 teaspoon extra virgin olive oil
- 1/2 teaspoon salt
- 1/4 teaspoon freshly ground black pepper
- 10 cups mixed greens
- 1 cup red seedless grape, halved
- 1/4 cup shredded Cheddar cheese
- 3 tablespoons pecans, toasted
- 1 medium pear
- 1 medium McIntosh apple

Instructions
At Home Preparation: Place the apple juice in a small saucepan and bring to a boil over medium-high heat. Cook until reduced to about 3 tablespoons (about 10 minutes). Combine reduced apple juice, vinegar, oil, salt and pepper, stirring with a whisk. Place in a container. Wash and dry the greens, roll in paper towels and place in a perforated zip top bag. Wash the grapes and cut in half. Place in a container. Toast the pecans by placing on a baking sheet and toasting in a toaster oven at 350° until lightly browned. Cool completely, chop and place in a container.

On Board Preparation: Core the apple and cut into 18 wedges. Core the pear and cut into wedges. Combine the greens, grapes, apple and pear in a large bowl. Drizzle with the apple juice mixture and toss gently to coat. Sprinkle with cheese and nuts. *Serves: 6.*

Apple, Spinach and Blue Cheese Salad

- 2 tablespoons fresh orange juice
- 2 tablespoons fresh lime juice
- 2 teaspoons Dijon mustard
- 2 teaspoons honey
- 1/4 teaspoon salt
- 1/8 teaspoon ground black pepper
- 1/2 cup thinly sliced red onion
- 1 large apple
- 1/4 cup crumbled blue cheese
- 8 cups baby spinach, washed

Instructions
At Home Preparation: Combine the first six ingredients in a bowl and whisk to blend thoroughly. Place in a container. Slice the onion and place in a container.

On Board Preparation: Let the dressing come to room temperature. Core and thinly slice the apple. Combine the onion, spinach and apple in a large bowl. Drizzle with the dressing and toss gently to coat. Sprinkle with the cheese.
Serves: 6.

Arugula and Grilled Fig Salad

1/3	cup crumbled gorgonzola cheese
1	tablespoon butter, softened
12	medium figs, halved
	cooking spray
2	tablespoons balsamic vinegar
1	tablespoon extra virgin olive oil
1/2	teaspoon salt
1/4	teaspoon ground black pepper
3	cups baby spinach
3	cups arugula
8	pieces Boston lettuce
2	tablespoons chopped green onions
3	slices peasant bread

Instructions

At Home Preparation: Combine the cheese and butter in a small bowl. Place in a container. Whisk together vinegar, oil, salt, and pepper in a small bowl and place in a container. Chop the green onions and place in a container. Grill the bread slices on each side until golden, about 5 minutes. Cool and place in a container.

On Board Preparation: Prepare the grill. Bring the butter/cheese mixture to easy spreading temperature. Spread each bread slice with about 1 teaspoon butter/cheese spread. Thread 4 fig halves lengthwise onto each of 6 skewers. Coat with cooking spray. Grill for 4 minutes on each side. Cool slightly, and remove from the skewers. Place the spinach and arugula in a large bowl and add the dressing. Toss gently to coat. Divide evenly among 8 serving plates. Top with figs and lettuce leaves, sprinkle with onions. Serve with the toast.
Serves: 8.

Asparagus and Orange Salad, Asian Style

      2 large oranges
      1 tablespoon vegetable oil
      6 cups asparagus, sliced diagonally
      1 clove garlic, thinly sliced
      2 teaspoons low sodium soy sauce
    1/4 teaspoon dark sesame oil
      1 tablespoon sesame seed, toasted
      8 Napa cabbage leaves

Instructions

At Home Preparation: Peel and section the oranges over a bowl, reserving 1 teaspoon of the juice. Place the sections and juice in a container.   Clean and diagonally slice the asparagus and place in a container. Slice the garlic and place in a container. Combine the soy sauce and sesame oil and place in a container. Toast the sesame seeds, cool and place in a container.

On Board Preparation: Heat the vegetable oil in a large skillet over medium heat. Add the asparagus and garlic and sauté 5 minutes. Pour the soy sauce mixture over the asparagus and toss well. Cool to room temperature. Stir in the sesame seeds, orange sections and 1 teaspoon juice. Serve on the cabbage leaves if desired. *Serves: 8.*

Balsamic Onion and Mozzarella Salad

        3 large sweet onions, sliced
      1/3 cup balsamic vinegar
      1/4 cup olive oil
    1 1/2 teaspoons paprika
        1 teaspoon salt
      1/2 teaspoon pepper
        8 ounces fresh mozzarella, sliced
       12 large basil leaves
        4 slices tomatoes

Instructions

At Home Preparation: Slice the onions into 8, 1/2 inch slices. Place in a single layer in a 13x9 airtight plastic container. Stir together the vinegar, olive oil, paprika, salt and pepper. Pour over the onion slices. Place in a container and chill for 8 hours, turning once. Slice the mozzarella into 4, 1/2 inch slices and place in a container.

On Board Preparation: Remove the onion slices from the vinegar marinade after 8 hours, using a slotted spatula and reserving the marinade. Prepare the grill and grill the onion slices 2 minutes on each side or until crisp-tender over medium-high heat. Layer an onion slice, cheese slice, tomato slice and 2 basil leaves, and top with an onion. Garnish with additional basil leaves if desired.   *Serves: 4.*

Beef, Grilled Onion and Sweet Potato Salad

   1   teaspoon crushed coriander seed
1 1/8 teaspoons ground pepper
   1   teaspoon chopped fresh thyme
 1/4 teaspoon salt
   1   pound flank steak, trimmed
   2   large sweet onions, sliced
   2   large sweet potatoes
   4   cups arugula
     For Dressing:
 1/3 cup fresh orange juice
 1/4 cup finely chopped shallot
   1   teaspoon chopped fresh parsley
   1   tablespoon extra virgin olive oil
   2   teaspoons low sodium soy sauce
   1   teaspoon stone ground mustard
 1/4 teaspoon salt

Instructions

At Home Preparation: Crush the coriander seeds. Chop the thyme. Combine the coriander seed, 1 teaspoon pepper, thyme, and 1/8 teaspoon salt. Place in a container. Slice the onions 1/2-inch thick and place in a container. Peel and slice the sweet potatoes 1/2-inch thick and place in a container. Prepare the dressing by combining the ingredients and stirring with a whisk. Place in a container.

On Board Preparation: Prepare the grill. Rub the spice mixture on both sides of the flank steak and set aside. Sprinkle the onion slices with 1/8 teaspoon pepper and 1/8 teaspoon salt and spray with cooking spray. Thread the onion slices onto skewers or arrange in a grilling basket coated with cooking spray. Grill for 5 minutes on each side or until just tender. Remove from skewers or basket and place in a large bowl. Lightly coat the sweet potatoes with cooking spray and grill for 5 minutes on each side or until lightly browned. Cool slightly and cut into 1/4 inch strips. Add to the onions in the bowl and toss gently to combine. Place the steak on the grill coated with cooking spray and grill 4 minutes on each side or until desired degree of doneness. Place on a cutting board and let rest for 5 minutes. Cut diagonally across the grain in thin slices. Place the greens in a large bowl, drizzle with 1/4 cup dressing, tossing gently to coat. Place on 4 plates and top each with 1 cup onion mixture. Arrange 3 ounces steak over each serving and drizzle with 1 tablespoon dressing. Serve immediately.
Serves: 4.

Best Ever Coleslaw

4 tablespoons finely chopped onion
1/2 cup mayonnaise
1/2 cup sour cream
3 tablespoons cider vinegar
1 tablespoon Dijon mustard
1 teaspoon dill seed
1 teaspoon Worcestershire sauce
1/4 teaspoon ground pepper
4 cups shredded cabbage

Instructions

At Home Preparation: Chop the onion and place in a container. Wash, thoroughly dry and shred the cabbage and place in a container.

On Board Preparation: Mix together all ingredients except the cabbage, seasoning to taste with pepper. Soak the cabbage in ice cold water for 15-30 minutes. Drain thoroughly, tossing to get completely dry. Toss with the dressing, cover and chill for at least one hour before serving.
Serves: 6.

BLT Salad

8 slices bacon
3/4 cup mayonnaise
1/4 cup milk
1 teaspoon garlic powder
1/8 teaspoon pepper
1/4 teaspoon salt
1 head romaine lettuce, torn
2 large tomatoes, chopped
2 cups seasoned croutons

Instructions

At Home Preparation: Cook the bacon slices, cool, crumble and place in a container. In a medium bowl, whisk the mayonnaise, milk, garlic powder and pepper and salt to taste. Place in a container. Wash, dry and tear the romaine. When it is completely dry, roll in paper towels and place in a perforated zip top bag. Chop the tomatoes and place in a container.

On Board Preparation: Place the romaine in a large bowl. Add the tomatoes and crumbled bacon. Toss with the dressing until evenly coated. Sprinkle with croutons and serve.
Serves: 4.

Caribbean Shrimp and Black Bean Salad

15	ounces black beans, rinsed & drained
1	small green pepper, finely chopped
1/2	cup sliced celery
1/2	cup sliced purple onion rings
2	tablespoons chopped fresh cilantro
2/3	cup mild salsa
1/4	cup fresh lime juice
2	tablespoons vegetable oil
2	tablespoons honey
1/4	teaspoon salt
3	cups water
2	pounds shrimp, unpeeled
4	cups field greens
1	cup cherry tomato

Instructions

At Home Preparation: Slice the celery and onions, separating the onion into rings. Combine the black beans, green pepper, celery, onion rings, cilantro, salsa, lime juice, vegetable oil, honey and salt. Place in a container and toss gently. Bring the water to a boil. Add the shrimp and cook 3 to 5 minutes until pink. Drain well and rinse with cold water. Chill until cool enough to handle. Peel and devein. Place in a container and refrigerate.

On Board Preparation: Place the lettuce or greens evenly on 4 plates. Arrange the shrimp around the edge of the lettuce. Spoon the black bean mixture into the center of each plate. Garnish with cherry tomatoes.
Serves: 4.

GALLEY TIP
When measuring honey or syrup, dip the spoon in oil first and the honey or syrup will slide right off, giving you a correct measure.

Chicken Salad with Feta

        8   cups leafy lettuce
        1   cup orange bell pepper, julienne
        1   cup cherry tomato
      1/2   cup matchstick carrot
      1/2   cup crumbled feta cheese
      1/4   cup chopped green onion
        2   tablespoons sliced almonds
        3   tablespoons frozen orange juice concentrate, thawed
        1   tablespoon white vinegar
        1   tablespoon olive oil
      1/8   teaspoon salt
      1/8   teaspoon pepper
       11   ounces mandarin orange sections, drained
        1   pound chicken breasts, boneless & skinless
            cooking spray

Instructions
At Home Preparation: Wash and tear the lettuce. Pat dry with paper towels. Core the bell pepper and cut into strips. Halve the cherry tomatoes. Chop the green onions. Toast the almonds. Place all in individual containers. (Do not refrigerate the almonds.) Combine the orange juice concentrate (undiluted), vinegar, oil, salt and pepper in a bowl and whisk to blend. Place in a container.

On Board Preparation: Remove the dressing from the refrigerator and allow to warm to room temperature. Prepare the grill and spray the rack with cooking spray. Grill the chicken breasts for 6 minutes on each side or until done. Cut into 1/2 inch thick slices. Set aside. Combine the lettuce, bell pepper strips, cherry tomatoes, matchstick carrots, feta and green onions in a large bowl. Shake or whisk the dressing and drizzle over the lettuce mixture. Toss to coat. Divide the lettuce mixture among 4 plates. Top evenly with chicken, oranges, and almonds.
Serves: 4.

Chicken Souvlaki Salad

        2   teaspoons minced garlic
        1   teaspoon fresh lemon juice
        1   teaspoon extra virgin olive oil
      1/2   teaspoon oregano
      1/4   teaspoon salt
      1/4   teaspoon pepper
        1   pound chicken breasts, boneless & skinless
        3   cups peeled & cubed cucumber
      1/2   cup sliced red onion
      1/2   cup crumbled feta cheese

2 tablespoons kalamata olives, pitted, chopped
2 medium tomatoes, cut into 1" thick pieces
1/2 cup plain yogurt
1/4 cup grated cucumber
1 teaspoon white wine vinegar
1/2 teaspoon garlic powder
1/4 teaspoon salt
1/4 teaspoon ground red pepper
1/4 teaspoon pepper

Instructions

At Home Preparation: Peel and cube the 3 cups cucumber and place in a container. Slice the red onion and place in a container. Pit and chop the olives and place in a container. Core and chop the tomatoes and place in a container.

On Board Preparation: Prepare the grill. Combine 1 teaspoon garlic and the next 6 ingredients (through chicken breasts) in a large zip top plastic bag. Seal and shake to coat. Remove the chicken from the bag and grill 5 minutes on each side or until done. Cut into 1 inch pieces. Combine the chicken, cubed cucumber, onion, feta cheese, olives and tomatoes in a large bowl. Combine the yogurt and remaining ingredients in a small bowl (be sure to include the remaining 1 teaspoon garlic!). Pour over the chicken mixture and toss to coat well.
Serves: 4.

GALLEY TIP

If you are using dried herbs, soak them in hot water for a minute or so before adding to sauces or mayonnaise.

Chinese Chicken Salad

4 chicken breasts halves
2 whole scallions, trimmed
2 slices fresh ginger
1 teaspoon salt
6 whole scallions, thinly sliced
8 ounces water chestnuts, drained
For Dressing:
2 tablespoons sesame seeds
1 tablespoon finely chopped fresh ginger
1 teaspoon mustard powder
1 tablespoon brown sugar
1/4 cup rice wine vinegar
1/2 cup vegetable oil
2 tablespoons sesame oil
1/2 teaspoon salt
4 dashes pepper
4 cups shredded romaine lettuce

Instructions

At Home Preparation: Put the chicken in a large skillet with the whole scallions and ginger. Add water to barely cover the chicken and bring to a boil over high heat. Add the salt and lower the heat. Simmer, partially covered, for about 20 minutes, or until the chicken is tender. Remove from the heat and let the chicken cool in the broth. Remove the meat and discard the skin and bones. Tear the meat into shreds and place in a container. Combine the dressing ingredients and place in a container. Shred the lettuce and place in a perforated zip top plastic bag wrapped in paper towel. Slice the scallions and place in a container. Drain the water chestnuts and place in a container.

On Board Preparation: Toss the chicken meat with the sliced scallions and water chestnuts. Shake the dressing to thoroughly blend. Pour half the dressing onto the chicken and toss to coat. Spoon onto a bed of shredded lettuce or cabbage and drizzle with the remaining dressing. Sprinkle with sesame seeds.
Serves: 4.

Corn and Walnut Salad

16 ounces canned corn, drained
1 medium green pepper, seeded & chopped
3 medium scallions, sliced thin
3 tablespoons fresh lime juice
2 teaspoons sugar
1 cup sour cream
4 tablespoons vegetable oil

2   dashes Tabasco sauce
1/4   teaspoon salt
1/8   teaspoon pepper
1   large tomato
1/2   cup coarsely chopped walnuts

Instructions

At Home Preparation: Drain the corn and place in a container. Chop the green pepper and place in a container. Peel and slice the scallions and place in a container. Cut the tomato into wedges and place in a container. Chop the walnuts and place in a container.

On Board Preparation: Mix the corn, bell pepper and scallions in a bowl. Add the lime juice, sugar, sour cream, and oil. Salt to taste and add a few drops of Tabasco to taste if desired. Chill and serve garnished with tomato wedges and sprinkled with the walnuts.
Serves: 4.

Crab Stuffed Avocado

8   ounces crabmeat
6   tablespoons mayonnaise
3   tablespoons sour cream
2   teaspoons Dijon mustard
2   teaspoons sherry
3   teaspoons brandy
1/2   teaspoon paprika
4   medium avocados
1   teaspoon lemon juice
1   large lemon, sliced

Instructions

At Home Preparation: Clean crab meat if necessary and place in a container. Mix together the mayonnaise, sour cream and mustard. Stir in the sherry, brandy; add paprika. Place in a container. Refrigerate at least one hour. Slice the lemon and place in a container.

On Board Preparation: Halve and peel the avocados. Sprinkle with a little lemon juice to prevent browning and place 2 halves each on a serving plate. Divide the crab meat evenly between the avocado halves. Top with the sauce. Garnish with lemon slices.
Serves: 4.

Crab Stuffed Tomatoes

```
4   medium tomatoes
8   ounces crabmeat
2   tablespoons minced onions
1   tablespoon minced celery
1   teaspoon Salad Supreme
1   teaspoon lemon juice
1/4 cup mayonnaise
1/2 teaspoon salt
1/4 teaspoon pepper
8   large lettuce leaves
1   large lemon, sliced
```

Instructions

At Home Preparation: Mince the onion and celery and place in a container. Wash the tomatoes, remove stems, dry thoroughly and place in a container. Drain and clean the crab meat of any shell pieces, then place in a container. Wash and thoroughly dry the lettuce leaves. Gently roll in paper towels and place in a perforated zip top bag. Slice a lemon into thin slices and place in a container.

On Board Preparation: In a bowl, combine the crab meat, onion, celery, Salad Supreme, lemon juice, and salt and pepper to taste; toss. Add mayonnaise and combine thoroughly. Chill for 30-45 minutes. Cut the tomatoes into sections without cutting all the way through at the base. Place lettuce leaves on 4 serving plates and set tomatoes in the middle, opening the sections. Fill each with crab meat mixture and garnish with lemon slices.
Serves: 4.

Recipe Notes
Salad Supreme can be found in the spice section of the grocery store.

Crab, Shrimp and Coconut Salad

```
1/2 pound shrimp
1/2 teaspoon salt
1   cup frozen corn, thawed
1/3 cup finely chopped onion
1/3 cup chopped fresh cilantro
1/3 cup diced avocado
1/2 pound lump crab meat
1   medium chopped jalapeno pepper
3   tablespoons fresh lemon juice
2   teaspoons extra virgin olive oil
6   cups torn leafy lettuce
1/4 cup flaked coconut
```

Instructions

At Home Preparation: Peel and devein the shrimp. Place in a container. Chop the onion and jalapeno and place each in a container. (Seed the jalapeno for milder heat.) Toast the coconut by placing in a toaster oven at 350° until lightly browned. Cool and place in a container. Wash thoroughly dry, and tear the lettuce, wrap in paper towels and place in a perforated zip top plastic bag. Combine the juice, olive oil and 1/4 teaspoon salt, stirring with a whisk. Place in a container.

On Board Preparation: Peel and dice the avocado. Chop the cilantro. Heat a medium nonstick skillet over medium-high heat. Coat the pan with cooking spray. Add the shrimp and 1/4 teaspoon salt. Cook for about 4 minutes until the shrimp are done, turning once. Remove from the pan and coarsely chop. Combine the corn, onion, cilantro, avocado, crab meat and jalapeno in a medium bowl. Gently stir in the shrimp. Drizzle with the juice mixture and toss gently to coat. Divide the lettuce among 4 plates and top with the shrimp mixture. Sprinkle with the toasted coconut. ***Serves: 4.***

Dilled Potato Salad with Feta

2	pounds red potatoes, unpeeled
1/3	cup red wine vinegar
1/3	cup vegetable oil
1	tablespoon dried dill
1	teaspoon salt
1/2	teaspoon pepper
1	large red bell pepper, chopped
1	large cucumber
1/2	cup sliced green onion
4	ounces crumbled feta cheese

Instructions

At Home Preparation: Place potatoes in a large pan and cover with water. Bring to a boil and cook 25-30 minutes or just until tender. Drain and cool. Cut into quarters and place in a container. Core and chop the bell pepper and place in a container. Cut the cucumber in half (do not peel) and slice thin. Place in a container. Slice the green onions and place in a container.

On Board Preparation: Whisk together the vinegar, oil, dill, salt and pepper. Pour over the potatoes. Stir in the bell pepper, cucumber, green onions and feta cheese. Cover and chill at least 2 hours. ***Serves: 6.***

Recipe Notes

This entire recipe can be prepared at home if desired. Choose small red potatoes for the best results.

Feta, Olive and Tomato Salad

5 medium tomatoes
6 ounces crumbled feta cheese
1/4 teaspoon fresh dill
1 teaspoon fresh parsley
1/4 cup olive oil vinaigrette
1 can Greek olives, oil cured

Instructions

At Home Preparation: Cut each tomato into thick slices and place in a container. Crumble the feta, if necessary, and place in a container. Wash the dill and parsley, dry completely, and place in a container.

On Board Preparation: Place the tomato slices on a platter. Sprinkle the feta over the tomatoes. Tear the herbs and sprinkle on the tomatoes. Drizzle with the vinaigrette to taste.
Serves: 4.

Greek Pasta Salad

3 cups farfelle (bow tie) pasta, uncooked
8 ounces tuna steak, cut 3/4 inch thick
1/8 teaspoon salt
1 1/2 cups peeled & sliced cucumbers
3/4 cup crumbled feta cheese with peppercorns
1/4 cup red onion
1/4 cup kalamata olives, pitted, sliced
1/4 teaspoon ground pepper
12 medium cherry tomatoes, halved
For Dressing:
1/4 cup fresh lemon juice
2 teaspoons extra virgin olive oil
1 teaspoon dried oregano
1/4 teaspoon fresh pepper
1/8 teaspoon salt

Instructions

At Home Preparation: Prepare the dressing by mixing the ingredients in a bowl with a whisk. Place in a container. Peel and slice the cucumber and place in a container. Chop the red onion and place in a container. Cook the pasta according to package directions, drain and rinse with cold water. Drain and place in a container.

On Board Preparation: Prepare the grill. Sprinkle the tuna with 1/8 teaspoon salt and grill for 5 minutes on each side or until desired degree of doneness. Cool slightly and cut into 1-inch pieces. Combine the pasta, tuna, cucumber, feta, chopped onion, olives black pepper and tomatoes in a large bowl. Drizzle with the dressing and toss to coat.
Serves: 4.

Italian Bread Salad

    4 cups cubed French bread
    6 tablespoons olive oil
    3 tablespoons red wine vinegar
    2 cloves garlic, minced
    1 teaspoon dried oregano
    1 teaspoon salt
  3/4 teaspoon freshly ground black pepper
  1/8 teaspoon crushed red pepper
    1 large romaine lettuce head, chopped
    5 large plum tomatoes, chopped
    2 cups chopped prosciutto
    8 ounces fresh mozzarella, cubed
    3 whole green onions, chopped

Instructions

At Home Preparation: Preheat oven to 325°. Cube the French bread and place on a cookie sheet. Bake for 15 minutes until lightly browned. Cool completely and place in a container. Whisk together the olive oil, vinegar, minced garlic, oregano, salt, black pepper and red pepper. Place in a container. Chop the lettuce, tomatoes, green onions and prosciutto. Place each in a container. Cube the mozzarella and place in a container.

On Board Preparation: Reserve one cup of the bread cubes. Spread the remaining bread cubes in a large bowl. Top with the lettuce, tomatoes, chopped prosciutto and mozzarella. Drizzle with the dressing and toss. Let stand for 15 minutes before serving. Place on a large platter or divide among 4 plates. Top with the reserved bread cubes and green onions.
Serves: 4.

Mixed Apple Salad Over Greens

1/4 cup fresh lemon juice
2 tablespoons honey
1 teaspoon olive oil
1 dash salt
1 dash freshly ground pepper
2 cups chopped Granny Smith apples
2 cups chopped Brae Burn apples
1/4 cup crumbled blue cheese
2 slices bacon, cooked
4 cups mixed greens

Instructions
At Home Preparation: Combine the lemon juice, honey, olive, salt and pepper in a small bowl and whisk to combine. Place in a container. Cook the bacon, cool, crumble and place in a container.

On Board Preparation: Chop the apples. Combine with the cheese and bacon. Drizzle the dressing over the apple mixture and toss gently. Serve over greens.
Serves: 4.

Mixed Greens with Vanilla-Pear Vinaigrette

15 ounces canned pears halves, do not drain
1/3 cup white wine vinegar
1 tablespoon honey
3/4 cup kosher salt
1/4 teaspoon freshly ground pepper
1/4 teaspoon vanilla extract
1 dash red pepper
1 cup sliced red onion, sliced vertically
20 ounces mixed greens
1/4 cup walnuts, chopped and toasted

Instructions
At Home Preparation: Slice the onions and place in a container. Toast the chopped walnuts until lightly toasted. Cool and place in a container. Drain the pears, reserving 1/3-cup juice. Make the vinaigrette by combining the pears, 1/3 cup juice, vinegar, and remaining ingredients in a blender; process until smooth. Place 2/3 cups in a container and reserve the remaining for another use.

On Board Preparation: Combine the greens and sliced onions in a large bowl. Drizzle with the Vinaigrette and toss well. Sprinkle with the walnuts.
Serves: 8.

Pickled Beet and Onion Salad

   2 medium sliced red onions
 1/4 cup cider vinegar
 1/4 cup water
   1 teaspoon salt
 1/2 teaspoon dried oregano
   1 teaspoon crushed red pepper
   1 pound beets, cooked and sliced
   5 tablespoons vegetable oil
 1/4 teaspoon salt
 1/8 teaspoon pepper
 1/4 cup coarsely chopped walnuts
   1 cup sour cream

Instructions

At Home Preparation: Slice the onion and put in a large bowl. Cover with boiling water and let stand for 5 minutes. Drain. Place in a tight sealing container and add the vinegar, water, salt, oregano and red pepper. Allow to marinate at least 1 hour or up to one week. When desired, remove from marinade and reserve 3 tablespoons in a container. Place the onions in a container.   Cook the beets, drain and place in a container. Chop the walnuts and toast in the oven at 350° for about 3-5 minutes or until just beginning to brown. Cool completely and place in a container.

On Board Preparation: Place the beets in a large bowl. Add 3 tablespoons of the marinade from the onions, toss well and set aside for at least 15 minutes. Season with salt and pepper.   Arrange the beets on a platter then scatter the onions on top. Sprinkle with the walnuts and place dollops of sour cream around the edge, if desired.
Serves: 4.

Recipe Notes
This is also good made with canned beets.

GALLEY TIP
Leafy greens wrapped in a damp towel and placed in a perforated plastic bag will keep up to a week.

Potato Salad with Peas

2 pounds red potatoes
1 cup frozen green peas
3 tablespoons chopped fresh parsley
2 tablespoons chopped fresh chives
2 tablespoons chopped fresh basil
1/2 cup tarragon vinegar
1 tablespoon sugar
1/2 teaspoon salt
1/8 teaspoon freshly ground pepper
1 clove garlic, minced

Instructions

At Home Preparation: Prepare the ingredients by shelling the peas and chopping the herbs and garlic. Cover the potatoes with water in a large saucepan. Bring to a boil. Reduce heat and simmer, partially covered for about 25 minutes or until tender. Add the peas and cook one additional minute. Drain and cool slightly until the potatoes are comfortable to handle. Slice the potatoes into 1/4 inch slices. Combine the potatoes, peas, parsley, chives and basil in a large bowl. Place in a container. Combine the vinegar, sugar, salt, pepper and garlic in a small bowl and whisk. Place in a container.

On Board Preparation: About an hour before serving, toss the potato mixture with the dressing and chill.
Serves: 6.

Recipe Notes
Use fresh shelled peas if you can find them or a high quality frozen.

Potato Salad with Prosciutto and Truffle Oil

2 pounds Yukon gold potato, peeled, sliced into 1/4-inch pieces
2 1/2 cups chicken broth
2 tablespoons butter
3 ounces chopped prosciutto
1 cup chopped celery
1/2 cup chopped sweet onion
1/2 cup chopped fresh chives
1 tablespoon truffle oil
1 tablespoon fresh lemon juice

Instructions

At Home Preparation: Place the sliced potatoes in a large saucepan. Add the chicken broth and bring to a boil. Reduce heat to medium and simmer, partially covered, until potatoes are just tender, about 6 minutes. Drain, reserving the broth. Place the potatoes in a large bowl and return the broth to the saucepan. Boil until reduced to 1/3 cup, about 13 minutes. Pour over the potatoes and toss gently until the broth is absorbed. Melt the butter in a medium nonstick skillet over medium heat. Add the prosciutto and sauté until crisp, about 6 minutes. Add to the potatoes. Chop the celery, onions and chives and place each in a container. Whisk the truffle oil and lemon juice in a small bowl to blend and place in a container. (Take along a small amount of additional truffle oil.)

On Board Preparation: Add the celery, onions and chives to the potatoes and prosciutto. Drizzle the truffle oil mixture over the potato mixture and toss to coat. Season with salt, pepper and additional truffle oil to taste. Let stand until room temperature.
Serves: 6.

Roasted Garlic Potato Salad

- 3 pounds red potatoes, quartered
- 1 tablespoon vegetable oil
- 1 tablespoon stone ground mustard
- 2 teaspoons crushed coriander seed
- 6 cloves garlic, halved
- 1/2 cup chopped fresh parsley
- 1/2 cup plain yogurt
- 1/3 cup thinly sliced green onion
- 3/4 teaspoon salt
- 1/4 teaspoon freshly ground pepper
- 8 whole green onions

Instructions

At Home Preparation: Preheat the oven to 400°. Combine the first 5 ingredients in a large bowl, tossing to coat the potatoes. Place in a shallow roasting pan and bake at 400° for 30 minutes or until tender, stirring occasionally. Cool to room temperature. Place in a container. Chop the parsley. Crush the coriander seeds with a mortar and pestle. Peel and halve the garlic. Thinly slice 1/3 cup green onions. Place each in a container.

On Board Preparation: Combine the parsley, yogurt, sliced green onions, salt and pepper in a large bowl. Add the potato mixture and toss gently. Serve at room temperature or chilled. Garnish with the whole green onions if desired.
Serves: 8.

Romaine and Endive with Stilton and Toasted Walnuts

- 1/2 clove garlic
- 1/4 teaspoon anchovy paste
- 1 egg yolk
- 1/2 cup buttermilk
- 4 ounces Stilton cheese
- 4 ounces olive oil
- 1/4 lemon, juiced
- 1/4 teaspoon salt
- 1/8 teaspoon pepper
- 1/2 cup walnuts, toasted and chopped
- 2 head hearts of romaine
- 1 head Belgian endive
- 1 large pear or apple

Instructions

At Home Preparation: Toast the walnuts by placing them in a 350° oven, toasting just until they begin to brown. Cool, lightly chop and place in a container. Mash the garlic and anchovy in a mortar and pestle with a pinch of salt and pepper. Transfer to a bowl and stir in the egg yolk followed by the buttermilk and cheese. Slowly whisk in the olive oil and finally the lemon juice. Adjust salt and pepper to taste. Place in a container. Cut the romaine leaves from the head; wash and dry, roll in paper towels and place in a perforated zip top bag. Cut the outer leaves from the endive. Place in a container.

On Board Preparation: Chop the first third of the stem ends of both types of leaves into 1/4 inch strips. Place them in a bowl with the remaining tips and drizzle with the vinaigrette. Toss well to coat. Remove the core and slice the pear or apple into thin slices. Arrange them around the plates, alternating with the romaine and endive tips. Place the chopped greens in the center and sprinkle with the toasted walnuts.

Serves: 4.

Salad Nicoise

- 3/4 pound small, whole boiling potatoes
- 3 tablespoons olive oil
- 2 teaspoons wine vinegar
- 1 clove garlic, minced
- 1/4 teaspoon salt
- 1/8 teaspoon pepper
- 1 teaspoon chopped fresh chives
- 3 1/2 ounces albacore tuna in water
- 3/4 cup shredded ham

1/3 cup julienne green peppers
1/3 cup julienne red bell peppers
1/2 head romaine lettuce
1/2 head iceberg lettuce
  1 large tomato, cut into wedges
  1 small red onion, thinly sliced
  2 tablespoons olive oil
1/4 teaspoon salt
  2 large eggs, hard cooked and sliced
  2 ounces oil-cured anchovy fillets, drained
  1 medium lemon, thinly sliced
  2 tablespoons mixed fresh herbs
  1 can kalamata olives, pitted
  1 large egg
  1 large egg yolk
  2 tablespoons fresh lemon juice
2/3 cup olive oil
  3 tablespoons whipping cream
  1 tablespoon wine vinegar
1/4 teaspoon salt
1/8 teaspoon pepper
  1 tablespoon capers, drained

Instructions

At Home Preparation: Make the dressing by placing the 1 large egg and egg yolk in a blender. Mix briefly. Blend in the 2 tablespoons lemon juice. With the blender running add the 2/3 cup olive oil in a slow steady stream. Transfer to a small bowl and add the 3 tablespoons whipping cream, 1 tablespoon wine vinegar, capers, salt and pepper. Place in a container. For the salad, peel the potatoes and cook in boiling salted water for 15 minutes or until just tender. Be careful not to overcook. Cool slightly and slice. Cool completely and place in a container. Drain the tuna and place in a container. Julienne the peppers and place in a container. Wash the lettuce and dry completely. Roll in paper towels and place in a perforated zip top bag. Cut the tomato into wedges and place in a container. Slice the onion and place in a container. Hard cook the eggs, peel and cool. Slice and place in a container. Drain the anchovy fillets. (Soak them in milk for about 15 minutes after draining to take away the strong fishy taste, then drain.) Place in a container. Thinly slice the lemon and place in a container. Chop the herbs and place in a container.

On Board Preparation: Combine 3 tablespoons olive oil, vinegar and garlic in a medium bowl. Add the potatoes and stir very gently to coat. Season with salt and pepper and sprinkle with chives. Combine the tuna, ham and peppers in a small bowl. Cover with half of the dressing. Arrange lettuce on a platter. Place tuna mixture in the center. Drizzle the remaining dressing around edge of the platter. Place the potatoes on one end, then the tomatoes, and onion rings. Drizzle with olive oil and sprinkle with salt and a little freshly ground black pepper. Place the sliced eggs on the other side of the platter and garnish with the anchovy strips. Add the lemon slices as additional garnish. Sprinkle entire salad with the fresh herbs and garnish with olives.   *Serves: 4.*

Shrimp and Broccoli Pasta Salad

1/2 pound fresh spinach pasta
  1 pound shrimp
  1 cup broccoli florets
1/3 cup sliced and pitted kalamata olives
  1 teaspoon chopped fresh basil
  2 tablespoons chopped fresh parsley
  2 tablespoons lemon juice
1/3 cup olive oil
1/4 teaspoon salt
1/8 teaspoon pepper
  1 lemon, sliced
  8 sprigs parsley (optional)

Instructions
At Home Preparation: Cook the pasta 2-3 minutes in boiling water or until al dente. Rinse under cold water; drain. Sprinkle with 2 teaspoons olive oil and toss to coat. Place in a container. Peel and devein the shrimp. Cook in salted boiling water 3-5 minutes or until they turn pink. Do not over cook. Drain and place in ice water to cool. Drain and place in a container. Blanch the broccoli florets for 3 minutes. Cool completely and place in a container. Chop the basil and parsley and place in a container.

On Board Preparation: Combine the pasta, shrimp, broccoli, olives, basil and parsley. Sprinkle with lemon juice and remaining olive oil. Toss to coat; salt and pepper to taste. Serve at room temperature, garnished with lemon slices and fresh parsley (optional).
Serves: 4.

Shrimp Salad

  1 pound shrimp, cooked
 15 ounces artichoke hearts, quartered
  8 ounces black olives, quartered lengthwise
  1 shallot, minced
  1 clove garlic, minced
1 1/2 teaspoons fresh dill
1/2 teaspoon paprika
  1 teaspoon Dijon mustard
1/2 cup mayonnaise
  2 tablespoons sour cream
  1 head Belgian endive
  1 small red bell pepper
  1 small jar marinated asparagus

Instructions

At Home Preparation: Peel the shrimp and cook in boiling water until just turned pink. Cool completely and place in a container. Drain the artichoke hearts, quarter and place in a container. Mince the shallot, garlic and fresh dill and place each in a container. Clean the endive leaves, dry thoroughly and roll in paper towels. Place in a perforated zip top bag. Cut the red pepper into strips and place in a container. Drain the marinated asparagus and place in a container.

On Board Preparation: In a large bowl, combine the shrimp, artichoke hearts and olives. Add the shallot, garlic, dill and paprika. Toss until well blended.   In a small bowl combine mustard, mayonnaise and sour cream.   Add to the shrimp mixture and combine thoroughly. Chill for about an hour. Serve on a bed of endive, garnished with the red pepper strips and asparagus spears.
Serves: 4.

Spicy Carrot Salad

    4 cups diagonally cut carrots
    8 cloves garlic, halved
    2 cups thinly sliced onions
    2 cups cider vinegar
    1 cup water
  1/2 cup sliced pickled jalapeno peppers
  1/2 teaspoon salt
    8 cups thinly torn iceberg lettuce

Instructions

At Home Preparation: Place the carrots and garlic in a large pan, cover with water and bring to a boil. Cover, reduce heat, and simmer for 5 minutes or until just crisp-tender. Drain thoroughly. Cut the lettuce and place in a container. Combine the carrot mixture with the onions, vinegar, water, jalapenos and salt in a large plastic bowl. Stir well and place in a container. Refrigerate at least 8 hours.

On Board Preparation: Arrange the lettuce on one large or 8 individual serving plates. Spoon the carrot mixture into the center using a slotted spoon.
Serves: 8.

Spinach and Goat Cheese Salad

    2 slices prosciutto, cut into 1/2-inch strips
2 1/2 tablespoons balsamic vinegar
    1 teaspoon extra virgin olive oil
1/4 teaspoon salt
1/4 teaspoon freshly ground black pepper
  10 ounces fresh spinach
1/2 cup crumbled goat cheese

Instructions

At Home Preparation: Preheat the oven to 400°. Arrange the prosciutto slices on a baking sheet. Bake at 400° for 6 minutes or until crisp. Cool completely and place in a container. Combine vinegar, olive oil, salt and pepper in a small bowl and whisk to blend. Place in a container. Wash the spinach, dry, wrap in paper towels and place in a perforated zip top plastic bag.

On Board Preparation: Combine the prosciutto and spinach in a large bowl. Drizzle with the vinegar mixture and toss gently to coat. Sprinkle with the goat cheese and serve immediately.
Serves: 8.

Spinach Salad

1/4 cup diced shallots
1/2 cup olive oil
1/4 cup balsamic vinegar
1/2 cup sugar
1/4 teaspoon salt
1/8 teaspoon pepper
  8 slices Applewood smoked bacon
  1 large Granny Smith apple, sliced
  2 packages prewashed baby spinach

Instructions

At Home Preparation: Sweat the shallots in olive oil. Add remaining ingredients and bring to a boil; simmer approximately 2 minutes. Cool completely and place in a container. Cook the bacon, cool, and place in a container.

On Board Preparation: Bring the dressing back to warm-hot. Core and slice the apple. (Sprinkle with a little lemon juice to prevent oxidation.) Toss the warm dressing with the spinach. Place on serving plates and garnish with the bacon and sliced apple.
Serves: 4.

Spinach Salad with Orange Dressing

    6 cups fresh spinach
    4 large eggs, hard cooked
  1/2 cup chopped walnuts
  1/2 cup thinly sliced red onion
  1/4 cup raisins
   11 ounces mandarin orange sections, drained
  1/2 cup grated Parmesan cheese
   11 ounces mandarin orange sections, drained
    5 cloves garlic
    2 tablespoons low sodium soy sauce
    2 tablespoons balsamic vinegar
    1 tablespoon extra virgin olive oil

Instructions

At Home Preparation: Wash the spinach, remove stems and dry completely then roll in paper towel and place in a perforated zip top plastic bag. Hard boil the eggs, remove the shells, lightly chop and place in a container. Chop the walnuts and place in a container. Slice the red onion and place in a container. Prepare the dressing by placing 11 ounces of mandarin oranges, 5 cloves garlic, 2 tablespoons soy sauce, 2 tablespoons balsamic vinegar and 1 tablespoon olive oil in a blender and blend for 30 seconds to 1 minute. If you prefer a creamier texture continue to blend for about another minute. Place in a container.

On Board Preparation: Combine all the ingredients in a large bowl and toss well with the dressing
Serves: 4.

> ## GALLEY TIP
> *Store tomatoes stem down in a cool place to keep them fresh longer. Warmth ripens tomatoes.*

Spinach-Pear Salad

2 large Bosc pears, thinly sliced
6 ounces fresh baby spinach
3 tablespoons water
2 tablespoons balsamic vinegar
1 teaspoon sugar
5 teaspoons extra virgin olive oil
1 1/2 teaspoons stone ground mustard
3/4 teaspoon salt
1/2 teaspoon freshly ground black pepper
1/4 cup shaved Parmigiana-Reggiano cheese

Instructions
At Home Preparation: Combine the water, vinegar, sugar, olive oil, mustard, salt and pepper and whisk. Place in a container. Shave the cheese and place in a container. Wash the spinach, dry completely, wrap in paper towel and place in a perforated zip top plastic bag.

On Board Preparation: Let the dressing come to room temperature. Core and slice the pears. Place the spinach and pear slices in a large bowl. Drizzle the dressing over the salad and toss gently. Sprinkle with the cheese.
Serves: 12.

Steak Salad with Caper Vinaigrette

1 pound beef tenderloin
4 cups water
3 cups green beans, cut into 1" thick pieces
4 cups watercress, trimmed
1 cup halved grape tomatoes
3/4 cup thinly sliced red onions
8 ounces mushrooms, sliced
7 3/4 ounces hearts of palm, rinsed & drained
For Dressing:
1/4 cup red wine vinegar
1 1/2 tablespoons fresh lemon juice
1 tablespoon capers
1 tablespoon honey mustard
2 teaspoons extra virgin olive oil
1/2 teaspoon sugar
1/2 teaspoon salt
1/8 teaspoon freshly ground black pepper

Instructions
At Home Preparation: Bring the water to a boil in a large saucepan and add the

beans. Cover and cook 3 minutes or until crisp-tender. Rinse with cold water and drain well. Cool completely and place in a container. Halve the grape tomatoes, place in a container. Slice the onion and place in a container. Wash the mushrooms, slice, sprinkle with a little lemon juice (to prevent oxidation) and place in a container. Drain and rinse the hearts of palm, dry thoroughly and place in a container. To prepare the dressing, combine all ingredients in a bowl and whisk well. Place in a container.

On Board Preparation: Remove the dressing from the refrigerator and let it warm slightly. Prepare the grill and spray with cooking spray. Grill the steak about 7 minutes on each side or until desired doneness. Let it stand 10 minutes then slice diagonally across the grain into thin slices. Place in a large bowl. Add the beans, watercress, tomatoes, onion, mushrooms and hearts of palm and toss gently. Drizzle the dressing over the salad mixture and toss gently to coat.
Serves: 4.

Strawberry-Chicken Salad

3/4	cup pear nectar
1/3	cup vegetable oil
1/3	cup raspberry vinegar
3	tablespoons chopped fresh basil
1	tablespoon sesame oil
1/2	teaspoon freshly ground black pepper
1/4	teaspoon salt
1/2	small sweet onion, diced
1/2	cup pecan halves, toasted
4	chicken breast halves, boneless & skinless
8	cups mixed greens
1	quart strawberries, sliced
2	pears, sliced
2	avocados, peeled

Instructions
At Home Preparation: Combine the first 7 ingredients in a plastic container and shake vigorously to combine. Refrigerate. (Will keep for up to 2 weeks.) Dice the onion and place in a container. Toast the pecans in the toaster oven at 350° for about 10 minutes stirring occasionally until just beginning to brown. Cool completely and place in a container.

On Board Preparation: Combine the chicken with 1/2 of the raspberry vinaigrette in a zip top bag. Seal and chill for 1 hour. Prepare the grill. Remove the chicken and discard the marinade. Grill the chicken covered over medium-high heat for 4 minutes on each side or until done. Let stand for 10 minutes. Slice the strawberries, pears and avocados. Place the salad greens, strawberries, pears, avocados, onions and pecans in a large bowls and gently toss. Divide among 4 servings plates. Slice the chicken and place atop the salad. Serve with the remaining raspberry vinaigrette.
Serves: 4.

Strawberry-Orange Chicken Salad

- 1 package mixed greens
- 1 pint strawberries, sliced
- 2 large navel oranges, sectioned
- 1 medium red onion, thinly sliced
- 1 1/2 cups strawberry preserves
- 1/4 cup white balsamic vinegar
- 1/4 cup olive oil
- 1/4 teaspoon crushed rosemary
- 1/4 teaspoon salt
- 1/4 teaspoon pepper
- 4 whole boneless chicken breasts
- 1/4 teaspoon salt
- 1/8 teaspoon pepper

Instructions

At Home Preparation: Wash the strawberries but do not slice. Place in a container. Peel and section the oranges and place in a container. Slice the onion and place in a container. Combine the strawberry preserves, balsamic vinegar, olive oil, rosemary, 1/4 teaspoon salt and 1/4 teaspoon pepper in a blender and pulse until smooth. Place in a container.

On Board Preparation: Prepare the grill. Salt and pepper the chicken breasts and grill covered on medium-high heat for 5-7 minutes on each side or until done. Set aside and let stand for at least 10 minutes. While the chicken is cooling, slice the strawberries. Divide the field greens among four plates. Top with the sliced strawberries, orange sections and red onion slices. Cut the chicken into 1/2 inch slices and add to the salads. Drizzle with the dressing.
Serves: 4.

Tomato and Cantaloupe Salad

- 2 pints cherry tomatoes
- 1 medium cantaloupe
- 1/2 cup crumbled feta cheese
- 1 bunch arugula
- 1 small lemon peel, grated
- 1/4 cup olive oil
- 2 tablespoons balsamic vinegar
- 1 bunch fresh basil
- 1/4 teaspoon salt
- 1/8 teaspoon pepper

Instructions

At Home Preparation: Wash the tomatoes, dry and place in a container. Using a melon ball tool or a teaspoon, make melon balls out of the cantaloupe and place in a container. Wash the arugula, dry thoroughly, tear, and place in a container. Zest the lemon and place in a container. Wash, dry and chop the basil and place in a container. In a small bowl, whisk together the olive oil, vinegar, basil, salt and pepper. Place in a container.

On Board Preparation: Cut the tomatoes in half. In a large bowl, mix the tomatoes and melon balls gently. Add the feta cheese, arugula and lemon zest and gently mix well. Pour the dressing over the salad just before serving and toss to coat well.

Serves: 8.

Recipe Notes
This is also good made with mixed field greens in place of the arugula.

Tomato Basil Mozzarella Salad

  3   large tomatoes
  8   ounces fresh mozzarella
 12   fresh basil leaves
1 1/2 tablespoons olive oil
1 1/2 tablespoons fresh lemon juice
 1/4   teaspoon salt
 1/4   teaspoon freshly ground black pepper

Instructions

At Home Preparation: Slice the tomatoes into 1/2 inch slices and place in a container. Slice the fresh mozzarella into 1/4 inch slices and place in a container. Wash the basil leaves, thoroughly dry, and place in a container.

On Board Preparation: Arrange the tomato and mozzarella slices alternately on a large plate or on individual serving plates. Tuck the basil leaves in attractively. Combine the olive oil and lemon juice and brush on the slices and basil leaves. Sprinkle with salt and pepper and refrigerate until ready to serve.

Serves: 4.

Recipe Notes
This one is so easy you can prepare it entirely on board!

Tortellini Salad

1/3 pound spinach tortellini
1 medium red bell pepper, chopped
1/2 medium Bermuda onion, chopped
1/2 cup pimento stuffed green olives, sliced
1/4 pound Genoa salami, diced
2 tablespoons chopped fresh basil
3 tablespoons chopped fresh parsley
1 dash thyme
1/4 teaspoon salt
1/8 teaspoon pepper
2 tablespoons olive oil
1/4 cup mayonnaise

Instructions

At Home Preparation: Cook tortellini according to package directions. Drain and sprinkle with a little olive oil, tossing to coat. Cool completely and place in a container. Chop the red pepper and onion and place each in a container. Slice the olives and dice the salami and place each in a container. Chop the fresh basil and fresh parsley and place in a container.

On Board Preparation: In a bowl, mix the tortellini with the red pepper, onion, olives, salami, basil, parsley, thyme, salt and pepper to taste. Sprinkle with olive oil. Add mayonnaise. Combine thoroughly. Chill for 30-60 minutes before serving.
Serves: 2.

Walnut Chicken Salad

4 cups cooked chicken
1 cup chopped celery
4 scallions, thinly sliced
1/4 teaspoon salt
1/8 teaspoon pepper
3/4 cup mayonnaise
3/4 cup sour cream
2 tablespoons lemon juice
2 dashes nutmeg
1 cup coarsely chopped walnuts
1/2 cup raisins

Instructions

At Home Preparation: Dice the cooked chicken into bit size pieces and place in a container. Chop the celery and place in a container. Slice the scallions and place in a container. Use your hands to coarsely break up the walnuts and place in a container.

On Board Preparation: Combine the chicken, celery, and scallions in a bowl and season to taste with salt and pepper. Add the mayonnaise, sour cream, and lemon juice and toss gently, combining well. Sprinkle with a little nutmeg and fold in the nuts and raisins. Cover and chill until ready to serve.
Serves: 4.

<u>Sandwiches</u>

Asian Chicken Burgers

         2   tablespoons peanut butter
         2   teaspoons low sodium soy sauce
   1 1/2   teaspoons dark sesame oil
         1   teaspoon water
         2   teaspoons rice vinegar
         1   clove garlic, minced
      1/2   green onion, finely chopped
         1   tablespoon chili paste
         2   teaspoons grated fresh ginger
         2   teaspoons low sodium soy sauce
      1/4   teaspoon salt
         1   pound boneless skinless chicken breast halves, chopped
             cooking spray
         4   hamburger buns
         1   cup alfalfa sprouts

Instructions
At Home Preparation: Combine the first 6 ingredients, whisking until smooth. Place in a container. Place the onions and next 5 ingredients in a food processor and process until coarsely ground. Shape into 4 patties and place in a container. (Can be frozen.)

On Board Preparation: Prepare the grill. Coat the grill rack with cooking spray. When it is heated, place the patties on the grill and cook approximately 4 minutes on each side or until done. Place the buns on the grill cut side down for about 1 minute or until toasted. Place each patty on a bun and top with 1/4 cup sprouts and about 1 tablespoons sauce.
Serves: 4.

Balsamic Burgers

   1   pound lean ground beef
   2   tablespoons balsamic vinegar
   2   tablespoons soy sauce
   1   teaspoon minced garlic
   4   hamburger buns

Instructions
At Home Preparation: Shape the ground beef into 4 patties, individually wrap and place in a container. (Can be frozen.) Combine the balsamic vinegar, soy sauce and garlic and place in a container.

On Board Preparation: Prepare the grill. Place the patties (thawed if you froze them) in a shallow dish or zip top bag and add the marinade. Marinate for 5 minutes. Grill to desired doneness, flipping once during cooking. Place each patty on a hamburger bun.
Serves: 4.

Beef, Orange and Gorgonzola Sandwich

2	tablespoons cider vinegar
1 1/2	teaspoons extra virgin olive oil
1/2	teaspoon grated orange zest
1/8	teaspoon salt
1/8	teaspoon ground pepper
1	cup orange section
4	French rolls
2	cups flank steak, grilled
1	cup baby spinach
1/4	cup gorgonzola cheese

Instructions
At Home Preparation: To prepare the vinaigrette combine the first 5 ingredients, stirring with a whisk. Place in a container. Peel and section the oranges and place in a container. Wash the spinach, dry completely, wrap in paper towel and place in a perforated zip top plastic bag.

On Board Preparation: Prepare the grill. Grill the flank steak seasoned with salt and pepper about 7 minutes on each side or until desired doneness. Cool slightly and thinly slice on the diagonal. Slice the rolls in half. Layer the bottom of each roll with 1/2 cup flank steak, 1/4 cup baby spinach, 1 tablespoon cheese and 1/4 cup orange sections. Drizzle each with about 2 teaspoons vinaigrette. Top with the top half of the roll.
Serves: 4.

GALLEY TIP
If green leafy vegetables become a bit wilted, add a little lemon juice to a bowl of cold water and soak for about an hour.

Chicken and Blueberry-Chipotle Wraps

        4 cups fresh blueberries
        1 cup finely chopped Granny Smith apple
      1/2 cup white wine vinegar
      1/3 cup sugar
      1/3 cup honey
        3 tablespoons grated orange peel
        1 tablespoon mustard seed
        2 tablespoons chopped chipotle peppers in adobo sauce
      1/2 teaspoon salt
      1/2 teaspoon ground ginger
        4 pounds chicken pieces, skinned & boned
      1/2 cup olive oil
      1/2 teaspoon salt
      1/4 teaspoon pepper
       16 ounces goat cheese
       16 flour tortillas

Instructions

At Home Preparation: Combine the blueberries and the next 9 ingredients in a large saucepan and bring to a boil. Reduce the heat and simmer, uncovered, for 25 minutes or until thick, stirring frequently. Cool and pour into a container. Refrigerate (for up to two months).

On Board Preparation: Prepare the grill. Place the olive oil, salt and pepper in a zip top bag. Toss the chicken pieces in the olive oil mixture. Grill the chicken pieces until done. Remove from the grill and cut into smaller pieces about one inch square. Warm the tortillas by placing on the grill and turning quickly just to warm. Spread each tortilla with about 1 ounce goat cheese. Place about 4 ounces of chicken on the goat cheese and top with desired amount of sauce.
Serves: 8.

Chicken Salad with Bacon and Blue Cheese Pitas

      3/4 cup plain yogurt
      1/4 cup crumbled blue cheese
        2 tablespoons mayonnaise
      1/2 teaspoon pepper
        3 cups shredded romaine lettuce
    1 1/2 cups cooked chicken
        4 slices bacon, cooked
        2 medium tomatoes, seeded & chopped
        4 whole pita breads, halved

Instructions

At Home Preparation: Combine the yogurt, blue cheese, mayonnaise and pepper, stirring well. Place in a container. Wash, pat dry and shred the romaine, dry thoroughly, wrap in paper towels and place in a perforated zip top bag. Cook the chicken (or use prepared chicken), shred and place in a container. Cook the bacon, cool, crumble and place in a container. Seed and chop the tomatoes and place in a container.

On Board Preparation: Combine the lettuce, chicken, bacon and tomatoes in a medium bowl, stirring well. Drizzle with the yogurt mixture and toss gently to coat. Spoon 1/2 cup chicken mixture into each pita half. Serve immediately.
Serves: 4.

Chipotle Cheddar Stuffed Burgers

7   ounces chipotle peppers in adobo sauce
2   pounds lean ground beef
2   teaspoons steak seasoning
4   slices Cheddar cheese
4   hamburger buns

Instructions

At Home Preparation: Place the chipotle peppers in a blender or food processor and process until smooth. Measure 4 teaspoons of this puree and reserve the remainder for another use. Combine the puree, ground beef, and steak seasoning in a large bowl until blended. (Using your hands works best so you do not overwork the meat.) Shape into 8 patties and place in a container. (Can be frozen.)

On Board Preparation: Place a slice of cheese between two patties, pressing the edges to seal. Chill about 30 minutes while the grill is heating. Grill over medium-high heat (350-400) about 7-8 minutes on each side or until no longer pink. (Always cook ground meat thoroughly.) Serve on the buns with desired toppings.
Serves: 4.

GALLEY TIP
When cooking with mustard, add it last minute for a sharper flavor, or earlier for a milder more blended flavor.

Classy Club Sandwich

  3 ounces cream cheese, softened
  2 ounces blue cheese, crumbled
  1 teaspoon minced onion
  1 dash Worcestershire sauce
  1 tablespoon mayonnaise
 12 slices wheat berry bread
  2 large tomatoes
  8 slices cooked chicken
  4 slices Swiss cheese
  8 slices bacon, cooked & drained
  4 pieces leafy lettuce
  4 teaspoons mayonnaise, optional

Instructions

At Home Preparation: Combine the cream cheese, blue cheese, minced onion, Worcestershire and 1 tablespoon mayonnaise. Place in a container. Slice the tomatoes into 8 slices and place in a container. Cook the bacon, drain on paper towels, cool complete and place in a container. Wash the lettuce leaves, dry thoroughly wrap in paper towels and place in a perforated zip top bag.

On Board Preparation: Toast the bread slices. Spread the cream cheese mixture on 4 slices of the toast. Top each with 2 slices tomato, 2 slices chicken or turkey, 1 slice cheese. Sprinkle with salt and pepper to taste. Add a second slice of toast and top with 2 slices of bacon and a lettuce leaf. Spread the remaining slices of toast with mayonnaise to taste and place on top of the sandwich. Secure each with 4 toothpicks and cut into 4 triangles.
Serves: 4.

Country Club Hamburgers

 1 1/2 pounds ground round
   1/2 teaspoon salt
   1/4 teaspoon pepper
     3 tablespoons crumbled blue cheese
     1 tablespoon butter, softened
     2 teaspoons Worcestershire sauce
     1 teaspoon Dijon mustard
     2 teaspoons minced fresh chives
     4 hamburger buns
   1/2 pound bacon

Instructions

At Home Preparation: Season the meat with salt and pepper and form into 8 thin patties. Place in a container. Mince the chives and place in a container.

On Board Preparation: Prepare the grill. Mix the cheese and the butter until blended. Add the Worcestershire sauce, mustard and chives and mix well. Spread evenly over the meat patties. Combine two patties, cheese sides together. Wrap each with bacon and secure with toothpicks. Grill about 4 minutes on each side or until desired doneness. (Some cheese mixture may leak out.) Toast the buns and serve.
Serves: 4.

Fried Oyster Sandwich

      1 pound French bread
    1/4 cup butter, softened
     24 ounces oysters, drained
      1 cup cornmeal mix
      3 cups vegetable oil
    1/3 cup mayonnaise
  2 1/2 tablespoons sweet pickle relish
      1 tablespoon lemon juice
    1/8 teaspoon hot sauce
      1 cup shredded lettuce
      1 large tomato, thinly sliced

Instructions

At Home Preparation: Slice off the top third of the French bread loaf. Hollow out the bottom section, reserving what is removed for another use. Place the hollowed out loaf and top in a container. Drain the oysters and place in a container. Wash and shred the lettuce, wrap in paper towels and place in a perforated zip top bag. Slice the tomato and place in a container.

On Board Preparation: Spread the inside surface of the bread loaf with butter. Toast or broil until lightly browned; set aside. Dredge the oysters in the cornmeal mix and fry in deep hot oil (375°) until they float to the top and are golden brown. Drain well on paper towels and keep warm. Combine the mayonnaise, pickle relish, lemon juice, and hot sauce, stirring well. Stir in the shredded lettuce. Spread the lettuce mixture in the hollowed bread loaf. Top with tomato slices, oysters, and the top of the loaf. Cut into servings.
Serves: 4.

Recipe Notes
A round loaf of French bread works best for this sandwich. If you would rather fry the oysters at home, wrap them in foil and reheat in the oven when you are on board.

Garlic Burgers

1 pound lean ground beef
2 tablespoons red wine
2 tablespoons soy sauce
2 teaspoons minced garlic
4 hamburger buns

Instructions

At Home Preparation: Shape the ground beef into 4 patties, individually wrap and place in a container. (Can be frozen.) Combine the red wine, soy sauce and garlic and place in a container.

On Board Preparation: Prepare the grill. Place the patties (thawed if you froze them) in a shallow dish or zip top plastic bag and add the marinade. Marinate for 5 minutes. Grill to desired doneness, flipping once during cooking. Place each patty on a hamburger bun.
Serves: 4.

Goat Cheese with Pepper and Onion Jam Sandwiches

2 teaspoons olive oil
3 cups thinly sliced onions
1 1/2 tablespoons balsamic vinegar
1 1/2 tablespoons currants
1 whole French bread baguette
4 ounces goat cheese
2 tablespoons olivada (black olive spread)
7 ounces roasted red peppers
1 1/2 cups arugula
1/8 teaspoon pepper
1/8 teaspoon salt

Instructions

At Home Preparation: In a heavy nonstick skillet, heat the oil over low heat. Add onions and cook, stirring often, until they are very tender and light golden, about 15-20 minutes. (If they brown too quickly, add 1 or 2 tablespoons water.) Remove from the heat and stir in vinegar, currants, salt and pepper. Let cool and place in a container. Drain and slice the roasted red peppers and place in a container. Wash the arugula, dry completely and place in a perforated zip top plastic bag wrapped in paper towel.

On Board Preparation: Slice the baguette into four equal pieces. Split each piece horizontally. Spread the bottoms with goat cheese and the tops with olivada. Spoon the onion mixture over the goat cheese, spreading evenly. Top with roasted peppers and arugula. Top with the olivada half.
Serves: 4.

Grilled Chicken Sandwiches

- 1/4 cup lime juice
- 2 tablespoons minced shallots
- 2 tablespoons dry white wine
- 1 teaspoon dried whole thyme
- 2 teaspoons vegetable oil
- 1/2 teaspoon sugar
- 1/2 teaspoon dried whole marjoram
- 1/4 teaspoon freshly ground black pepper
- 6 chicken breast halves, boneless & skinless
- 3 tablespoons mayonnaise
- 1 teaspoon spicy brown mustard
- 6 hamburger buns
- 6 pieces leafy lettuce
- 1 small purple onion, sliced
- 2 large tomatoes, sliced

Instructions
At Home Preparation: Combine the first 8 ingredients and place in a container. Slice the onion, separate into rings and place in a container. Slice the tomatoes into 6 slices and place in a container.

On Board Preparation: Place the chicken in the marinade and refrigerate 1-4 hours. Remove from the marinade; place the liquid in a small saucepan and bring to a boil. Reduce heat and simmer 5 minutes. Prepare the grill. Combine the mayonnaise and mustard, set aside. Place the chicken on the grill and cook 5-6 minutes on each side or until done, basting frequently with the marinade. Spread the mayonnaise mixture on the bottom halves of the buns. Place the grilled chicken on top. Top each with a lettuce leaf, onion rings, and tomato slice. Place the bun top on the sandwich.
Serves: 6.

Grilled Flank Steak Sandwich

1 1/2   pounds flank steak
1/2   cup dry white wine
2   tablespoons balsamic vinegar
2   teaspoons freshly ground black pepper, coarsely ground
2   teaspoons minced garlic
1   teaspoon dried whole oregano
4   teaspoons olive oil
1   cup thinly sliced green pepper
1   cup thinly sliced red bell pepper
1/2   cup thinly sliced onion
1/2   teaspoon minced garlic
1/4   teaspoon sugar
1/4   teaspoon salt
8   sandwich rolls

Instructions

At Home Preparation: Trim any excess fat from the flank steak and place in a container. Combine the wine, vinegar, pepper, garlic and oregano and place in a container. Slice the green and red pepper and place in a container. Slice the onion and place in a container. Mince the garlic and place in a container.

On Board Preparation: Place the flank steak in the marinade and refrigerate 8 hours, turning occasionally. In a skillet coated with the olive oil, heat over medium-high heat until hot. Place the peppers, onion and garlic in the skillet and sauté 4 minutes. Sprinkle with sugar and salt; sauté an additional 2 minutes or until crisp tender. (Be careful not to over cook.) Remove from the heat and keep warm. Prepare the grill. Remove the steak from the marinade and bring the marinade to a boil in a small saucepan. Reduce heat and simmer 5 minutes. Coat the grill rack with cooking spray. Place the steak on the rack and cook 6-7 minutes on each side over medium-high heat, or until desired doneness. Baste frequently with the marinade during cooking. Slice the steak diagonally across the grain into 1/4-inch slices. Toast the sandwich buns if desired. Divide the steak among the buns. Spoon the pepper mixture over the steak and top with the bun tops.
Serves: 8.

Ham and Cheese Roll-Ups

8   slices whole-grain bread
1/2   cup mayonnaise
1   teaspoon tarragon
8   slices Jarlsberg cheese
8   slices ham
8   stalks asparagus spears
1/4   cup champagne mustard

Instructions

At Home Preparation: Cut the crusts from the bread and place in a container, discarding the crust or reserving for another use. Combine the mayonnaise and tarragon, stirring well and place in a container. Cook the asparagus stalks until just crisp-tender. Cool completely and place in a container.

On Board Preparation: Spread the bread slices with the tarragon mayonnaise. Top each bread slice with a slice of ham and a slice of cheese. Place an asparagus stalk at one end of each and roll tightly. Secure with toothpicks. Serve with Champagne mustard for dipping.
Serves: 4.

Ham and Pepper Sandwich

1	pound Italian bread loaf, round or oval
3	tablespoons honey mustard
2	medium green onions, chopped
3	ounces cream cheese, softened
1	tablespoon mayonnaise
1	pound ham, thinly sliced
1/4	cup pickled banana peppers, drained
6	ounces Swiss cheese slices
4	ounces American cheese, sliced
1	large tomato, sliced
4	large lettuce leaves

Instructions

At Home Preparation: Chop the green onions. Stir together onions, cream cheese and mayonnaise and place in a container. Wash the lettuce, dry thoroughly, wrap in paper towels and place in a perforated zip top bag. Wash and slice the tomato and place in a container.

On Board Preparation: Cut off the top third of the bread loaf. Spread the cut side of the top with honey mustard. Set aside. Scoop out the soft center of the remaining bread, leaving about 1/4 inch thick shell. Spread the bottom with the cream cheese mixture. Layer the ham, peppers and cheeses on top of the cream cheese mixture. Top with the lettuce and tomato slices. Place the top of the bread on and cut into 4 wedges.
Serves: 4.

Ham Salad Sandwiches

1 1/2 cups coarsely ground ham
8 ounces crushed pineapple, drained
1/4 cup mayonnaise
1 tablespoon horseradish
1 teaspoon mustard
8 slices rye bread

Instructions

At Home Preparation: Grind the ham in a meat grinder or in a food processor and place in a container. Drain the pineapple thoroughly and place in a container.

On Board Preparation: Combine all ingredients except the rye bread and mix well. Refrigerate for one hour or up to 2 days. When ready to serve, spread evenly on 4 of the bread slices. Top with the remaining slices and cut in half or quarters.
Serves: 4.

Monte Cristo Sandwich

8 slices white bread
4 slices turkeys
4 slices ham
4 slices Swiss cheese
1 tablespoon Dijon mustard
3 large eggs
1/2 cup milk
1 dash nutmeg
4 tablespoons butter

Instructions

Spread 4 slices of bread with Dijon mustard. Layer the meats and cheese on top. Top with the remaining bread slices. Beat eggs with milk and nutmeg. Melt the 4 tablespoons butter in a large skillet. Dip each sandwich in the egg mixture. Sauté until golden brown and cheese begins to melt. Turn and brown the other side.
Serves: 4.

Recipe Notes

This recipe can be made entirely on board or can be made entirely at home and frozen. Reheat in a medium oven for 20 minutes, wrapped in foil.

Mozzarella and Tomato Sandwiches

1	pound fresh mozzarella, thinly sliced
1/4	teaspoon freshly ground pepper
1/8	teaspoon crushed red pepper
1	loaf French bread
5	medium plum tomatoes
4	servings mixed greens
1/4	cup red wine vinegar
2	large garlic cloves, crushed
1	tablespoon finely chopped shallots
1/2	teaspoon dried oregano
2	tablespoons finely chopped parsley
3/4	cup olive oil

Instructions

At Home Preparation: Combine the red wine vinegar, garlic shallot, oregano, parsley and olive oil, whisking well and place in a tight sealing shaker container. After about 2 hours, taste and remove garlic if it is to your liking. (Do not leave garlic in for too long.)   Slice the mozzarella and place in a container. Slice the bread lengthwise and place in a container. Slice the tomatoes and place in a container. Wash the lettuce, dry completely and place in a perforated zip top bag wrapped in paper towels.

On Board Preparation: Shake the vinaigrette vigorously to mix. Layer the cheese in a bowl with about 3 tablespoons of the vinaigrette and season with the fresh ground pepper and red pepper. Open the bread and hollow out slightly by removing some of the soft center. Brush the inside generously with the vinaigrette. Place overlapping slices of tomatoes and cheese on one side of the bread and sprinkle with a little vinaigrette. Cover with the lettuce. Close the sandwich and wrap tightly in wax paper or aluminum foil. Let sit for about one hour. Slice crosswise into pieces.
Serves: 4.

GALLEY TIP
To avoid "onion tears", light a candle next to your cutting surface. The candle will draw the fumes that create the "tears".

Nutty Banana Sandwich

- 4 slices whole-grain bread
- 2 tablespoons peanut butter
- 1 large banana, halved and sliced lengthwise
- 2 tablespoons honey
- 1 tablespoon chopped walnuts

Instructions
Slice the bananas into 8 pieces. On 2 slices of bread, spread 1 tablespoon of peanut butter on each and place the banana slices on top, divided evenly between the two sandwiches. On the other slices of bread, spread each with 1 tablespoon honey and sprinkle walnuts on top. Place on top of the peanut butter banana slice and cut in half.
Serves: 2.

Recipe Notes
This is also really good made with almond or cashew butter!

Peanut Butter and Banana Split Sandwich

- 4 slices firm white bread
- 2 teaspoons butter, softened
- 2 tablespoons creamy peanut butter
- 4 teaspoons honey
- 1 teaspoon mini semisweet chocolate chips
- 2 large strawberries, thinly sliced
- 1 small banana
- 2 tablespoons pineapple jam

Instructions
At Home Preparation: Combine the peanut butter and honey and place in a container. Clean the strawberries and place in a container.

On Board Preparation: Slice the banana lengthwise into 3 slices. Slice the strawberries. Spread one side of each bread slice with 1/2 teaspoon butter. Spread the plain (unbuttered) side of 2 of the slices with the peanut butter/honey mixture. Sprinkle each with 1/2 teaspoon of the chocolate chips. Top evenly with strawberry slices and banana slices. Spread the plain side of the remaining bread slices with the pineapple jam. Carefully assemble the sandwiches. Heat a nonstick skillet over medium-high heat. Add the sandwiches and cook about 2 minutes on each side or until lightly browned.
Serves: 2.

Shrimp and Remoulade Sandwich

1 1/2 cups cooked & chopped shrimp
1/3 cup chopped celery
3 tablespoons mayonnaise
1 teaspoon chopped green onion
1 teaspoon capers
1/2 teaspoon tarragon vinegar
1/4 teaspoon salt
1/4 teaspoon horseradish
4 slices oatmeal bread
1 1/2 cups shredded romaine lettuce

Instructions

At Home Preparation: Cook and coarsely chop the shrimp and place in a container. Chop the celery and place in a container. Chop the green onions and place in a container. Wash, thoroughly dry, and shred the romaine and place in a perforated zip top plastic bag wrapped in paper towel.

On Board Preparation: Combine the shrimp, celery, mayonnaise and green onions, stirring well. Add the capers, vinegar, salt and horseradish stirring until combined. Toast the bread and place on a work surface. Divide the lettuce among the bread slices. Spoon the shrimp mixture evenly over the lettuce.
Serves: 4.

GALLEY TIP
Tomatoes should not be refrigerated until they are fully ripened.

Smoked Mozzarella and Tomato Sandwiches

2/3 cup sun-dried tomato (not oil packed)
1 clove garlic, crushed
1/4 teaspoon salt
2 tablespoons extra virgin olive oil
1 tablespoon lemon juice
1/8 teaspoon red pepper flakes
2 tablespoons chopped black olives
8 slices sourdough bread
4 ounces fresh smoked mozzarella, sliced 1/4-inch
1/8 teaspoon freshly ground black pepper
3 medium tomatoes, sliced
2 teaspoons balsamic vinegar
1 cup fresh basil leaf

Instructions

At Home Preparation: Place sun-dried tomatoes in a bowl and cover with boiling water. Let plump for 10 minutes. Mash the garlic and salt into a paste with a mortar and pestle. Transfer to a bowl and whisk in 1 tablespoon of the oil, lemon juice and red-pepper flakes. Drain the sun-dried tomatoes and chop fine. Add to the oil/garlic dressing along with the olives; mix well. Place in a container. Slice the mozzarella and place in a container. Slice the tomatoes and place in a container. Wash and completely dry the fresh basil leaves and place in a container.

On Board Preparation: Spread the olive mixture over 4 of the bread slices. Brush 1 tablespoon oil over the remaining bread slices. Arrange cheese slices on top and sprinkle with black pepper. Place tomato slices on top and season with salt and vinegar. Top with several basil leaves and set the remaining bread slices on top. *Serves: 4.*

Spinach Salad Sandwich

1/4 cup mayonnaise
1 1/2 tablespoons catsup
8 slices rye bread
4 slices Swiss cheese
2 large eggs, hard cooked
2 cups torn spinach
1 cup sliced mushrooms

Instructions

At Home Preparation: Combine the mayonnaise and catsup until blended and place in a container. Hard cook the eggs, peel, thinly slice and place in a container. Wash the spinach, pat dry with paper towels, and tear into bit sizes pieces. Pat dry again to be sure spinach is thoroughly dry, wrap in paper towel and place in a perforated zip top bag. Wash and slice the mushrooms sprinkle with a little lemon juice to prevent browning and place in a container. (Or purchase mushrooms already sliced.)

On Board Preparation: Spread the mayonnaise mixture evenly on the bread slices. Top 4 pieces of bread each with a slice of cheese. Arrange even amounts of egg, spinach, and mushrooms over cheese. Top with remaining bread slices. Cut in half and serve.
Serves: 4.

Tenderloin Sandwiches with Horseradish Sauce

> 2/3 cup sour cream
> 1/4 cup Dijon mustard
> 2 tablespoons minced fresh tarragon
> 2 tablespoons horseradish
> 1 1/2 pounds beef tenderloin, trimmed
> 1/2 teaspoon freshly ground black pepper
> 2 tablespoons lemon juice
> 3 cups mixed greens
> 4 French rolls
> 2 tablespoons capers
> 1/2 cup shaved Parmesan cheese

Instructions

At Home Preparation: Combine the first four ingredients, stirring well with a whisk. Place in a container and chill. Shave the parmesan and place in a container.

On Board Preparation: Prepare the grill for cooking the tenderloin. If you prefer, the beef can be prepared in a large skillet coated with cooking spray. Secure the tenderloin at approximately 2-inch intervals with twine. Sprinkle with the pepper. Once the grill has come up to temperature, place the tenderloin on the grill and cook to desired degree of doneness, approximately 15 minutes for medium rare, turning to cook all sides. Let rest for about 15 minutes before cutting into about 16 slices. Arrange the greens on the French rolls. Place 4 slices of beef and about 4 tablespoons of the chilled sauce on each. Sprinkle with Parmesan and capers.
Serves: 4.

Tex-Mex Chipotle Sloppy Joes

    1   teaspoon olive oil
    1/2 cup chopped onion
    1   tablespoon minced garlic
    2   teaspoons minced jalapeno peppers
    1   teaspoon sugar
    1   teaspoon ground cumin
    1   teaspoon chili powder
    1/2 teaspoon ground coriander
    1/4 teaspoon chipotle Chile powder
    1   pound ground turkey breast
  1 1/2 cups mild salsa
    1   tablespoon chopped fresh cilantro
    4   Kaiser rolls, cut in half

Instructions
At Home Preparation: Chop the onion. Mince the jalapeno and place both in a container. Chop the cilantro and place in a container.

On Board Preparation: Heat the oil in a large nonstick skillet over medium-high heat. Add the onion, jalapeno and garlic and sauté 2 minutes until soft. Add sugar and next 5 ingredients (through turkey), cook 5 minutes or until turkey is browned, stirring to crumble. Stir in salsa; cook 4 minutes or until slightly thick. Stir in cilantro. Spread about 3/4 cup turkey mixture on bottom half of each roll; cover with top half of roll.
Serves: 4.

Tuna and Swiss Roll-Ups

    12   ounces albacore tuna in water, drained
    2   tablespoons mayonnaise
    1   teaspoon minced garlic
    2   ounces chopped water chestnuts
    1   stalk celery, chopped
    1/4 teaspoon salt
    1/8 teaspoon pepper
    2   large flour tortillas
    1/2 cup grated Swiss cheese

Instructions
At Home Preparation: Chop the water chestnuts and celery. Mix the tuna, mayonnaise, garlic, water chestnuts, celery, salt and pepper, blending well. Place in a container.

On Board Preparation: Spread the tuna mixture evenly on each of the tortillas. Sprinkle evenly with the Swiss cheese. Roll the tortillas, tucking in the ends.
Serves: 2.

Tuna Soufflé Sandwich

    8 slices white bread
    7 ounces tuna
  1/4 cup chopped celery
  1/4 cup chopped green pepper
  1/2 cup chopped Cheddar cheese
1 1/2 cups milk
    3 large eggs, beaten
    1 teaspoon salt
  1/8 teaspoon paprika

Instructions

At Home Preparation: Trim the crusts from the bread slices and place in a container. Chop the celery and green pepper and place in a container. Shred the Cheddar and place in a container. Drain the tuna and place in a container.

On Board Preparation: Preheat the oven to 325°. Place 4 slices of bread in a greased 8-inch square baking dish. Combine the tuna, celery, and green pepper and spread over the bread. Sprinkle the cheese over all. Top with the remaining slices of bread. Combine the milk, eggs and salt, mixing well. Pour over the bread and sprinkle with paprika. Bake 40 minutes.
Serves: 4.

Seafood Main Dishes

Champagne and Lobster

1 1/2   pounds lobster meat, cooked
1   tablespoon butter
1   medium tomato
1   tablespoon chopped chives
1/4   cup Champagne
1/4   cup heavy cream
1/2   teaspoon salt
1/4   teaspoon pepper
8   sprigs parsley

Instructions
At Home Preparation: Cook the lobster and remove from the shell. Cut into large chunks. Cool and place in a container. Wash the tail shells thoroughly and place in a container. Peel, seed and chop the tomato and place in a container. Chop the chives and place in a container.

On Board Preparation: Melt butter in a skillet. Add the tomato, chives and lobster meat: heat thoroughly. Add the champagne and cook to reduce the liquid to 1 tablespoon. Add the cream. Cook until reduced by half and thickened. Salt and pepper to taste. Arrange the meat and sauce in the tail shells, garnish with fresh parsley and serve immediately.
Serves: 4.

Cheesy Baked Mussels

2   pounds mussels, scrubbed
2   cloves garlic, crushed
2   tablespoons butter
2   tablespoons olive oil
1/4   cup Worcestershire sauce
2   teaspoons fresh lemon juice
1/4   cup grated Parmesan cheese
1/4   cup grated Cheddar cheese
1/4   cup chopped parsley
1/2   cup fresh bread crumbs

Instructions
At Home Preparation: Grate the cheeses and place in a container. Make fresh bread crumbs by placing bread in a food processor fitted with the blade and pulse until soft crumbs are formed. Place in a container. Scrub and de-beard the mussels, then place in a container.

On Board Preparation: Preheat oven to 350°. Steam the mussels in water until they just open. Remove and discard the half shell. Loosen the mussels. In a skillet,

sauté the garlic in butter and oil, then add the Worcestershire, lemon juice, cheese, parsley and bread crumbs. Stir to mix well. Spoon 2 teaspoons of the bread crumb mixture onto each mussel and place on a baking tray. Bake for 10 minutes until golden brown.
Serves: 4.

Crab and Corn Pancakes

    1/2 pound crabmeat
      2 small potatoes, grated
      1 medium carrot, grated
      1 large egg
      4 ounces cream style corn
      4 ounces canned corn
      3 medium scallions, chopped
      2 tablespoons sour cream
      2 tablespoons vegetable oil
      1 tablespoon chopped parsley

Instructions
At Home Preparation: Clean and drain the crab meat. Place in a container. Grate the potato and carrot and place each in a container. Chop the scallions and place in a container.

On Board Preparation: Make sure there is no excess liquid in the crab meat, potato and carrots. Lightly beat the egg. Mix the crab, carrot and potatoes together with the corn, scallions, egg, parsley and cream. Heat the oil in a skillet and pour in 1/4 cup of the mixture. Flatten out to form a patty. Cook on medium heat 5 minutes per side, turning once during the cooking. Sprinkle with parsley. Drain on a paper towel. Repeat until all mixture is used.
Serves: 4.

Crab Claws in Lemon Butter Sauce

     12 large stone crab claws
      2 sticks butter
      2 tablespoons fresh lemon juice
      2 dashes Tabasco sauce

Instructions
If crab is frozen, thaw completely. Place the crab claws on a baking dish and heat 15 minutes in a 300° oven or on a grill. Prepare the sauce by melting the butter and adding the lemon juice and Tabasco to taste. Divide among 4 individual dipping bowls and serve with the crab.
Serves: 4.

Crabmeat Fritters

- 3/4 cup self rising flour
- 1 cup cooked rice
- 1 large egg
- 1 cup milk
- 2 medium spring onions
- 1 pound crabmeat
- 2 tablespoons vegetable oil

Instructions
At Home Preparation: Cook the rice according to package directions. Cool completely and place in a container. Chop the spring onions and place in a container. Clean and drain the crab meat and place in a container.

On Board Preparation: Sift the flour into a bowl and add the cooked rice. Form a well in the mixture and stir in the egg and milk, spring onions and crab meat. Preheat a skillet over medium-high heat with the cooking oil. Drop about a tablespoon of the mixture in the skillet and cook each side until golden brown.
Serves: 4.

Greek Style Shrimp

- 2 medium onions, thinly sliced
- 1/2 cup olive oil
- 2 pounds tomatoes, peeled & chopped
- 2 teaspoons salt
- 1 teaspoon parsley
- 1/2 teaspoon freshly ground black pepper
- 2 cloves garlic, minced
- 2 tablespoons fresh basil, cut in strips
- 1/2 pound crumbled feta cheese
- 8 ounces large shrimp, cooked
- 4 cups saffron rice, cooked
- 1/2 cup peas, cooked & drained

Instructions
At Home Preparation: Slice the onions and place in a container. Peel, seed and coarsely chop the tomatoes and place in a container. Mince the garlic and place in a container. Cut the basil into thin strips and place in a container. Cook, cool and peel the shrimp and place in a container. Cook the rice, cool and place in a container. Cook, drain and cool the peas and place in a container.

On Board Preparation: Sauté the onions in olive oil until tender. Add the tomatoes, parsley, salt pepper, garlic and basil. Cover and simmer for one hour, stirring occasionally. Add the shrimp and simmer 5 minutes. Combine the rice and peas and reheat. Serve the shrimp over the rice, sprinkled with feta cheese.
Serves: 4.

Grilled Grouper with Mango Salsa

3	medium mangos, peeled & chopped
1/2	large Vidalia onion, chopped
1	large tomato, seeded & chopped
3	tablespoons chopped fresh cilantro
3/4	teaspoon garlic salt
2	pounds grouper fillets
1/4	cup olive oil
1/2	teaspoon salt
1/4	teaspoon pepper

Instructions
At Home Preparation: Combine the mangos, onion, tomato, cilantro and garlic salt. Place in a container and chill.

On Board Preparation: Prepare the grill. Brush the grouper fillets with olive oil seasoned with salt and pepper. Grill the grouper until flaky and cooked through. Top the grouper with the salsa and serve.
Serves: 4.

GALLEY TIP
Always add oil or cooking spray to a heated pan or grill to prevent sticking. Do not add it while the pan is still cold.

Grilled Salmon

4   8 oz. servings fresh salmon
1   large lemon
1/4   cup soy sauce
1/2   teaspoon salt
1/4   teaspoon pepper
1/4   cup sesame oil
2   teaspoons ground ginger
1   large lemon

Instructions

At Home Preparation: Cut 1 lemon into wedges and place in a container. Rinse the salmon in cold water and pat dry thoroughly. Place in a container.

On Board Preparation: In a flat dish, place the salmon steaks and squeeze the lemon juice over the steaks. Add the soy sauce, salt and pepper to taste, the sesame oil and ginger. Cover and refrigerate 2 hours or preferably overnight. Soak the hickory chips in water for 30-45 minutes. Prepare the grill adding hickory chips just before grilling. (The hotter the grill and the denser the smoke the more intense the smoky flavor.) Grill the salmon for 5-8 minutes per side until desired doneness. Garnish with lemon wedges.
Serves: 4.

Recipe Notes
Use hickory chips to grill this salmon dish.

Grilled Shrimp with Kiwi-Cucumber Salsa

3   tablespoons fresh lime juice
1   tablespoon seeded & chopped jalapeno pepper
2   teaspoons minced ginger
1   teaspoon lime zest
2   cups peeled & chopped kiwi fruit
1   cup seeded & chopped cucumber
1   cup peeled & chopped cantaloupe
1/2   medium green onion, thinly sliced
2   tablespoons chopped fresh mint leaves
2   pounds large shrimp
1/4   cup olive oil
1   dash lime juice

Instructions

At Home Preparation: Combine the lime juice, jalapeno, ginger and lime peel in a medium bowl and whisk until blended. Add the remaining ingredients and toss. Season with salt and pepper as desired. Place in a container and chill.

On Board Preparation: Prepare the grill. Peel the shrimp, toss in the olive oil and lime juice. Grill just until pink and curled. Spoon salsa over shrimp and serve. *Serves: 4.*

Grilled Shrimp with Southwest Marinade

1/3	cup lime juice
1/3	cup olive oil
2	tablespoons tequila
2	tablespoons chopped fresh cilantro
1	clove minced garlic
1	medium seeded & chopped jalapeno pepper
1/4	teaspoon salt
1/4	teaspoon pepper
1	pound large shrimp, peeled

Instructions
At Home Preparation: Combine all the ingredients except the shrimp. Place in a container. Peel and devein the shrimp and place in a container.

On Board Preparation: Pour the marinade over the shrimp and refrigerate 2 hours. Prepare the grill and grill the shrimp until they turn pink. Brush with marinade as they cook if desired.
Serves: 2.

Recipe Notes
These shrimp are great tossed with pasta and a little olive oil or make additional marinade to toss. As an appetizer, serve over field greens, or on crackers or toast points.

GALLEY TIP
Toss fruits and vegetables that oxidize quickly with a little lemon or orange juice to keep them looking fresh.

Grilled Swordfish

4 servings swordfish steaks
1/2 cup vegetable oil
3 tablespoons soy sauce
2 tablespoons dry sherry
1 1/2 teaspoons ginger root, grated
1 teaspoon orange peel, grated
1/4 teaspoon freshly ground black pepper

Instructions

At Home Preparation: Peel the ginger root (but do not grate) and place in a container. Grate the orange peel and place in a container.

On Board Preparation: Place the swordfish steaks in a flat dish. Grate the ginger root and add it to the oil, soy sauce, sherry, orange peel and pepper. Pour over the fish and marinate, covered, in the refrigerator overnight, turning occasionally. Prepare the grill and coat the rack with cooking spray. Grill the swordfish, basting with the marinade for 4-5 minutes per side or until firm to the touch.
Serves: 4.

Grouper Cakes

2 tablespoons butter
2 tablespoons olive oil
1 1/2 cups chopped celery
3/4 cup chopped red onion
1/2 cup chopped red bell pepper
1 tablespoon capers, drained
1 teaspoon Creole seasoning
1/2 teaspoon Worcestershire sauce
1/2 teaspoon Tabasco sauce
1/2 teaspoon salt
1/2 teaspoon freshly ground black pepper
1/2 pound grouper fillets
1/2 cup Panko bread crumbs
1/2 cup mayonnaise
2 teaspoons Dijon mustard
2 large eggs, lightly beaten
1/4 cup olive oil

Instructions

At Home Preparation: Finely chop the celery red onion and red pepper and place each in a container. Bake the grouper fillets in a 350° oven until cooked through. Cool, flake, and place in a container. Heat the butter and 2 tablespoons olive oil in a skillet over medium heat. Sauté the celery onion, bell pepper, parsley and capers for 10 minutes or until tender. Stir in the Creole seasoning, Worcestershire, Tabasco and salt and pepper. Remove from heat and let cool. Place in a container.

On Board Preparation: Put the flaked grouper in a bowl. Add the bread crumbs, mayonnaise, Dijon mustard and 2 beaten eggs. Fold in the vegetable mixture gently just until combined. Cover and chill for 30 minutes. Shape into 12 cakes for a main course or 24 for appetizers. Heat the 1/4 cup olive oil in a non-stick skillet over medium-high heat. Place the grouper cakes in the skillet and cook until golden brown on each side. Remove to paper towels to drain. Serve with your favorite cocktail or tartar sauce if desired.
Serves: 6.

Grouper with Honey-Jalapeno Sauce

1	cup honey
1/4	cup white wine vinegar
1 1/2	teaspoons cinnamon
4	ounces sliced jalapeno peppers in juice
1/2	cup light brown sugar
3	dashes Tabasco sauce
1/4	cup cornstarch
32	ounces grouper fillets
1	large red bell pepper

Instructions

At Home Preparation: In a saucepan, bring the honey vinegar, cinnamon, jalapenos and their juice, 1/2 cup water, brown sugar and Tabasco to a gentle boil. Place the cornstarch in a cup and add 1/2 cup cold water to dilute, stirring to dissolve. With a whisk, slowly add the cornstarch mixture to the honey mixture. Cook over medium heat to thicken slightly. Strain, discarding solids. Place in a container and refrigerate up to 2 days. (The flavor improves as it sits.) Cut the red pepper into julienne strips and place in a container.

On Board Preparation: Prepare the grill and spray the rack with cooking spray. Heat the sauce. Grill the grouper fillets until done. Top with the sauce and pepper strips.
Serves: 4.

Herbed Mussels

    2 tablespoons olive oil
    1 medium onion, finely chopped
    1 teaspoon dried oregano
    3 tablespoons chopped fresh parsley
    1 clove garlic, finely chopped
  1/2 cup white wine
    3 dozen mussels, scrubbed
    1 loaf French bread

Instructions

At Home Preparation: Chop the onion and place in a container. Chop the parsley and garlic and place each in a container. Scrub and debeard the mussels and place in a container. Slice the French bread, if desired, and place in a container.

On Board Preparation: Heat the oil in a large saucepan or pot over medium heat, then add the onion and sauté until soft, about 5 minutes. Stir in the herbs and garlic, wine and mussels. Cover and increase the heat to high. Steam until the mussels open, about 5 minutes. With a slotted spoon, transfer the mussels to a large bowl, discarding any that are unopened. Pour the cooking sauce over the mussels being careful not to pour in any sandy residue from the bottom of the pan. Serve with the French bread to soak up the sauce.
Serves: 6.

Island Grouper

    1 large mango
    1 large papaya
  1/4 large pineapple
    2 medium jalapeno peppers
  1/2 large tomato, peeled & chopped
  1/3 cup red wine vinegar
  1/2 large red onion, diced
    1 tablespoon olive oil
  1/3 cup fresh coarsely chopped cilantro
    1 cup peanut oil
  1/3 cup soy sauce
    1 large orange
   10 whole peppercorns, lightly crushed
    2 large bay leaves
    4 servings grouper fillets, cut on the bias

Instructions

At Home Preparation: Peel the papaya and mango, remove the seeds and cube into small pieces. Cube the pineapple. Wearing plastic gloves, remove the stems, seeds and ribs from the jalapenos and chop fine. Combine the papaya, mango, pineapple, jalapenos, tomato, vinegar, onion, olive oil and cilantro. Toss gently to combine and place in a container. (Can be kept at room temperature up to 6 hours. If preparing well ahead, refrigerate and bring back to room temperature for 6 hours before serving.) Juice the orange and place in a container.

On Board Preparation: Prepare the grill and coat the rack with cooking spray. Combine the peanut oil, soy sauce, orange juice, peppercorns and bay leaves; keep at room temperature. Place the grouper fillets in the marinade for about 3-5 minutes. Grill the fish until just cooked through, basting with the marinade frequently during cooking. To serve, top with the salsa.
Serves: 4.

Jalapeno and Shrimp on a Skewer

- 3/4 cup unsweetened orange juice
- 2 tablespoons minced fresh parsley
- 1 tablespoon minced jalapeno pepper
- 1 tablespoon peeled & grated ginger root
- 1/4 teaspoon crushed red pepper
- 1 large garlic clove, minced
- 1 1/2 pounds large shrimp

Instructions

At Home Preparation: Combine first 6 ingredients in a bowl, stirring well, then place in a container. Peel and devein the shrimp leaving the tails intact and place in a container.

On Board Preparation: Place the shrimp in the marinade and return to the refrigerator for 1 hour, stirring occasionally. Remove shrimp from the marinade; bring marinade to a boil, and set aside. Thread 6 shrimp onto each of 8 skewers, piercing tail and neck of the each shrimp. Coat the grill rack with cooking spray, and place on the grill over medium-hot heat or coals. Place skewers on rack and cook about 3 to 4 minutes on each side; basting frequently with the marinade.
Serves: 4.

Jamaican Jerk Shrimp with Pineapple Salad

   3 tablespoons lime juice, freshly squeezed
   1 teaspoon grated lime zest
   1 tablespoon canola oil
   2 cloves garlic, finely chopped
1/2 teaspoon dried thyme leaf
   1 cup unsweetened pineapple juice
1/2 teaspoon dried oregano
1/4 teaspoon cinnamon
1/4 teaspoon ground allspice
   2 tablespoons Jamaican jerk sauce
 20 large shrimp, peeled
   3 cups cooked white rice
 16 ounces black beans, drained and rinsed
1/2 teaspoon sea salt
1/2 teaspoon freshly ground black pepper
   2 cups fresh pineapple chunks
   6 large scallions, cut in 2" lengths
   1 head Boston lettuce
   1 medium lime, sliced

Instructions

At Home Preparation: In a small saucepan, bring pineapple juice to a boil over medium-high heat; cook until reduced to 1/3 cup, about 8-10 minutes. Remove from the heat and whisk in lime juice and zest, oil, garlic, thyme, oregano, cinnamon and allspice. Let cool to room temperature and place in a container. Peel and devein the shrimp. Place in a container. Cook the rice and cool to room temperature, then place in a container. Cut the pineapple into chunks and place in a container. Trim and cut the scallions and place in a container. Wash, completely dry and tear the lettuce. Roll in paper towels and place in a perforated zip top bag. Slice the lime for garnish and place in a container.

On Board Preparation: In a shallow dish just large enough to hold the shrimp, whisk together jerk sauce and 1/4 cup of the pineapple juice marinade. Add shrimp and turn to coat. Cover and refrigerate for 30 minutes. In a large bowl, toss rice and black beans with the remaining marinade. Season with salt and pepper and set aside. Prepare a medium-hot grill. Remove the shrimp from the marinade. Add pineapple chunks and scallions to the marinade, turning to coat. Thread 4 long or 8 short skewers with shrimp, pineapple and scallions; brush with the remaining marinade. Grill, turning once or twice, until the shrimp are cooked through, 6-10 minutes. Arrange a bed of lettuce on a large platter or individual plates. Spoon the rice and bean mixture on top then slide the shrimp, pineapple and scallions on top.
Serves: 4.

Recipe Notes
Buy a good quality commercially prepared Jamaican jerk sauce.

Lemon Pasta with Shrimp

- 1   pound large shrimp
- 1/2 pound fresh linguini
- 1   teaspoon olive oil
- 1   small thinly sliced red onion
- 1/2 cup chopped fresh parsley
- 2/3 cup kalamata olives, pitted
- 3   tablespoons fresh lemon juice
- 1/3 cup olive oil
- 1/2 teaspoon salt
- 1/4 teaspoon pepper
- 4   servings field greens
- 1   medium lemon, thinly sliced

Instructions

At Home Preparation: Peel and devein the shrimp. Cook in boiling water just until they turn pink and begin to curl. Drain and cool completely and place in a container. Cook the pasta in boiling water just until tender. Drain and rinse. Drizzle with a few drops, up to 1 teaspoon olive oil and toss to coat. Cool completely and place in a container. Chop the parsley and place in a container. Slice the lemon into thin slices and place in a container.

On Board Preparation: Toss the pasta, shrimp, onion, parsley and olives together in a bowl. Mix the lemon juice and olive oil in a small bowl. Drizzle over the pasta and toss to coat. Salt and pepper to taste. On four serving plates, place a "nest" of field greens. Place equal portions of the pasta mixture on each and garnish with the lemon slices.

Serves: 4.

Recipe Notes
Use any of your favorite pasta to substitute for the linguini for this dish.

GALLEY TIP
Poke a hole in the center of a hamburger patty to cook faster.
The hole disappears when the meat is done.

Lobster Éclairs

        1 cup water
      1/2 cup butter, cut in pieces
      1/4 teaspoon salt
        1 cup flour
        4 large eggs
        2 tablespoons heavy cream
    1 1/2 cups lobster meat, cooked and cubed
      1/2 cup mayonnaise
        2 tablespoons finely minced celery
        2 teaspoons curry powder
        4 servings watercress
        2 medium lemons, thinly sliced

Instructions

At Home Preparation: Preheat oven to 400°. Prepare the pate choux: In a heavy saucepan bring water, butter and salt to a boil over high heat. Lower heat and add flour all at once. With a wooden spoon, beat the mixture until it leaves the sides of the pan and forms a ball. Transfer the dough to the bowl of an electric mixer. With the mixer at high speed, beat in 3 eggs, one at a time, beating thoroughly after each addition. The batter should be just thick enough to hold peaks. If it is too thick, add another egg to bring batter to the right consistency. Butter a large baking sheet. To make the éclairs, fill a pastry bag fitted with a 1/3 inch plain tube with the pate choux. Pipe out about 16 strips, 3 inches long, onto the baking sheet about 1 inch apart. Beat 1 egg with cream and brush tops of éclairs with egg mixture. Place the baking sheet in the center of the oven and bake éclairs for 10 minutes. Reduce the oven temperature to 350° and continue baking for another 10 minutes. Turn off the oven. With the tip of a sharp knife make 1 or 2 slits in each éclair and let the éclairs stand in the oven for 10 to 15 minutes or until they are dry. Transfer to a rack and cool completely. Place in a container. Cook and cube the lobster meat. Cool completely and place in a container. Mince the celery and place in a container. Wash the watercress and dry completely. Roll in paper towels and place in a perforated zip top plastic bag. Slice the lemons and place in a container.

On Board Preparation: Put the lobster meat in a bowl and fold in the mayonnaise celery and curry powder. Split the éclairs in half lengthwise and divide the lobster mixture among the bottom halves. Place watercress over the filling and replace the tops pressing them down slightly. Garnish with lemon wedges.
Serves: 4.

Lobster with Orange Butter

    1 1/8 cups dry white wine
      1/4 cup whipping cream
        4 sticks butter

  1/2 teaspoon salt
  1/4 teaspoon pepper
    1 cup frozen concentrate orange juice, thawed
    4 large lobster tails
    2 large oranges

Instructions

At Home Preparation: Cook the lobster tails and cool. Remove the meat from the shell and cut each tail into 5 slices, keeping each tail together. Place in a container. Peel and section the oranges and place in a container. Cook the orange juice in a small pan until reduced by half. Cool and place in a container.

On Board Preparation: Soften the butter to room temperature. In a saucepan over medium heat, reduce 6 tablespoons of wine to about 1-1/2 tablespoons. Reduce the heat and add the cream, cooking until thickened. Whisk in the butter, 1 tablespoon at a time. Remove from the heat and salt and pepper to taste. Whisk the reduced orange juice into the butter mixture and heat until warm; remove from heat and keep warm. Place the prepared lobster in a skillet with enough wine to cover the bottom. Cover and warm the lobster over low heat. To serve, transfer the lobster to plates; top each with the orange butter and garnish with orange sections.
Serves: 4.

Marinated Grilled Fish Kabobs

     3 pounds fresh tuna
     2 cloves garlic, crushed
     1 medium onion, finely chopped
     1 teaspoon dried oregano
     1 teaspoon coarsely ground pepper
 1 1/2 cups red wine
   1/2 cup olive oil
     1 large bay leaf
     1 piece orange peel, 2-inch
     3 medium zucchini, cut crosswise into 1/2-inch rounds

Instructions

At Home Preparation: Trim any excess fat from the fish. Cut into 1-1/2 inch cubes and place in a container. Crush the garlic and chop the onion and place in a container. Cut the rind from an orange in a 2-inch strip and place in a container. Wash the zucchini and cut into 1/2 inch rounds. Place in a container.

On Board Preparation: Place the fish in a nonmetallic bowl and add the garlic, onion, oregano and pepper. Toss well with your hands, rubbing the seasoning into the fish. Add the wine, oil, bay leaf and the orange rind, turning the fish to coat. Marinate for 30 minutes at room temperature. Prepare the grill. Thread alternating pieces of tuna and zucchini snugly on skewers. Grill about 5 minutes on each side, brushing occasionally with the marinade until lightly browned.
Serves: 6.

Mussels with Garlic Basil and Tomatoes

        5 pounds mussels
        4 cups dry vermouth
        4 cloves garlic, crushed
        1 teaspoon dried basil
        1 cup chopped tomato

Instructions

At Home Preparation: Scrub and debeard the mussels, discarding any that are open, and place in a container. Mince the parsley and place in a container. Crush the garlic and place in a container.

On Board Preparation: In a large stockpot, combine the vermouth, garlic and basil. Place over high heat and add the mussels. Cover and steam until mussels open, about 5 minutes, shaking the pot frequently. Remove with a slotted spoon to a serving dish, discarding any that did not open. Add tomatoes to remaining stock and simmer for a few minutes, just until heated. Pour over mussels.
Serves: 4.

Poached Salmon with Remoulade

        4 8 oz. fresh salmon steaks
        1 cup dry white wine
        1 cup mayonnaise
        2 cloves garlic, minced
    1 1/2 teaspoons finely chopped tarragon
        1 teaspoon mustard powder
        1 tablespoon capers
        3 large eggs, hard cooked (one for garnish)
        1 tablespoon minced fresh parsley
        8 sprigs fresh dill (for garnish)

Instructions

At Home Preparation: Put 1 inch of water in a skillet, add the wine and bring to a boil. Add the salmon and cook 10 minutes for each inch of salmon steak thickness. Drain and chill. Place in a container. Chill at least 4 hours before serving. Mince the garlic and place in a container. Hard cook the eggs. Cool and peel. Finely chop 2 of the eggs. Place in a container. Slice the third egg for garnish and place in a container. Mince the fresh parsley and place in a container.

On Board Preparation: Prepare the sauce by combining all ingredients except the salmon and garnish (sliced egg and dill sprigs). Let stand in the refrigerator for 2-3 hours before serving. Serve the salmon with some of the sauce on top and garnish with the sliced egg and dill sprigs.   *Serves: 4.*

Prawns in Garlic

1 1/2   pounds king prawns
1/2   cup olive oil
3   teaspoons chopped garlic
1/2   teaspoon chili sauce
1/4   teaspoon saffron strands
1/4   teaspoon salt
1   loaf crusty bread

Instructions

At Home Preparation: Shell and devein the prawns, leaving the tails on. Place in a container. Chop the garlic and place in a container. Pound the saffron strands in a mortar and pestle and place in a container.

On Board Preparation: Dissolve the saffron in a tablespoon of hot water. Heat the oil and cook the garlic, chili, and saffron in a heavy skillet until garlic is soft. Add the prawns and cook, turning until cooked through, about 3 to 4 minutes. Place the prawns in ramekins and pour over the juice. Serve with crusty bread for dipping.
Serves: 4.

GALLEY TIP

It's okay to replace eggs with egg substitute in most recipes which call for the eggs to be beaten. However, you will sacrifice a little taste.

Salmon in a Rosemary Cream Sauce

    16 ounces fish stock
     1 sprig fresh rosemary
     7 ounces heavy cream
     3 ounces butter
   1/4 teaspoon salt
   1/8 teaspoon pepper
   1/8 teaspoon white pepper
     1 tablespoon sunflower oil
     4 fresh salmon fillets, 6-ounces each
     4 sprigs fresh rosemary

Instructions

At Home Preparation: Rinse the salmon and remove any bones. Pat dry with a paper towel and place in a container. Place the fish stock and rosemary sprig in a saucepan and bring to a boil. Reduce heat and simmer until reduced to one half. Add the cream and continue to cook on simmer until reduced by one half again. Discard the rosemary. Whisk in 2 ounces of the butter and season to taste with salt and white pepper. Cool and place in a container.

On Board Preparation: Melt the remaining 1 ounce butter and the oil in a skillet over medium heat. Season the salmon and place flesh side down in the pan. Cook for 2-3 minutes, carefully turn to the skin side down and cook an additional 2-3 minutes. Reheat the sauce over low heat and spoon onto 4 plates. Place the salmon fillet on top and drizzle with a little more sauce. Garnish with the rosemary sprigs.
Serves: 4.

Salmon with Champagne Sauce

     6 ounces fresh salmon, cooked
     1 large egg
   1/4 teaspoon salt
   1/8 teaspoon pepper
   3/4 cup heavy cream
     2 sheets frozen puff pastry
     2 pounds fresh salmon fillets
     1 whole egg, beaten
   1/2 bottle Champagne
     2 medium shallots, minced
     3 cups heavy cream

Instructions

At Home Preparation: Mince the shallots and place in a container. Cook the 6 ounces salmon and cool. Make the mousse by processing the 6 ounces salmon in the blender until smooth. Add the egg, salt and pepper and pulse to mix. Slowly add the cream while processing until smooth. Place in a container and chill. Butterfly the fillet lengthwise to create a pocket and place in a container. Roll out the pastry sheets and place in a container.

On Board Preparation: Place the 2 pound salmon fillet on 1 sheet of pastry and trim the pastry to fit. Spoon the chilled mousse into the pocket of the fillet and press gently to close. Season the salmon with salt and pepper. Brush the edges of the pastry with some of the beaten egg. Place the other pastry sheet on top, trim and press together to seal. (Use the scrap pieces to make decorative shapes for the top of the salmon, if desired.) Brush the entire top with the remaining beaten egg. Place on a baking sheet cover and chill for at least 1 hour. Preheat the oven to 400°. Bake for 20 minutes or until golden. Combine the 1/2 bottle Champagne and shallots in a saucepan and heat on medium until reduced to a glaze. Add the 3 cups heavy cream and cook until the sauce coats a spoon. Season with salt and pepper. Slice the salmon and spoon some sauce over each.
Serves: 8.

GALLEY TIP
If you make sandwiches ahead, be sure to put ingredients such as mayo, mustard etc. between the meat and/or cheese to keep the bread from getting soggy.

Salmon with Radish Dill Sauce

- 1/2 cup dry white wine
- 1/2 cup heavy cream
- 1 medium shallot, finely chopped
- 1 cup unsalted butter
- 1/4 teaspoon white pepper
- 1/2 teaspoon salt
- 8 large radishes, trimmed
- 3 tablespoons chopped fresh dill
- 1 tablespoon horseradish, drained
- 1 tablespoon unsalted butter
- 1 tablespoon vegetable oil
- 4 fresh salmon fillets, 8 oz. each
- 1 cup milk
- 1/2 cup all-purpose flour
- 1/4 teaspoon salt
- 4 sprigs fresh dill

Instructions

At Home Preparation: Chop the shallot and place in a container. Trim and wash the radishes and place in a container. Chop the dill and place in a container. Drain the horseradish and place in a container. In a saucepan, combine the wine, cream and shallots. Bring to a boil; cook over medium heat until reduced to 1/2 cup. Reduce to low and whisk in 1 cup butter, 1 tablespoons at a time. Season with white pepper and salt. Remove from heat. Cut about 12 thin slices of radish and place in a container. Finely chop the remaining radishes and add to the sauce. Stir in the dill and horseradish; cool and place in a container.

On Board Preparation: In a skillet, melt 1 tablespoon butter with oil over medium-high heat. When it begins to sizzle, dip each salmon fillet in milk, dust lightly with flour and add to the skillet. Sauté, turning once until lightly browned, about 3 minutes per side. Reduce to medium and continue cooking, turning no more than twice, until it has almost lost its translucency in the thickest part. Season with salt. Bring the sauce back up to heat by placing over low heat. Divide among four plates placing salmon on top. Garnishing with reserved radish slices and dill sprigs. ***Serves: 4.***

Scallops in Cognac Over Lime Rice

- 4 cups cooked rice
- 1 medium lime peel, grated
- 1/4 cup fresh lime juice
- 2 tablespoons olive oil
- 1 medium red bell pepper
- 6 medium green onions

> 1 tablespoon dry white wine
> 1 pound scallops
> 2 tablespoons cognac
> 2 teaspoons chopped fresh tarragon
> 1/4 teaspoon salt
> 1/8 teaspoon pepper

Instructions

At Home Preparation: Cook the rice according to package directions, cool, and place in a container. Grate the lime peel and place in a container. Squeeze the lime juice and place in a container. Cut the red pepper into 1-inch julienne strips and place in a container. Chop the green onions, including about half of the green tops into 1-inch pieces and place in a container. Chop the tarragon and place in a container.

On Board Preparation: Place the rice in the top of a double boiler or in the microwave and reheat. Add the lime rind and 2 tablespoons of the lime juice and stir. Keep warm while cooking the scallops. In a large skillet heat 1 tablespoon oil over medium heat. Sauté the red pepper and green onions about 5 minutes stirring occasionally. Add the wine and cook 3 more minutes. Remove from the heat and place in a bowl. Heat the remaining oil in the same pan over medium-high heat; add scallops, Cognac, 2 tablespoons lime juice and the tarragon. Cook about 2 minutes, shaking pan frequently. Add the red pepper mixture and cook 1 minute. Season with salt and pepper to taste and serve over the rice.
Serves: 4.

Scallops in Lemon Butter

> 1 pound bay scallops
> 3 tablespoons butter
> 1 tablespoon olive oil
> 1 tablespoon lemon juice
> 1/4 teaspoon freshly ground black pepper
> 1 pound linguini

Instructions

At Home Preparation: Rinse the scallops and pat dry with a paper towel. Place in a container. (Freeze if desired.) Cook the linguini according to package directions, drain and rinse. Allow to cool, then place in container.

On Board Preparation: Reheat the linguini by placing in the microwave for 30-60 seconds or place in a pan with a few drops of water and heat over medium heat. In a medium saucepan, heat the butter and olive oil until the butter has melted over medium heat. Add the lemon juice and black pepper. Add the scallops and stir well. Heat over medium heat for just a few minutes, stirring to distribute the sauce. Scallops are properly cooked when the center is opaque. Be careful not to over cook. Divide the linguini between four plates and top with an equal portion of scallops. Pour the lemon butter over and serve.   *Serves: 4.*

Scallops with Red Pepper Coulis

   8 large scallops
   2 limes
   3 ounces olive oil
 1/4 teaspoon sea salt
 1/8 teaspoon pepper
   8 fresh coriander leaves
   6 ounces roasted red peppers
   1 clove garlic, coarsely chopped
   4 ounces olive oil
   1 teaspoon lime juice

Instructions

At Home Preparations: Prepare the scallops by separating the corals and trimming any rubbery muscles. Cut each into 2 or 3 disc slices and place in a container. In a bowl, whisk together the lime juice and all but 1 tablespoon of the olive oil. Season with freshly ground pepper to taste. Place in a container. To make the coulis, drain the peppers and place in a blender with the garlic and 4 ounces olive oil; puree. Strain if necessary, and season to taste with salt and pepper. Thin with a little lime juice if necessary and place in a container.

On Board Preparation: Place the scallops and corals in a glass or stainless steel bowl. Pour the olive oil mixture over the scallops, cover and marinate for 30 minutes. Drain the scallops and corals and pat dry with a paper towel. Heat the remaining olive oil in a non-stick skillet until hot. Add the scallops and sear quickly over high heat until light brown on both sides, 2-3 minutes total cooking time. To serve, arrange the scallops and corals on plates and grind a little sea salt and pepper over them. Spoon the coulis in the middle and garnish with coriander leaves.
Serves: 4.

Scotch Salmon

   1 pound fresh salmon steaks
   2 tablespoons Scotch
   2 tablespoons lemon juice
   1 teaspoon Italian seasoning
   1 dash salt
   1 dash pepper

Instructions

At Home Preparation: Cut the salmon into servings and place in a container. Combine the remaining ingredients and place in a container.

On Board Preparation: Place the salmon in a bowl and cover with the marinade. Cover and place in the refrigerator to marinate for 1-2 hours. Prepare the grill. Grill the salmon for about 10 minutes basting with the marinade during cooking.
Serves: 2.

Sea Bass Crusted with Potato and Green Onion

   4 servings sea bass, 8 ounces each
   2 medium Yukon gold potatoes, shredded
   2 stalks green onions, cut into 1" thick pieces
   2 cloves garlic, chopped
   1 tablespoon sesame oil
1/2 cup flour
1/4 teaspoon salt
1/8 teaspoon pepper

Instructions
At Home Preparation: Peel and shred the potatoes. Place on paper towels to allow excess moisture to absorb into the paper towels. Place in a container. Chop the green onions and place in a container.

On Board Preparation: Combine the potatoes, green onions, garlic, sesame oil, and salt and pepper. Coat one side of the sea bass pieces with the potato mixture. Heat a non-stick frying pan over medium heat. (Make sure the pan is hot before adding the fish.) Sauté potato side down over medium heat until golden brown. Gently turn and lightly brown on the uncoated side. Turn the heat down, cover and finish cooking until the fish flakes with a fork.
Serves: 4.

Recipe Notes
This is an easy dish but very elegant and delicious. You can also use other cuts of fish so experiment with some of your favorites.

GALLEY TIP
Store celery stalks in a paper bag to maximize freshness.

Shrimp and Blue Cheese

      8   ounces blue cheese
      8   ounces cream cheese
      1   tablespoon chopped chives
      1   tablespoon chopped parsley
      1   clove finely chopped garlic
    1/4   cup dry white wine
      2   pounds shrimp, peeled and deveined
      1   medium lemon, sliced

Instructions

At Home Preparation: Chop the chives and parsley and place in a container. Chop the garlic and place in a container. Peel and devein the shrimp and place in a container. Slice the lemon and place in a container.

On Board Preparation: Soften the blue cheese and cream cheese by bringing to room temperature. Preheat the oven to 400° or prepare grill. Blend the blue cheese, cream cheese, chives, parsley and garlic together in a bowl, using an electric mixer or mixing vigorously with a wooden spoon. Add the wine and blend thoroughly. Cut four large squares of aluminum foil; divide the cheese mixture evenly on each. Top each with shrimp and a lemon slice. Fold up ends to make a tight package. Place on a baking sheet and bake 20 minutes or grill, making sure the grill temperature is equivalent.
Serves: 4.

Shrimp and Olives

    1 1/2   pounds jumbo shrimp, cooked
      1/2   pound kalamata olives, pitted & drained
        1   cup fresh lime juice
        1   cup orange juice
      1/2   cup water
        4   cloves garlic, chopped
        2   tablespoons fennel seeds
        1   lime peel, julienne
        1   orange peel, julienne
        4   servings mixed greens
        1   small avocado, sliced

Instructions

At Home Preparation: Cook, peel and devein the shrimp. Cool and place in a container. Combine the remaining ingredients except the lime and orange peel and the avocado slices. Remove about 4 tablespoons and place in a separate container. Add the peel to the remaining liquid and place in a container.

On Board Preparation: Combine the marinade and the shrimp and chill for at least 24 hours. Just before serving, peel and slice the avocado. Drain the shrimp, reserving the marinade. Divide the field greens and the shrimp between four plates and garnish with avocado slices. Drizzle very lightly with the reserved marinade. *Serves: 4.*

Shrimp and Scallops

3/4	pound sea scallops
3/4	pound shrimp
2/3	cup dry vermouth
1/2	teaspoon salt
1/2	teaspoon white pepper
1	medium onion, chopped
1/2	pound mushrooms, sliced
4	ounces fresh Parmesan cheese, grated
1/4	cup dry grated Parmesan cheese
1/2	stick butter
2	tablespoons flour
1/4	cup cream
1	cup Panko bread crumbs

Instructions
At Home Preparation: Grate the fresh Parmesan and place in a container. Rinse the scallops and cut in half if too large. Place in a container. Peel and devein the shrimp and place in a container. Sauté the onions and mushrooms until tender. Cool and place in a container.

On Board Preparation: Preheat the oven to 350°. Combine the scallops, shrimp, vermouth, salt and pepper in a pan and cook until tender, about 5 minutes. Drain, reserving the liquid. Blend the reserved liquid with flour and add the cream. Add the dry Parmesan and stir over low heat until thickened. Butter 6 ramekins. Divide the shrimp and scallops evenly amongst the ramekins. Mix the onion and mushroom mixture into the sauce. Spoon evenly into the ramekins. Sprinkle with the freshly grated cheese and Panko bread crumbs. Bake until bubbly, about 10 minutes. *Serves: 6.*

Shrimp and Scallops ala Orange

- 1 lemon
- 12 large shrimp, peeled and deveined
- 16 sea scallops, cleaned
- 1/4 cup all-purpose flour
- 4 tablespoons butter
- 2 shallots, finely chopped
- 2 cloves garlic, minced
- 2 tablespoons butter
- 1/4 cup dry vermouth
- 2/3 cup fresh orange juice
- 1 cup heavy cream
- 4 fresh basil leaves, chopped
- 1 cup mandarin orange sections

Instructions

At Home Preparation: Peel and devein the shrimp and place in a container. Mince the parsley and place in a container. Clean the scallops and place in a container. Finely chop the shallots and place in a container. Mince the garlic and place in a container. Chop the basil and place in a container.

On Board Preparation: Squeeze a little lemon juice on the shrimp and scallops and toss them lightly in the flour. In a large skillet sauté them in 4 tablespoons butter; set aside. In a skillet sauté the shallots and garlic in 2 tablespoons butter. Pour in vermouth and cook to reduce by one half. Add the orange juice and reduce by one half. Add the cream and cook about 10 minutes. Add the basil, shrimp and scallops. Heat just until heated through and serve garnished with the mandarin orange slices.
Serves: 4.

Shrimp in Sauterne Sauce

- 1 1/2 cups olive oil
- 1 1/2 cups Sauterne
- 4 bay leaves, crushed
- 3 cloves garlic, minced
- 1 medium green pepper, chopped
- 3 ribs celery, chopped
- 1/2 medium onion, chopped
- 1/4 teaspoon salt
- 1/8 teaspoon pepper
- 2 pounds jumbo shrimp
- 1 loaf French bread

Instructions

At Home Preparation: Mince the garlic and place in a container. Chop the green pepper and celery and place in a container. Chop the onion and place in a container.

On Board Preparation: Bring all ingredients except the shrimp to a boil in a large stock pot. Add the shrimp and cook on medium heat for 10-15 minutes or until the shrimp turn pink. Divide shrimp among individual serving bowls and pour the sauce evenly over each. Serve with the French bread for dipping.
Serves: 4.

Shrimp Steamed in Beer

- 1 can beer
- 2 pounds shrimp, in shells
- 1/2 teaspoon thyme
- 1/2 teaspoon mustard powder
- 1 bay leaf
- 1 clove garlic, chopped
- 1 tablespoon salt
- 1 tablespoon chopped parsley
- 1/4 teaspoon pepper
- 1/2 teaspoon chopped chives
- 4 tablespoons butter
- 2 tablespoons lemon juice
- 1 tablespoon chopped parsley
- 1 tablespoon chopped chives
- 1 teaspoon salt

Instructions

At Home Preparation: Chop the garlic, parsley and chives and place each in a container.

On Board Preparation: Make the sauce by melting the 4 tablespoons butter in a saucepan and adding the 2 tablespoons lemon juice 1 tablespoon chopped parsley, 1 tablespoon chopped chives and 1 teaspoon salt. For the shrimp, combine the beer, shrimp and spices in a covered pan. Cover tightly and bring to a boil. Reduce heat and simmer for 3 minutes or just until pink. Do not over cook. Add the sauce to the shrimp mixture. Peel and eat.
Serves: 4.

Shrimp with Tomatoes and Feta

   2 pounds jumbo shrimp
   4 tablespoons extra virgin olive oil
   4 medium tomatoes, peeled, seeded and chopped
   2 cloves garlic, minced
   1 tablespoon chopped fresh basil
   4 ounces crumbled feta cheese
1/4 teaspoon salt
1/8 teaspoon pepper
 12 kalamata olives, pitted

Instructions

At Home Preparation: Peel and devein the shrimp. Place in a container. Peel, seed and chop the tomatoes and place in a container. Mince the garlic and place in a container.

On Board Preparation: Heat the olive oil in a skillet and sauté the shrimp about 5 to 6 minutes, until they turn pink. Add the tomatoes, garlic, basil and feta cheese. Stir over medium heat for about 5 minutes. Salt and pepper to taste. Serve garnished with the Greek olives.
Serves: 4.

Spicy Shrimp with Coconut Sauce

  1/2 cup coconut milk
    1 tablespoon lime juice
    1 teaspoon minced ginger
    1 teaspoon low sodium soy sauce
    1 teaspoon honey
  1/2 teaspoon cornstarch
  1/2 teaspoon chili paste with garlic
  1/2 teaspoon minced garlic
  1/4 teaspoon salt
    2 teaspoons canola oil
1 1/2 pounds jumbo shrimp, peeled and deveined
    2 tablespoons chopped green onions
  1/2 teaspoon crushed red pepper
    2 cups jasmine rice

Instructions

At Home Preparation: Combine the first 9 ingredients in a medium bowl, stirring well, and place in a container. Chop the green onions and place in a container. Cook the rice, cool completely, and place in a container. Peel and devein the shrimp and place in a container.

On Board Preparation: Reheat the rice by adding a few drops of water and microwave on high for about 2 minutes. Keep warm until ready to serve. Heat the canola oil in a large nonstick skillet over medium-high heat. Add the shrimp and sauté for 2 minutes. Add the green onions and red pepper and cook an additional minute. Add the coconut milk mixture and bring to a boil. Reduce heat and simmer 1 minute or until shrimp turn pink. Serve immediately with the rice.
Serves: 4.

Spinach Fettuccini with Scallops

2	tablespoons butter
2	tablespoons olive oil
3/4	pound bay scallops
1/2	green pepper, diced
1	large tomato, seeded & chopped
4	green onions, chopped
10	large mushrooms, sliced
2	cups heavy cream
1/4	cup grated Parmesan cheese
9	ounces spinach fettuccini
5	ounces boursin cheese with garlic
1/4	teaspoon salt
1/8	teaspoon pepper

Instructions

At Home Preparation: Seed and chop the green pepper and place in a container. Mince the parsley and place in a container. Seed and dice the tomato and place in a container. Mince the parsley and place in a container. Chop the green onions, including part of the green tops and place in a container. Slice the mushrooms and place in a container. Grate the Parmesan and place in a container. Cook the fettuccini according to package directions until al dente, drain, cool and place in a container.

On Board Preparation: In a large skillet over medium heat, melt the butter and oil. Add the scallops and sauté 2-3 minutes until opaque. Stir in the green pepper, tomato, green onions and mushrooms. Sauté for 4 minutes. Add the cream and Parmesan and stir until blended. Reduce heat and simmer until sauce thickens, about 10 minutes. Add the Boursin cheese and stir until blended. Reheat the fettuccini by adding a few drops of water and microwaving about 1 minute or until hot. Toss the fettuccini and the scallop mixture to coat. Season with salt and pepper to taste.
Serves: 4.

Stir Fried Spinach and Shrimp

1/4 pound baby spinach
1/2 small onion, finely chopped
1/2 teaspoon turmeric
  1 red hot chili, chopped
1/2 teaspoon salt
  1 pound jumbo shrimp
  2 tablespoons olive oil

Instructions

At Home Preparation: Wash and dry the spinach, if needed. Roll in a paper towel and place in a perforated zip top bag. Chop the onion and place in a container. Chop the chili pepper and place in a container. Peel and devein the prawns, chop and place in a container.

On Board Preparation: Mix all ingredients except the oil together in a bowl. Heat the oil in a skillet or wok and add the mixture. Stir fry for 6-7 minutes.
Serves: 4.

Tropical Snapper

  1 cup pineapple juice
1/2 cup white wine
1/4 cup Worcestershire sauce
  2 tablespoons brown sugar
  1 large whole snapper
1/2 cup flour
1/4 teaspoon salt
1/8 teaspoon pepper
  2 tablespoons olive oil
  2 tablespoons mustard
  1 tablespoon Worcestershire sauce
1/2 cup pineapple, crushed
  1 tablespoon chopped mint leaf

Instructions

At Home Preparation: Combine the pineapple juice, white wine, 1/4 cup Worcestershire and sugar. Mix well and place in a container. Salt and pepper the flour, mixing well and place in a container. Chop the fresh mint and place in a container.

On Board Preparation: Make 1 or 2 cuts into the thickest parts of the fish flesh. Place in a shallow pan and cover with the marinade. Marinate overnight. Remove the fish from the marinade and reserve the liquid. Pat the fish dry with a paper towel. Coat the fish with the seasoned flour and dust off the excess. Heat the oil in a skillet and cook the fish about 4 to 5 minutes on each side until crisp and golden brown. Remove and keep warm. Place the marinade in a saucepan, add the mustard and additional 1 tablespoon Worcestershire and gently cook until reduced by one third. Add the crushed pineapple and mint and heat for about a minute more. Pour the sauce over the fish.

Serves: 4.

Soups and Stews

Asparagus Soup

- 4 tablespoons butter
- 3 cups asparagus, cut into 1" thick pieces
- 1 1/2 cups scallions
- 3 cups chicken broth
- 1/4 cup dry sherry
- 8 asparagus spears
- 1 cup half & half
- 1/2 teaspoon salt
- 1/4 teaspoon white pepper

Instructions

At Home Preparation: Cut the scallions in 1/2 inch pieces. Melt butter in a heavy saucepan over medium-high heat. Add 3 cups asparagus and scallions. Cook 5 minutes, stirring occasionally. Add broth and sherry. Reduce heat to medium, cover and cook until asparagus is tender, 2-3 minutes. Remove from heat and cool slightly. Puree asparagus mixture in a food processor or blender. Place in a container. Clean and trim the 8 fresh asparagus spears. Place in a container.

On Board Preparation: Cook the 8 asparagus spears in boiling water until crisp tender, about 5 minutes. Drain well and pat dry. Add the half-and-half to the chilled puree. Season to taste with salt and white pepper. Divide evenly between 4 serving bowls. Garnish each with 2 spears asparagus.
Serves: 4.

Baked Potato Soup

- 4 large baking potatoes
- 2/3 cup butter
- 2/3 cup all-purpose flour
- 6 cups milk
- 1 cup chopped green onion
- 3/4 teaspoon salt
- 1/2 teaspoon pepper
- 12 slices bacon
- 5 ounces Cheddar cheese, shredded
- 8 ounces sour cream

Instructions

At Home Preparation: Bake the potatoes 1 hour in a 400° oven. Cool until you can handle them. Scoop out the inside of the potatoes and place in a container, uncovered, and cool completely. Cover. Chop the green onions and place in a container. Partially cook the bacon until just starting to brown. Cool and place in a container.

On Board Preparation: Melt the butter in a large skillet over medium low heat. Stir in the flour to make a roux. Cook about 1 minute, stirring constantly. Gradually pour in the milk while stirring until all the milk has been added. Bring the heat to medium and continue stirring until the soup mixture starts to get thick. Add the potatoes, green onions, salt, ground black pepper, bacon and cheese. Stir well and continue to heat for about 15 minutes, allowing the flavors to blend. Stirring well, mix in the sour cream until well blended. Serve immediately.
Serves: 6.

Bay Scallop Chowder

        1   tablespoon butter
        2   tablespoons water
      1/2   cup chopped celery
        1   medium carrot, grated
        1   medium onion, chopped
        1   cup chopped potatoes
        1   pint half & half
      1/2   teaspoon salt
      1/4   teaspoon pepper
        3   drops Tabasco sauce
        1   pound bay scallops

Instructions
At Home Preparation: Chop the celery and place in a container. Peel and grate the carrot and place in a container. Peel and chop the onion and place in a container. Peel and chop the potatoes and place in a container.

On Board Preparation: In a large saucepan, heat the butter and 2 tablespoons water. Add the celery, carrots and onions and cook about 10 minutes over medium-low heat. Add the potatoes and cook an additional 10 minutes. Add the half-and-half, salt, pepper and Tabasco; cook 20-25 minutes. Add the scallops; cook 5-10 minutes.
Serves: 4.

GALLEY TIP
Cook fish 10 minutes per inch, measured at the thickest part of the piece.

Beer and Cheese Soup

    1 stick butter
  3/4 cup diced celery
  1/4 cup diced yellow onion
  1/4 cup flour
    2 pounds Velveeta cheese
    1 teaspoon white pepper
    8 cups chicken stock
  3/4 cup beer
    5 ounces Ro-Tel tomatoes with green chilies

Instructions

At Home Preparation: Dice the celery and onion and place each in a container. Cut the Velveeta into cubes and place in a container.

On Board Preparation: Bring the beer to room temperature. In a large saucepan, melt the butter over medium heat; add the celery and onion; sauté 3 minutes. Add the flour and whisk to combine. Cook 2 minutes. Add the Ro-Tel tomatoes, Velveeta, pepper and chicken stock. Cook, stirring occasionally, until the cheese melts and the soup thickens. Just before serving, slowly pour in the beer and mix.   *Serves: 8.*

Black Bean and Chorizo Chili

      7 ounces chipotle peppers in adobo sauce
        cooking spray
  2 1/2 cups chopped onions
  1 1/2 cups chopped green peppers
  1 1/2 cups chopped red bell peppers
      5 cloves garlic, minced
  6 1/2 ounces chorizo sausages
  1 1/2 tablespoons chili powder
      1 tablespoon ground cumin
  1 1/2 teaspoons dried oregano
      1 tablespoon lime juice
   1/8 teaspoon cinnamon
   45 ounces canned black beans
   42 ounces canned whole tomatoes, chopped
  8 1/2 ounces whole kernel canned corn, drained
  1 1/2 ounces Mexican chocolate, chopped
   3/4 teaspoon salt
   1/2 teaspoon pepper
   3/4 cup sour cream
    4 cups tortilla chips

Instructions

At Home Preparation: Remove two chiles from the can, reserving remaining chiles and sauce for another use. Finely chop the two chiles and place in a container. Chop the onions, green and red bell peppers and place each in a container. Dice the chorizo and place in a container.

On Board Preparation: Heat a large Dutch oven coated with cooking spray over medium-high heat. Add chiles, 1 3/4 cups onion, bell peppers, garlic and chorizo; sauté 5 minutes or until tender. Add chili powder and next 7 ingredients, stirring to combine. Bring to a boil. Reduce heat, and simmer, covered, 30 minutes, stirring occasionally. Remove from heat; stir in chocolate, salt and black pepper. Ladle 1 cup of chili into bowls. Top each with 1 tablespoon sour cream and 1 tablespoon onion. Serve with tortilla chips.
Serves: 12.

Recipe Notes
Be sure to use genuine Mexican chocolate. There is no substitute!

Black Bean and Shrimp Soup

1	medium onion, chopped
2	stalks celery, chopped
1	medium green pepper, chopped
2	medium carrots, chopped
29	ounces beef broth
2	cloves garlic, minced
1	can tomatoes, chopped
1	cup water
3	tablespoons dry sherry
1 1/2	teaspoons ground cumin
1/2	pound shrimp, cooked
1	tablespoon white wine vinegar
3/4	cup sour cream
32	ounces black beans, cooked

Instructions

At Home Preparation: Chop all the vegetables and place each in a container. Mince the garlic and place in a container. Rinse and drain the canned black beans and place in a container. Cook, shell and devein the shrimp and place in a container. (You can use frozen cooked shrimp as well.)

On Board Preparation: In a 5 quart microwave-safe casserole with lid, combine the onion, celery, green pepper, carrots, beef broth, garlic, tomatoes and water. Cover and cook in the microwave on high for 18 minutes. Stir in the black beans, sherry and cumin. Cover and cook on high for an additional 12 minutes. Place the shrimp evenly in soup bowls and ladle the soup over. Top each serving with a dollop of sour cream.
Serves: 4.

Brunswick Stew

4 1/2 pounds pork roast
4 1/2 pounds chicken
3 pounds canned tomatoes, chopped
8 ounces tomato sauce
3 large onions, diced
2 small green peppers, diced
3/4 cup cider vinegar
1/4 cup sugar
1/4 cup all-purpose flour
1 cup water
1 teaspoon salt
1/2 teaspoon pepper
1/2 teaspoon ground turmeric
2 tablespoons hot sauce
16 ounces frozen shoe peg corn

Instructions

At Home Preparation: Place the pork roast in a roasting pan, insert a meat thermometer being careful not to touch bone or fat. Bake at 325° about 30 minutes per pound or until the thermometer registers 160°. Cool completely. Trim any fat and cut into 2-inch pieces. Place the chicken in Dutch oven and cover with water. Bring to a boil; cover, reduce heat and simmer 2 hours or until tender. Remove from the broth and cool completely. (Reserve the broth for another use.) Remove the meat from the bone, discarding the chicken skin and cut into 2-inch pieces. Coarsely grind the pork and chicken in a food processor or meat grinder and place in a container. Chop the canned tomatoes, without draining, and place in a container. Dice the onion and green pepper and place each in a container.

On Board Preparation: Combine the ground meats, tomatoes, tomato sauce, onion, green pepper, vinegar and sugar in a large stock pot or Dutch oven. Combine the flour and water, stirring until smooth and stir into the meat mixture. Stir in the spices and hot sauce. Cook over medium heat 30 minutes, stirring occasionally. Add water if needed to reach desired consistency. Stir in the corn and cook an additional 10 minutes.
Serves: 12.

Caribbean Ceviche

1 pound grouper
1/2 cup fresh lime juice
1 pinch salt
1 cup coconut milk
1 teaspoon oregano
1 small onion, sliced thin
2 whole chiles, sliced thin

Instructions

At Home Preparation: Cut the fish into bite-size cubes and place in a container. Slice the chiles and onion and place each in a container.

On Board Preparation: Place the fish in a plastic bowl with the lime juice. Salt lightly and marinate for at least 1 hour, turning the pieces occasionally, until the fish "cooks" in the lime juice. Stir in the coconut milk, oregano, chiles and onion and marinate for 1 additional hour.
Serves: 6.

Recipe Notes
This recipe is also good made with any firm white fish or tuna.

Caribbean Shrimp Stew

1/4	cup minced fresh ginger
1/4	cup minced garlic
2	tablespoons olive oil
2	cups chopped onions
1/3	cup dark rum
3	cups chopped tomatoes
4	cans Thai coconut milk
1/2	tablespoon kosher salt
1/4	cup chopped jalapeno pepper
1/4	cup fresh lime juice
1/2	cup chopped cilantro
4	pounds large shrimp
2	cups cooked black beans
1/4	pound roasted peanuts, chopped
6	cups cooked rice

Instructions

At Home Preparation: Mince the ginger and garlic and place each in a container. Chop the onions, tomatoes, jalapeno and cilantro and place each in a container. If you are not using prepared black beans, cook the beans, cool, and place in a container. Chop the peanuts and place in a container. Cook the rice (about 6 cups), cool and place in a container.

On Board Preparation: In a heavy pot, sauté the ginger and garlic in a small amount of olive oil (about 2-3 tablespoons). Add the rum and simmer 3 minutes. Add the tomatoes, coconut milk, salt, jalapeno and lime juice; simmer 10 minutes. While simmering, peel and devein the shrimp. Reheat the rice by adding a few drops of water and microwaving about 1-2 minutes or until hot. Set aside. Add the cilantro, shrimp and beans to the stew pot; cook until shrimp are opaque. Serve immediately over hot rice, garnished with chopped peanuts. ***Serves: 12.***

Cauliflower-Cheddar Soup

2 tablespoons butter
1 medium onion, chopped
1/4 cup all-purpose flour
1/2 teaspoon salt
2 cups milk
13 3/4 ounces canned chicken broth
1 1/2 cups water
1 head cauliflower
8 ounces shredded sharp Cheddar cheese

Instructions

At Home Preparation: Chop the onion and place in a container. Wash dry and cut up the cauliflower into 1-inch pieces and florets (to make about 2 1/2 pounds) and place in a container. Shred the cheese and place in a container.

On Board Preparation: In a 4-quart saucepan, melt the butter over medium heat. Add the onion and cook until golden, about 10 minutes, stirring occasionally. Stir in the flour and salt; cook 2 minutes, stirring frequently. Gradually stir in the milk, chicken broth and water; add the cauliflower and heat to boiling over high heat. Reduce heat to low; cover and simmer until cauliflower is tender, about 10 minutes. Remove the center from the blender cover. Place the soup in the blender in small batches and process on low until very smooth. Return to the saucepan; heat over medium heat until hot, stirring occasionally. Remove from heat and stir in the mustard and 1-1/2 cups cheese until melted and smooth. If you want to make this ahead of time, refrigerate then reheat slowly before serving. Be careful not to heat too quickly or let it boil or the cheese may get stringy. Use the remaining cheese as a garnish by sprinkling over the top once ladled into the bowls.
Serves: 8.

Cheese Soup with Pumpernickel Croutons

3 slices pumpernickel bread, cubed
1 medium onion, peeled & quartered
1 medium carrot, peeled & quartered
1 stalk celery, quartered
1 teaspoon butter
3/4 cup all-purpose flour
32 ounces canned chicken broth
3 cups milk
1/2 teaspoon salt
1/2 teaspoon paprika
1/2 teaspoon pepper
1 1/2 cups shredded sharp Cheddar cheese

Instructions

At Home Preparation: Heat oven to 375°. Cube the bread and place on a jellyroll pan, and bake for 15 minutes or until toasted. Let cool completely and place in a container. Quarter the onion, carrot and celery, place in a food processor and pulse until chopped. Place in a container. Measure the flour and place in a container.

On Board Preparation: Melt the butter in a large saucepan over medium-high heat. Add the chopped vegetables and sauté 5 minutes or until tender. Gradually add 1 can of broth to flour in a medium bowl; stir well with a whisk. Add flour mixture to the saucepan. Stir in 1 can of broth; bring to a boil. Reduce heat to medium, and cook 10 minutes or until thick. Stir in milk, salt, paprika, and pepper; cook for 10 minutes. Remove from heat; add the cheese, and stir until cheese melts. Ladle into serving bowls and top with croutons.
Serves: 8.

Chilled Cantaloupe Soup

      3 medium cantaloupe
    1/4 cup dry sherry
      2 tablespoons dry sherry
    1/4 cup sugar
    3/4 cup orange juice
     12 whole mint leaves

Instructions

At Home Preparation: Cut each cantaloupe in half. Scoop out and discard the seeds from the cantaloupe and scoop the pulp out of the shells leaving 1/2 inch thickness. Cut a thin slice from each shell to form the bottom of the soup bowl. Place each shell in a container. Chop up the pulp and place in a container.

On Board Preparation: Combine the cantaloupe pulp, sherry, sugar and orange juice in the blender container and process until smooth. Chill thoroughly. Serve in the cantaloupe shells garnished with the mint leaves.
Serves: 6.

Chilled Cucumber Soup

    2 medium cucumbers, peeled & sliced
    4 large green onions, coarsely chopped
  1/2 cup water
    1 teaspoon salt
  1/4 teaspoon pepper
  3/4 cup cooked potatoes
    3 sprigs fresh mint leaves
    1 cup chicken broth
  1/2 cup heavy cream
  1/2 cup chopped cucumber (for garnish)
    8 sprigs fresh mint leaves (for garnish)

Instructions

At Home Preparation: Peel, seed and slice the cucumber. Coarsely chop the
green onions including most of the green. Cook the potatoes and rice (using a potato
ricer) or chop fine. Chop additional cucumber for garnish and place in a container.
Combine the first 5 ingredients in a saucepan and simmer for 20 minutes. Cool
completely and place in a container.

On Board Preparation: Place the cooked cucumber and onion mixture in the
blender container. Blend on high speed for 15 seconds, then add the potatoes. Cover
and blend on high. Remove the center of the blender cover and while still running,
add the remaining ingredients (except garnish) slowly. Chill for at least one hour.
Garnish with chopped cucumber and fresh mint.
Serves: 4.

Chilled Curried Pea Soup

     2 cups frozen green peas
     1 medium onion, sliced
     1 medium carrot, peeled & sliced
     1 small potato, peeled & sliced
     1 stalk celery, sliced
     1 clove garlic, minced
     1 teaspoon curry powder
   1/2 teaspoon salt
 10 3/4 ounces canned chicken broth
     1 cup milk
   3/4 cup whipping cream

216

Instructions

At Home Preparation: Slice the onion and place in a container. Peel and slice the carrot and potato and place each in a container. Slice the celery, including the leafy top and place in a container. Mince the garlic and place in a container.

On Board Preparation: Several hours before serving (or the day before), combine the peas, onion, carrot, potato, celery, garlic, curry powder and salt in a saucepan. Add 1 cup of the broth and bring to a boil. Cover; reduce heat; and simmer until the vegetables are tender, about 15 minutes. Cool slightly. Place in a blender with the remaining broth and process until smooth. Add the milk and cream; chill thoroughly before serving.
Serves: 4.

Chilled Fruit Soup

    6 medium peaches
  1/4 cup dry white wine
    6 tablespoons lemon juice
    2 tablespoons honey
  1/4 teaspoon cinnamon
    1 dash nutmeg
    1 cup fresh orange juice
    1 medium cantaloupe
    8 sprigs mint leaves

Instructions

At Home Preparation: Peel, pit and slice the peaches and place in a saucepan with the wine, lemon juice, honey cinnamon and nutmeg. Heat to boiling. Lower heat, cover and simmer for 10 minutes. Remove from the heat, cool to room temperature, puree in the blender and place in a container. Peel, seed and cut the cantaloupe into 1/2-inch pieces and place in a container.

On Board Preparation: Puree the orange juice and 3/4 of the cantaloupe in the blender until smooth. Combine with the peach mixture, stirring well. Cut the remaining cantaloupe into smaller pieces, if desire, and add to the soup. Cover and chill about 1 hour or until thoroughly chilled. Garnish with mint sprigs and serve.
Serves: 4.

Cold Blueberry Soup

  1 cup fresh blueberries
1/4 cup lemon juice
  1 stick cinnamon
  2 cups water
  1 pinch salt
1/4 cup sugar
  1 tablespoon cornstarch
  2 tablespoons water
1/4 cup heavy cream
1/3 cup sugar crystals
1/4 cup heavy whipping cream, whipped
1/4 cup fresh blueberries (optional garnish)

Instructions

At Home Preparation: Wash the 1 cup blueberries, remove any stems and place in a large saucepan with the lemon juice, cinnamon stick and 2 cups water. Cook at a simmer for 15 minutes or until berries are soft. Remove from the heat and stir in salt and sugar. Mix the cornstarch with the 2 tablespoons water and add to the blueberry mixture. Heat to boiling, reduce heat and simmer for 2 minutes. Remove from the heat and discard the cinnamon stick. Cool completely and place in a container. Chill thoroughly.

On Board Preparation: Puree the blueberry mixture in the blender. Stir in the 1/4 cup heavy cream and refrigerate until cold. Whip the remaining 1/4 cup heavy cream. Rim 4 champagne glasses with sugar crystals by dipping in a little water then in the sugar crystals. Pour the soup in the champagne glasses and top with the whipped cream and a few blueberries for garnish.   *Serves: 4.*

Crab Soup

    4 tablespoons butter
    1 medium yellow onion, diced
1 1/2 cups diced celery
  1/3 cup diced red bell pepper
  1/3 cup diced green pepper
  1/2 cup flour
    4 cups chicken stock
    4 cups milk
1 1/2 cups half & half
  1/3 cup sherry
  1/2 teaspoon salt
  1/4 teaspoon pepper
    1 pound lump crab meat
    4 tablespoons chopped celery

Instructions

At Home Preparation: Dice the onion, celery and bell pepper and place each in a container. Clean and pick over the crab meat and place in a container. Finely chop the parsley and place in a container.

On Board Preparation: In a large skillet melt the butter over medium heat and add the onion, celery and bell peppers cooking slowly, stirring occasionally until the vegetables are crisp-tender but not browned. Remove the skillet from the heat and sprinkle the vegetables with the flour and stir to blend. Return to medium-high heat and cook 6 to 8 minutes, stirring constantly until the flour is golden brown. Transfer to a 4-quart saucepan and gradually add the stock, stirring with a whisk until there are no lumps. Blend in the milk, cream and sherry. Bring quickly to a boil and continue boiling for 1 minute. Season to taste with salt and pepper. Add the crab meat and parsley and simmer for 5 minutes. If the soup is too thick, add a little more stock. Consistency should be creamy but not thick.
Serves: 6.

Creamy Crab Soup

1/2	pound lump crab meat
2	tablespoons butter
2	tablespoons all-purpose flour
3	cups half & half
1	teaspoon chicken bouillon granules
1/8	teaspoon white pepper
1/4	cup dry sherry

Instructions

At Home Preparation: Remove any cartilage or shell fragments from the crab meat and place in a container.

On Board Preparation: Melt the butter in a saucepan over low heat; add the flour, stirring until smooth. Cook 1 minute, stirring constantly. Gradually add the half-and-half and continue to cook over low heat, stirring constantly, until thickened and bubbly. Stir in the crab meat, bouillon and pepper. Cover and cook over low heat 10 minutes (do not boil), stirring frequently. Stir in the sherry and cook 1 minute.
Serves: 4.

Creamy Crab Stew

- 1 stick butter
- 3/4 cup finely chopped carrots
- 3/4 cup finely chopped celery
- 3/4 cup finely chopped onion
- 1/4 cup flour
- 4 cups milk
- 4 cups heavy cream
- 1 small bay leaf
- 1 tablespoon ground pepper
- 1 teaspoon salt
- 1/8 teaspoon cayenne pepper
- 1 teaspoon Old Bay seasoning
- 1 tablespoon Worcestershire sauce
- 1 pound lump crab meat

Instructions

At Home Preparation: Chop the carrot, celery and onion and place each in a container. Pick over the crab meat to remove shell fragments and cartilage and place in a container.

On Board Preparation: In a large saucepan, melt the butter over medium-low heat. Add the carrot, celery and onion and cook about 5 minutes, or until softened, stirring constantly. Add the flour and cook, stirring constantly for 3 minutes. Add the milk, cream, bay leaf, pepper, salt, cayenne, Old Bay and Worcestershire. Bring to a boil; reduce heat; simmer, stirring until slightly thickened, about 8 minutes. Add the crab meat and continue cooking and stirring for 1 minute. Remove the bay leaf. **Serves: 8.**

Creamy Gazpacho

- 2 cups vegetable juice cocktail
- 2 cups peeled & diced cucumbers
- 1 cup plain yogurt
- 3 large scallions, chopped
- 1/2 cup chopped parsley
- 1/2 medium jalapeno pepper, seeded & chopped
- 2 cloves garlic
- 1/2 teaspoon salt
- 1/2 teaspoon fresh pepper
- 2 tablespoons lemon juice
- 1 medium orange bell pepper, seeded & chopped
- 1 medium yellow bell pepper, seeded & chopped
- 2 medium tomatoes, seeded & chopped

Instructions

At Home Preparation: Prepare all of the vegetables by peeling, seeding and chopping and place each in a container. (Do not peel the bell peppers.)

On Board Preparation: Combine 1 cup of cucumber, scallions, parsley, jalapeno, garlic, salt, pepper and lemon juice in a food processor and pulse until well chopped. Add the vegetable juice and yogurt, pulse until ingredients are well blended, while leaving some texture to the vegetables. Transfer mixture to a large soup bowl. Add the peppers, tomatoes and remaining cup of cucumber. Stir well, Taste and season with additional salt and pepper if necessary. Chill. Serve chilled and topped with a dollop of plain yogurt and fresh parsley (if desired). Gazpacho is best if made and served the same day.
Serves: 8.

Cucumber-Dill Soup

2	medium cucumbers, peeled & chopped
1	medium green onion, coarsely chopped
1	tablespoon lemon juice
16	ounces sour cream
1	cup half & half
1	tablespoon minced fresh dill
1	teaspoon salt
1/4	teaspoon pepper
1/8	teaspoon hot sauce
8	sprigs fresh dill

Instructions

At Home Preparation: Process the cucumbers, green onion and lemon juice in a blender or food processor until smooth, stopping to scrape down the sides. Pour into a large bowl; stir in sour cream and next 5 ingredients. Place in a container and chill thoroughly.

On Board Preparation: Ladle into serving bowls and garnish with fresh dill sprigs.
Serves: 4.

Dark Beer Beef Stew

    3   pounds chuck steak, sliced
  1/2   teaspoon salt
  1/8   teaspoon pepper
  1/4   cup olive oil
    5   large onions, thinly sliced
    1   clove garlic, crushed
    1   medium bay leaf
    1   teaspoon thyme
    2   tablespoons all-purpose flour
    1   tablespoon brown sugar
   24   ounces dark beer

Instructions

At Home Preparation: Slice the chuck steak into 1/4-inch slices and place in a container. Slice the onions and place in a container.

On Board Preparation: Season the beef with salt and fresh ground pepper. Heat the oil in a large pot over medium high heat. Quickly brown the beef in batches and remove from the pot. Add the onions to the pot and reduce the heat to medium. Cover and cook the onions, stirring occasionally until they are soft and golden brown, about 15-20 minutes. Add the garlic, bay leaf, thyme and flour. Cook, stirring for 5 minutes. Ad the sugar and slowly add the beer, stirring constantly. Return the beef to the pot and cook, partially covered, about 1 hour, or until the beef is tender. Raise the heat and cook until the sauce thickens, about 5 minutes.
Serves: 6.

Galicia's Soup

    1/2   pound dried garbanzo beans
    1/4   pound lean salt pork, chopped
    1/4   pound smoked ham, chopped
    1/4   pound chorizo sausage, sliced
      1   large ham bone
  1 1/2   teaspoons ground cumin
    1/4   teaspoon fresh black pepper
     10   ounces frozen chopped spinach
      1   tablespoon butter
      4   small potatoes, peeled & cubed

Instructions

At Home Preparation: Cover the beans with cold, salted water and soak overnight. Drain and place in a container. Peel the potatoes, cube and place in a container.

On Board Preparation: In a large stock pot, sauté the salt pork until lightly browned. Add the ham and chorizo and cook over medium heat until lightly browned. Add the beans, 2 quarts water, ham bone, cumin and pepper. Cover and bring to a boil. Reduce heat and simmer until beans are tender, about 2 hours. While the soup simmers, heat the spinach with butter. Add the potatoes to the soup and cook 20 minutes. Add the spinach and cook 5 minutes. Remove the ham bone before serving.
Serves: 6.

Recipe Notes
This is a more delicately flavored version of the more traditional Caldo Gallego. It gets better as it refrigerates so it is a great make ahead soup.

Ham and Corn Chowder

3	tablespoons vegetable oil
8	ounces smoked ham, diced
3	medium onions, chopped
2	stalks celery, coarsely chopped
3	medium carrots, sliced
2	sprigs fresh thyme
1	small bay leaf
1	pound boiling potatoes, diced
2	cups chicken broth
3/4	teaspoon salt
2/3	cup heavy cream
1 1/2	cups milk
5	cups corn

Instructions
At Home Preparation: Peel and dice the potatoes, plunge into ice water for 3-5 minutes. Drain the corn (if using canned) or cook fresh corn and remove from the husk. Place in a container. Sauté the ham in the vegetable oil in a large skillet, remove and set aside. In the same oil, sauté the celery, carrots, thyme and bay leaf turning constantly until the vegetables are crisp-tender but not brown. Add the potatoes and chicken broth and simmer for 20-25 minutes until the potatoes are tender. Discard the thyme and bay leaf. Skim any remaining drippings and discard. Cool completely and place in a container.

On Board Preparation: In a large saucepan bring the cream and milk just to a boil. Add the corn and potato mixture stirring constantly and simmer 5 minutes. Remove the solids to a food processor and puree. Add the pureed vegetables to the cream mixture along with the sautéed ham, stirring constantly. If too thick, add a small amount of milk to reach desired consistency. Adjust seasoning and heat through.
Serves: 6.

Minted Kiwi Soup

        6   medium kiwi fruit
       10   whole mint leaves
        2   cups plain yogurt
      3/4   cup heavy cream
        3   tablespoons cider vinegar
        1   cup sugar
      3/4   cup apricot nectar
        1   cup heavy cream
      1/4   cup sugar
        8   sprigs mint

Instructions
At Home Preparation: Cut each kiwi in half and scoop out the fruit with a spoon discarding the skins. Put the kiwi and the mint leaves in the blender and puree. Add yogurt, 3/4 cup heavy cream, cider vinegar, 1 cup sugar and apricot nectar. Blend until smooth. Place in a container and refrigerate. (Can also be frozen.)

On Board Preparation: Whip the 1 cup heavy cream until it forms soft peaks, beating in 1/4 cup sugar. Fold into the kiwi mixture and chill. Serve garnished with mint sprigs.
Serves: 8.

Old English Cheese Soup

      1/4   cup butter
      1/2   cup finely diced onion
      1/2   cup finely diced carrots
      1/2   cup finely diced celery
      1/4   cup flour
    1 1/2   tablespoons cornstarch
        4   cups milk, room temperature
        4   cups chicken stock, room temperature
      1/8   teaspoon baking soda
        1   pound Old English Cheese, cubed
        1   teaspoon salt
        1   dash white pepper
        1   tablespoon dried parsley
        1   dash cayenne pepper
        2   dashes paprika, for garnish

Instructions

At Home Preparation: Dice the onion, carrot and celery and place in a container. Cube the cheese and place in a container.

On Board Preparation: Bring the milk and stock to room temperature. In a heavy saucepan, melt the butter and sauté the vegetables until tender-crisp. Stir in the flour and cornstarch and cook until bubbly. Add the stock and milk slowly blending until smooth. Add the baking soda and cheese. Stir and cook until thickened over low heat. Season to taste with salt and pepper and add the parsley and cayenne. This soup can be made ahead to this point and reheated just before serving in the top of a double boiler. Be careful not to let it boil. Garnish with paprika.
Serves: 6.

Peanut Butter Soup

1/2 cup chopped celery
1/4 cup chopped onion
  1 tablespoon butter, melted
  1 tablespoon all-purpose flour
 29 ounces chicken broth
1/2 cup creamy peanut butter
1/2 cup half & half
1/4 cup chopped chives

Instructions

At Home Preparation: Chop the celery and place in a container. Chop the onion and place in a container. Chop the chives and place in a container.

On Board Preparation: In a stockpot, sauté the celery and onion in the butter over medium heat until tender. Add the flour, stirring until smooth. Cook 1 minute, stirring constantly. Gradually add chicken broth and bring to a boil. Add the peanut butter and milk; reduce heat and simmer 5 minutes, stirring constantly. Do not let it boil. Serve immediately garnished with chopped chives.
Serves: 4.

Recipe Notes
Everyone will rave about this unusual soup!

Red Wine Beef Stew

```
 8   pounds beef chuck, cut in 2" pieces
1/2  teaspoon salt
1/4  teaspoon pepper
 1   cup vegetable oil
 8   onions, chopped
12   medium carrots, sliced 1/4-inch
 1   cup all-purpose flour
 1   tablespoon dried thyme
 1   tablespoon dried marjoram
 2   whole bay leaves
 6   cups dry red wine
 2   cups tomatoes, peeled, seeded and chopped
1/4  cup Dijon mustard
 3   pounds mushrooms
1/2  cup vegetable oil
1/4  cup unsalted butter
 1   cup chopped fresh parsley
 1   medium lemon peel, grated
```

Instructions

At Home Preparation: Cut the meat and place in a container. Chop the onions and place in a container. Cut the carrots and place in a container. Peel, seed and chop the tomatoes and place in a container. Chop the parsley and place in a container. Grate the lemon rind and place in a container. Cook the mushrooms in batches in a skillet with a mixture of oil and butter. Season with salt and pepper. When the mushrooms are tender, add the parsley and lemon rind. Cool completely and place in a container.

On Board Preparation: Pat any excess liquid from the beef and put into a bowl. Rub with salt and pepper. Heat the oil in a large pot. Brown the meat in batches. Add the onions and carrots to the pan and cook about 10 minutes, or until beginning to soften. Stir in the herbs, mix well, then add the meat. Add the wine gradually, stirring constantly. Add the tomatoes and mustard. Add enough water to just cover the meat, if necessary. Simmer until the meat is tender, about 2-1/2 hours. Skim any fat from the surface. Stir the mushroom mixture into the stew.
Serves: 12.

Spicy Tropical Gazpacho

```
 1   cup tomato juice
 1   cup pineapple juice
1/2  cup peeled & chopped mango
1/2  cup peeled & chopped papaya
1/2  cup chopped pineapple
```

1/2 cup seeded & chopped cucumber
1/4 cup chopped green pepper
1/4 cup chopped red bell pepper
  2 tablespoons minced fresh cilantro
1/4 teaspoon salt
  1 teaspoon hot sauce

Instructions
At Home Preparation: Peel and chop the mango, papaya and pineapple. Place each in a container. Peel, seed and chop the cucumber and place in a container. Chop the red and green bell pepper and place in a container. Mince the fresh cilantro and place in a container.

On Board Preparation: Combine all the ingredients in a food processor or blender and pulse 4 times or until combined. If you do not have a blender or food processor on board, or you prefer a chunkier soup, combine all the ingredients in a bowl and stir well. Cover and chill.
Serves: 4.

Spinach Bisque

10 ounces frozen chopped spinach, cooked
  2 tablespoons butter
  2 tablespoons finely chopped onions
  2 tablespoons flour
  2 cups half & half
10 ounces chicken broth
1/4 teaspoon salt
1/8 teaspoon pepper
1/2 teaspoon paprika

Instructions
At Home Preparation: Cook the spinach according to package directions, drain thoroughly, cool and place in a container. Chop the onion and place in a container.

On Board Preparation: In a medium saucepan, sauté the onion in the butter or medium heat. Stir in the flour and blend. Add the half and half, chicken broth and spinach. Season with salt, pepper and paprika.
Serves: 6.

Recipe Notes
This is really great with diced ham or chicken added.

Tex-Mex Seafood Soup

4 1/2 cups water
   1/2 pound small shrimp, unpeeled
   1/2 pound fresh bay scallops
     5 cups peeled & chopped tomatoes
     2 cups peeled & chopped cucumbers
     1 cup chopped red bell pepper
     3 tablespoons lime juice
     1 tablespoon minced jalapeno pepper
   1/2 teaspoon ground cumin
     1 clove garlic, thinly sliced
   16 ounces spicy vegetable juice cocktail
     1 tablespoon chopped cilantro

Instructions

At Home Preparation: Bring 4 cups of water to a boil; add shrimp, and cook 3-5 minutes. Drain well; rinse with cold water. Peel and devein shrimp and place in a container. Bring remaining 1/2 cup water to a boil; add scallops. Cover, reduce heat, and simmer 2 minutes. Drain well; rinse with cold water and place in a container. Peel and chop the tomatoes, divide and place 1 cup in a container. Peel and chop the cucumber, divide and place half in a container. Chop the red bell pepper, divide and place half in a container. Mince the jalapeno. Thinly slice the garlic. Combine 4 cups tomato, 1 cup cucumber, 1/2 cup bell pepper and next four ingredients in a blender; cover and process until smooth. Place in a container.

On Board Preparation: Pour the puree in a large bowl and stir in remaining 1 cup tomato, 1 cup cucumber, and 1/2 cup bell pepper. Chill at least 3 hours. Stir in chilled shrimp and scallops. Garnish with cilantro if desired.
Serves: 4.

Tomato and Mushroom Bisque

   3/4 pound fresh shiitake mushrooms
     2 dashes lemon juice
     3 tablespoons olive oil
     2 stalks celery, chopped
     1 small onion, chopped
     1 whole leek, chopped
     1 large shallot, chopped
     1 clove garlic, chopped
2 1/2 pounds tomatoes, peeled, seeded and chopped
     2 cups chicken stock
   3/4 cup dry white wine
   1/2 cup whipping cream
     1 tablespoon lemon juice

1 teaspoon dried thyme
1 small bay leaf
1 pinch saffron
1/4 teaspoon salt
1/8 teaspoon white pepper

Instructions

At Home Preparation: Remove the stems from the mushrooms, thinly slice and sprinkle with just a little lemon juice and toss to prevent brown spots. Place 1/3 in a container. Heat 2 tablespoons of the oil in a large saucepan over medium-high heat. Add the celery, onion, leek, shallots and garlic. Cook, stirring occasionally, until vegetables are translucent, about 7 minutes. Add two thirds of the mushrooms, sauté 5 minutes. Add the tomatoes, stock, wine, cream, lemon juice, thyme, bay leaf and saffron. Bring to a boil; reduce heat; simmer 30 minutes. Discard the bay leaf and puree in the blender until smooth. Season with salt and white pepper. Place in a container and refrigerate.

On Board Preparation: Just before serving, heat 1 tablespoon oil in a small skillet over medium-high heat. Add the reserved mushrooms and sauté 5 minutes. Season with salt and white pepper to taste. Put the soup into serving bowls and garnish with the sautéed mushrooms.
Serves: 12.

<u>Very Berry Soup</u>

10 ounces frozen raspberries
10 ounces frozen strawberries
2 cups frozen blueberries
24 ounces vanilla yogurt
1/4 cup honey
1 dash vanilla extract
16 sprigs fresh mint leaves

Instructions

At Home Preparation: Thaw the frozen berries. Place all the berries and the honey in a food processor or blender and process until they are the consistency of crumbs. Place in and refrigerate.

On Board Preparation: Combine the berry mixture with the yogurt and the dash of vanilla and stir well. Chill for about an hour or until ready to serve. Garnish with fresh mint leaves.
Serves: 8.

Vichyssoise

2 cups chopped leeks
3 cups peeled & sliced potatoes
3 cups water
4 chicken bouillon cubes
1/4 teaspoon white pepper
3 tablespoons butter
2 cups half & half
2 tablespoons chopped chives

Instructions

At Home Preparation: Chop the leeks, including the tops, and place in a container. Peel and slice the potatoes and place in a container. Chop the chives and place in a container.

On Board Preparation: Combine the leeks, potatoes, water, bouillon white pepper and butter in a stockpot and cook over medium heat until the vegetables are tender. Cool slightly and place in the blender jar. Puree until smooth. Stir in the half-and-half and chill completely before serving. Garnish with the chopped chives.
Serves: 6.

<u>Sweet Treats</u>

Almond-Filled Brownies

    4 eggs
    2 cups sugar
1/2 cup unsalted butter
    1 teaspoon vanilla extract
    1 cup flour
1/2 teaspoon baking powder
    6 ounces unsweetened baking chocolate
1/2 teaspoon salt
1/2 cup sliced almonds
    8 ounces almond paste
    1 whole egg
    1 teaspoon almond extract

Instructions

Preheat oven to 350°. Grease and flour a 13x9 pan. Melt the chocolate and butter and cool slightly. In a mixer bowl, beat together eggs , sugar, butter and chocolate at low-medium speed until blended. Add vanilla, flour, baking powder and salt, mixing after each addition. Set batter aside. In a small bowl, combine the almond paste 1 egg and almond extract. Pour half the chocolate batter in the prepared pan. Spread with the almond paste filling and sprinkle with the almonds. Pour the remaining chocolate batter over all. Bake for 25 minutes. Let cool 45 minutes before cutting. Store in an airtight plastic container.
Serves: 12.

Apricot Brandy Pound Cake

    1 cup unsalted butter, softened
    3 cups sugar
    6 large eggs
    1 cup sour cream
1/2 cup apricot brandy
    1 teaspoon vanilla extract
    2 teaspoons dark rum
    3 cups all-purpose flour
1/2 teaspoon salt
1/2 teaspoon baking soda

Instructions

Preheat the oven to 325°. In a large bowl, cream the butter and sugar. Beat until mixture is light and fluffy. Add eggs one at a time, beating well after each addition. Beat in sour cream, brandy, vanilla and rum. In another bowl, sift together the flour, salt and baking soda. Stir the flour mixture into the batter. Pour the batter into a buttered bundt pan and bake for 1 hour, or until a cake tester inserted in the center comes out clean. Cool the cake in the pan on a rack for 1 hour. Turn out of the pan

and continue to cool on the rack until cooled completely. Store in an airtight plastic container. If desired, cut into individual servings and freeze.
Serves: 10.

Recipe Notes
This recipe can be made entirely at home or on board. This cakes freezes well either whole or cut into individual servings.

Baked Bananas

1/2 pint orange juice
  1 tablespoon corn flour
  2 tablespoons honey
  3 tablespoons dark rum
  2 tablespoons demerara sugar
1/2 teaspoon ground allspice
1/8 teaspoon cinnamon
  4 bananas
  1 medium orange
  1 tablespoon grated orange peel

Instructions
At Home Preparation: Blend the orange juice and corn flour together. Put it and the next 5 ingredients in a saucepan, mix and bring to a boil, stirring constantly. Cool completely and place in a container. Grate the orange peel and place in a container, then peel and section the orange. Place the orange sections in a container.

On Board Preparation: Preheat oven to 350°. Peel the bananas and carefully make a slit in the length of each. Open slightly and lay each out on a piece of aluminum foil. Cover each with some of the sauce, reserving some sauce for serving. Seal each banana in the foil and place on a baking sheet. Bake for 10 to 15 minutes (or grill). While the bananas are baking, heat the reserved sauce over low heat. Remove the baked bananas from the foil and place each on a plate. Garnish with the orange sections. Pour some of the heated sauce over each and sprinkle with a orange peel.
Serves: 4.

Banana Crisp

    4   large bananas
    1   tablespoon lemon juice
  1/4   teaspoon nutmeg
    1   teaspoon grated orange peel
    3   tablespoons brown sugar
  1/4   cup all-purpose flour
  1/4   cup rolled oats
  1/4   cup brown sugar
  1/4   cup butter
    3   cups vanilla ice cream, optional

Instructions

At Home Preparation: To make the topping combine the flour, oats and 1/4 cup brown sugar and place in a container. Grate the orange rind and place in a container.

On Board Preparation: Preheat the oven to 400°. Butter a 9-inch pie plate. Peel the bananas and slice them on the diagonal in 1/4 inch pieces. Arrange in overlapping layers and sprinkle with the lime juice, nutmeg, orange rind and sugar. Combine the flour mixture and butter in a bowl. Blend until the mixture resembles coarse crumbs. Sprinkle evenly over the bananas. Bake until the juices are bubbly and topping is crisp and browned, about 20 minutes. Serve with a scoop of ice cream, if desired.
Serves: 6.

Bananas Flambé I

    4   large bananas
    5   tablespoons butter
  1/4   cup Grand Marnier
  1/2   teaspoon cinnamon

Instructions

Peel the bananas and cut in half lengthwise and crosswise. Melt the butter in a skillet over medium heat. Sauté the bananas in the melted butter until slightly brown, but not soft, about 1 minute per side. Add the Grand Marnier to the pan and flame. Divide amongst 4 serving plates and sprinkle with cinnamon.
Serves: 4.

Recipe Notes

You may want to use your grill for this one. If not, it is recommended that you flame the Grand Marnier out in the open.

Bananas Flambé II

  6 large bananas
  4 tablespoons unsalted butter
1/3 cup brown sugar
  2 tablespoons lime juice
1/4 teaspoon nutmeg
1/2 cup rum

Instructions

Peel the bananas and cut them in half crosswise. Melt the butter over medium-high heat in a large skillet. Add the bananas and cook, shaking the pan gently, until lightly browned. Add the sugar and lime juice and sprinkle lightly with nutmeg. Continue to shake the pan gently for a few minutes until the sugar dissolves. Add the rum. When it is warm, ignite the rum and shake the pan until the flames die out. Serve with the pan juices spooned over.
Serves: 6.

Recipe Notes
Take the pan out in the open air to flame for safety! You can also prepare on the grill.

Berries with Amaretto Cream

1 1/2 tablespoons Amaretto
    2 tablespoons dark brown sugar
  1/2 cup sour cream
    2 cups fresh strawberries and blueberries

Instructions

At Home Preparation: Wash the blueberries, dry and place in a container. Hull the strawberries (do not wash) and place in a container.

On Board Preparation: Wash the strawberries and cut into bite size pieces. Mix the blueberries and strawberries together gently. In a small bowl mix the Amaretto and brown sugar. Add the sour cream and mix well. Let sit for at least 2 hours, stirring occasionally to dissolve the brown sugar. Put the fruit into serving dishes and drizzle with the sauce.
Serves: 4.

Recipe Notes
This is also good with any fresh berries or a combination of fresh berries of your choice.

Blueberry Crisp

4 cups fresh blueberries
1/3 cup sugar
1/4 teaspoon grated lemon zest
3/4 cup all-purpose flour
1/4 cup rolled oats
1/3 cup firmly packed brown sugar
1/4 teaspoon cinnamon
5 tablespoons unsalted butter
1/2 cup sliced almonds
vanilla ice cream, optional

Instructions

At Home Preparation: Wash the blueberries and place in a container. Combine the flour, oats brown sugar and cinnamon and place in a container. Lightly toast the almond slices, cool, and place in a container.

On Board Preparation: Preheat the oven to 375°. Lightly butter a 1-quart baking dish. Mix the blueberries, sugar and lemon zest in the baking dish and spread evenly. Place the flour mixture in a bowl and cut in the butter until it is crumbly. Add the almonds and mix well. Sprinkle evenly over the blueberries. Bake for 30-40 minutes, until the top is golden brown and the juices are bubbly. Serve with ice cream, if desired.
Serves: 6.

Chocolate Walnut Upside Down Cake

10 tablespoons butter
1/4 cup firmly packed light brown sugar
2/3 cup light corn syrup
1/4 cup heavy cream
1 cup coarsely chopped walnuts
1 3/4 cups sifted cake flour
2 teaspoons baking powder
1/4 teaspoon salt
1 1/2 cups sugar
2 large eggs, separated
3 ounces unsweetened baking chocolate, melted
1 teaspoon vanilla extract
1 cup milk
1 cup sour cream

Instructions
At Home Preparation: Sift the flour, baking soda and salt together and place in a container. Coarsely chop the walnuts and place in a container.

On Board Preparation: Preheat the oven to 350°. Generously butter a 10-inch bundt pan. Melt 4 tablespoons of butter in a small saucepan; stir in brown sugar; heat just until bubbly. Stir in the corn syrup and cream; heat, stirring constantly to just boiling; do not over cook. (Mixture will be thin.) Add nuts; pour into the prepared Bundt pan and set aside while preparing the cake batter. In a large bowl, cream the remaining 6 tablespoons butter and granulated sugar. Beat in egg yolks, chocolate and vanilla, until thoroughly combined. Add the flour mixture alternately with milk, beginning and ending with flour. Beat egg whites in a small bowl until they form stiff peaks; fold into cake batter. Spoon batter evenly over nut mixture. Bake 45 minutes or until cake tester inserted in the center comes out clean. Loosen cake from edges with a small knife; invert onto serving plate. Remove any nuts and syrup clinging to pan with a spatula and spread over cake. Serve warm with a dollop of sour cream.
Serves: 10.

Recipe Notes
This is a little complex but well worth the effort. It can be made entirely at home and warmed before serving on board.

Coconut Custard

- 1 cup coconut juice
- 6 ounces sugar
- 2 cups coconut cream
- 6 large egg yolks
- 2 tablespoons rum
- 1 teaspoon vanilla extract
- 1 package ladyfingers
- 1/2 cup rum

Instructions
At Home Preparation: Separate the eggs, reserving the whites and place the yolks in a container. Sprinkle the ladyfingers lightly with the 1/2 cup rum (or to taste) and place in a container.

On Board Preparation: Put the coconut juice in a pan. Add the sugar and stir over high heat until the sugar dissolves. Boil hard for 5 minutes unit it reaches a syrupy stage. Remove the pan from the heat and pour in the coconut cream. Beat the egg yolks in a bowl, add 1/2 cup of the cream and syrup mix and stir well. Pour the mix back in the saucepan and cook over low heat for about 5 minutes until it forms custard like consistency. Remove from the heat and stir in the rum and vanilla. Spoon over the ladyfingers.
Serves: 4.

Recipe Notes
Sponge cake also works in place of the ladyfingers.

Coconut Delight Bars

        1/2 cup butter
          2 tablespoons powdered sugar
          1 cup cake flour
          2 large eggs
     1 1/4 cups light brown sugar
          1 teaspoon vanilla extract
          2 teaspoons all-purpose flour
        1/4 teaspoon salt
          1 teaspoon baking powder
          1 cup coarsely chopped pecans
          1 cup shredded coconut

Instructions
At Home Preparation: Sift together the all-purpose flour, salt and baking powder. Place in a container. Coarsely chop the pecans and place in a container.

On Board Preparation: Preheat oven to 350°. Line an 8-inch square pan with waxed paper. Blend together the butter, confectioner's sugar and cake flour. Spread evenly in the pan and bake for 15 minutes. Beat the eggs, brown sugar and vanilla. Add the all-purpose flour mixture to the egg mixture. Stir in the nuts and coconut. Spread over the crust. Bake for 30 minutes. Cool in the pan and cut into 16 bars.
Serves: 8.

Coconut Macaroon Cupcakes

     1 3/4 cups sugar
          1 cup butter
        1/2 teaspoon salt
          5 large eggs
        1/4 teaspoon almond extract
          2 cups all-purpose flour
          3 ounces coconuts, toasted

Instructions
Preheat oven to 350°. Line 24 muffin tins with paper baking cups. Set aside. In a large mixer bowl, cream together sugar, butter, and salt until light. Add eggs one at a time, beating well after each addition. Add the almond extract. Fold in the flour. Stir in the coconut. Fill the muffin cups 2/3 full with batter. Bake for 20-25 minutes or until done. Cool on a wire rack. Store in an airtight plastic container.
Serves: 12.

Crepes with Strawberry-Almond Filling

    1   cup all-purpose flour, sifted
    3   large eggs
3/4   cup milk
3/4   cup water
1/4   teaspoon salt
    2   tablespoons butter, melted
    2   cups sour cream
    3   tablespoons sugar
    2   tablespoons Amaretto
    2   cups strawberries
    2   tablespoons butter
1/3   cup powdered sugar

Instructions

At Home Preparation: Make the crepes by placing the first 6 ingredients in a blender container in the order given. Blend 30 seconds, stop and stir down the sides. Blend 30-60 seconds or until smooth. Cook crepes according to the crepe maker directions or in an 8-inch crepe pan over medium-high heat. Melt 1-teaspoon butter, add 2 tablespoons batter. Swirl batter around the pan as crepe cooks so it will be very thin. When the top is dry, turn and quickly cook the other side. Remove from the pan and repeat until all the batter is used. Cool completely and place in a container and freeze. Hull the strawberries and place in a zip top bag. To make the filling combine the sour cream, sugar and Amaretto. Place in a container.

On Board Preparation: Thaw the crepes at room temperature. Wash and slice the strawberries (reserving a few for garnish) and sweeten as needed. Spread the crepes evenly with the filling and top with sliced strawberries. Roll up and place in a shallow casserole. Cover and refrigerate at least one hour. To heat, melt butter in a skillet over medium-low heat. Add the crepes and heat, turning carefully. Halve the reserved strawberries and add. Heat a little longer, then remove from heat and sprinkle with confectioner's sugar.
Serves: 4.

GALLEY TIP

For fluffier rice, add one teaspoon lemon juice per quart of cooking water.

Decadent Brownies

- 1/3 cup dried apricots, chopped
- 1/4 cup rum
- 3 tablespoons unsalted butter
- 4 ounces semisweet chocolate
- 1 cup firmly packed brown sugar
- 1 teaspoon instant coffee
- 3 large eggs
- 1 teaspoon vanilla extract
- 3/4 cup all-purpose flour
- 1/4 teaspoon salt
- 1 cup semisweet chocolate chips
- 1 cup pecans

Instructions

At Home Preparation: Put the dried fruit and rum in a bowl and set aside until the fruit absorbs the liquid. Place in a container. Mix the brown sugar and instant coffee and place in a container. Combine the flour and salt and place in a container. Chop the pecans and place in a container.

On Board Preparation: Preheat the oven to 350°. Line an 8 ½ x 11 pan with overlapping sheets of foil and butter the foil lightly. Melt the butter and 4 ounces of semisweet chocolate in a large saucepan over simmering water. Stir until smooth and set aside to cool slightly. Beat the sugar and coffee into the chocolate. Add the eggs one by one, beat well after each addition. Add the vanilla, and the soaked fruit and liquid. Stir the flour and salt into the chocolate mixture, until just blended. Stir in the nuts and chocolate chips. Pour the batter into the prepared pan and smooth the top. Bake until the center is set but still slightly moist, about 25 minutes. Allow to cool at least 30 minutes before cutting into small squares.
Serves: 10.

Recipe Notes
Substitute currants for the apricots and/or Scotch for the rum for a different taste. These are also good made with walnuts or pistachios in place of the pecans.

Divine Chocolate Dessert

- 1/2 cup slivered almonds
- 12 ounces semisweet chocolate chips
- 3 tablespoons sugar
- 3 large egg yolks
- 3 large egg whites
- 2 cups heavy cream

   1 teaspoon vanilla extract
   8 ounce angel food cake
   2 tablespoons butter

Instructions

At Home Preparation: Lightly toast the almonds, cool and place in a container. Separate the eggs and place the yolks and whites in separate containers. Tear up the angel food cake into 1/2-inch pieces and place in a container. In a double boiler, melt the chocolate and sugar. Cool. Beat the egg yolks and mix into the chocolate. Place in a container.

On Board Preparation: Bring the chocolate mixture to room temperature. Stiffly beat the egg whites and gently fold into the chocolate mixture. Beat the cream to stiff peaks and gently fold in. Butter a 10-inch spring form pan and place half the cake pieces in the bottom. Cover with half the chocolate mixture. Layer remaining cake pieces and chocolate. Refrigerate at least 24 hours. Remove the spring form rim. Top with toasted almonds.
Serves: 10.

Easy Fudge

  12 ounces milk chocolate, chopped
1/4 cup heavy cream
1/8 teaspoon salt
1/2 teaspoon vanilla extract
3/4 cup chopped walnuts

Instructions

Lightly butter an 8-inch square baking pan. Combine the chocolate, cream and salt in a 1-quart glass measuring cup or other microwave safe container. Microwave on high until chocolate melts, about 2 - 2 1/2 minutes. Add vanilla and stir until smooth, about 2 - 3 minutes. Blend in chopped nuts. Pour fudge into the prepared pan. Cool until firm. Cut into 1 inch squares.
Serves: 8.

Recipe Notes
This fudge is also very good made with dark chocolate.

Fresh Blueberry Crisp

4 cups fresh blueberries
1/3 cup sugar
1/4 teaspoon grated lemon zest
3/4 cup all-purpose flour
1/4 cup rolled oats
1/3 cup packed brown sugar
1/4 teaspoon cinnamon
5 tablespoons unsalted butter
1/2 cup almonds, sliced
vanilla ice cream (optional)

Instructions

At Home Preparation: Wash the blueberries, dry, and place in a container. Combine the flour, oats brown sugar and cinnamon and place in a container. Toast the almond slices and place in a container.

On Board Preparation: Preheat the oven to 375°. Lightly butter a 1-quart baking dish. Mix the blueberries, sugar and lemon zest in the baking dish and spread evenly. Place the flour mixture in a bowl and cut in the butter until it is crumbly. Add the almonds and mix well. Sprinkle evenly over the blueberries. Bake for 30-40 minutes, until the top is golden brown and the juices are bubbly. Serve with ice cream, if desired.
Serves: 6.

Grilled Pineapple

1 large pineapple
5 tablespoons unsalted butter, melted
1 cup brown sugar
whipped cream

Instructions

At Home Preparation: Trim the pineapple and core. Cut crosswise into 1-inch slices, then into 4 wedges and place in a container.

On Board Preparation: Brush the pineapple slices lightly with the melted butter. Place the brown sugar in a shallow pan and place the buttered pineapple slices in it, turning to coat on both sides. Set aside for 15 minutes. Prepare the grill and grill 2-3 minutes on each side until lightly browned. Serve with whipped cream.
Serves: 4.

Recipe Notes
Substitute vanilla ice cream or crème fraîche for the whipped cream.

Grilled Pineapple with Rum and Toasted Coconut

1/4 cup packed light brown sugar
1/4 cup dark spiced rum
  1 large pineapple, cored
  1 tablespoon butter
  2 tablespoons coconut, toasted
    vanilla ice cream

Instructions

At Home Preparation: Combine the brown sugar and rum in a microwave safe bowl. Microwave on HIGH 1-1/2 minutes or until the sugar dissolves. Place in a container. Prepare the pineapple by coring, halving lengthwise and slicing into 12 wedges, and place in a container. Toast the coconut and place in a container.

On Board Preparation: Heat the butter in a grill pan over medium-high heat. Add the pineapple and grill for about 3 minutes on each side or until grill marks form and pineapple is thoroughly heated. Sprinkle with coconut. Serve with ice cream if desired.
Serves: 6.

Recipe Notes
You can substitute whipped cream for the vanilla ice cream for a little different taste.

GALLEY TIP
Kill the odor of cooking shrimp by adding caraway seeds to the water.

Orange Almond Mousse

         1   tablespoon unflavored gelatin
       1/4   cup cold water
         1   cup sugar
         3   tablespoons grated orange peel
       1/4   cup water
     1 1/4   cups fresh orange juice
         2   tablespoons fresh lemon juice
         1   cup heavy cream
         1   cup sliced almonds
         1   medium orange, sectioned

Instructions
At Home Preparation: Grate the orange peel and place in a container. Peel the orange, section and place in a container. Lightly toast the sliced almonds, cool and place in a container.

On Board Preparation: Stir gelatin into 1/4 cup cold water and let set for 15 minutes. In a small saucepan, combine sugar, orange peel and 1/2 cup water; bring to a boil. Boil 1 minute then stir in the softened gelatin until dissolved. Add the orange and lemon juice and mix well. Refrigerate until thickened to consistency of egg whites, about 45 minutes. (Be careful not to let it set completely.) Whip the cream to stiff peaks. Fold into the gelatin mixture and return to the refrigerator until set. Serve garnished with the toasted almonds and orange sections.
Serves: 6.

Peanut Butter Dip with Apples and Graham Crackers

       2/3   cup firm tofu, crumbled
       2/3   cup cottage cheese
         3   tablespoons creamy peanut butter
         1   tablespoon honey
         1   teaspoon vanilla extract
         2   medium apples
         4   whole graham crackers
         6   dashes cinnamon

Instructions
At Home Preparation: Position knife blade in food processor bowl; add first 5 ingredients. Top with cover and process until smooth. Place in a container and chill.

On Board Preparation: Slice the apples and sprinkle with a little lemon juice to prevent oxidation. Arrange apple slices and graham crackers on a plate with the dip. Sprinkle the dip with cinnamon and serve.   ***Serves: 4.***

Pears and Apples with Hard Sauce

   3 medium apples
   3 medium pears
   1 tablespoon lemon juice
   2 tablespoons unsalted butter
   2 tablespoons brown sugar
1/8 teaspoon cinnamon
   2 tablespoons rum
   3 tablespoons unsalted butter, softened
   1 cup powdered sugar
   1 tablespoon rum
   2 tablespoons heavy cream

Instructions

Prepare the sauce by beating the 3 tablespoons butter in a small bowl until creamy. Add the 1 cup powdered sugar gradually, beating constantly until smooth. Stir in the one tablespoon rum and 2 tablespoons heavy cream and mix well. Core and quarter the apples and pears. Heat the 2 tablespoons butter in a large skillet over medium-high heat. When it is foaming, add the fruit and cook shaking the pan to keep it from sticking, until the fruit is lightly browned on both sides, turning the fruit once during the cooking. Sprinkle the brown sugar, 1/8 teaspoon cinnamon, and 2 tablespoons rum over the fruit and cook until the juices bubble and thicken. Serve with the sauce.
Serves: 6.

Pineapple Casserole

   2 tablespoons flour
1/2 cup sugar
   3 large eggs
 20 ounces crushed pineapple in light syrup
   8 tablespoons butter, melted
 10 slices French bread, cubed (or brioche bread for a sweeter taste)

Instructions

At Home Preparation: Mix the flour and sugar together and place in a container. Cube the bread and place in a container.

On Board Preparation: Preheat the oven to 325°. Place the flour and sugar in a mixing bowl. Beat the eggs and add to the flour mixture along with the pineapple. Melt the butter and add to the mixture. Lightly grease a 9x9-inch baking dish and spread the bread cubes in the bottom. Pour the pineapple mixture over the bread. Bake, uncovered, for 30-40 minutes.   *Serves: 8.*

Poached Bananas with Chocolate-Orange Sauce

      4 ounces unsweetened baking chocolate
    1/4 cup butter
      3 large egg yolks
      6 tablespoons sugar
    1/2 cup milk
    1/3 cup orange juice
    1/4 teaspoon grated orange peel
      4 large bananas, cut in half
      2 cups dry white wine
    3/4 cup sugar
      1 tablespoon vanilla extract
      1 whole cinnamon stick

Instructions

At Home Preparation: Prepare the sauce by melting the chocolate and butter in a double boiler. Stir until blended. Add the egg yolks one at a time, beating after each addition. Add the sugar and milk. Cook, stirring, over simmering water until thickened. Add the orange juice and grated orange rind. Blend thoroughly. Cool completely and place in a container.

On Board Preparation: Cut the bananas in half lengthwise then crosswise. Combine the wine, sugar, vanilla and cinnamon stick in a saucepan. Simmer for 5 minutes. Add the bananas and cook 5 minutes at just below simmer. Remove from the heat and let stand 20 minutes. Meanwhile, reheat the chocolate sauce in a double boiler. Remove bananas from cooking liquid. Serve immediately with the chocolate sauce.
Serves: 4.

Recipe Notes
For best results, use barely ripe bananas.

Rum Cake

       1 cup pecans, toasted and chopped
  18 1/2 ounces yellow cake mix
   1 3/4 ounces instant vanilla pudding
       4 large eggs
     1/2 cup milk, chilled
     1/2 cup vegetable oil
     1/2 cup dark rum
       1 stick butter

1/4 cup water
1 cup sugar
1/2 cup dark rum

Instructions

Preheat the oven to 325°. Grease and flour a 12-cup Bundt pan. Sprinkle nuts on bottom of the pan. Combine the cake mix, instant pudding, eggs milk, vegetable oil and 1/2 cup dark rum. Beat for 2 minutes on high with an electric mixer. Pour into the prepared pan. Bake for 1 hour. Cool in the pan, invert on a serving plate. To make the glaze, melt the butter in a saucepan over low heat. Stir in the water and sugar. Boil 5 minutes, stirring constantly. Remove from the heat and stir in the rum. (The rum will cause it to steam so be careful not to burn yourself.)   Prick the top of the cake with a fork. Drizzle the glaze. Let cool and place in an airtight plastic container.
Serves: 10.

Recipe Notes

This cake gets better if it sits for 1-3 days. It also freezes very well. You can make it ahead, slice and freeze in a container.

Strawberries with Grand Marnier Cream

1 cup milk
1 cup heavy cream
1/2 teaspoon vanilla extract
4 large egg yolks
1/2 cup sugar
1/4 cup Grand Marnier
1 quart fresh strawberries

Instructions

At Home Preparation: Separate 4 eggs, reserving the whites for another use and set aside the yolks. Hull the strawberries and place in a container. In the top of a double boiler, scald the milk, cream and vanilla. In a small bowl, beat the egg yolks and sugar until light yellow. Add the egg mixture to the milk mixture very slowly, stirring constantly over low heat until thickened. Stir in the Grand Marnier. Pour into a container and refrigerate. (Can be made as much as a week in advance.)

On Board Preparation: Wash the strawberries and cut into bite size pieces. Bring the sauce to room temperature and mix with the strawberries.
Serves: 6.

Strawberry Tarts

  4 individual tart shells, unbaked
  8 ounces almond paste
  1 large egg
  3 tablespoons sugar
  1 teaspoon almond extract
1/2 pint fresh strawberries
1/2 cup apricot jam, strained

Instructions

At Home Preparation: Preheat the oven to 400°. Combine the almond paste, egg, sugar and almond extract in a food processor fitted with the metal blade. Divide the mixture equally among the tart shells. Bake for 15 minutes or until tart shells are lightly browned. Cool completely and place in a container. Hull the strawberries and place in a zip top bag. Strain the apricot jam and place in a container.

On Board Preparation: Wash and halve the strawberries. Arrange over the tarts. Brush with apricot jam. Refrigerate at least one hour before serving.
Serves: 4.

Warm Fruit Compote

  8 ounces pineapple chunks
16 ounces peaches in light syrup, sliced
16 ounces canned pears halves, sliced
16 ounces maraschino cherries
1/2 cup firmly packed brown sugar
  8 tablespoons butter
  2 tablespoons mustard

Instructions

At Home Preparation: Drain the pineapple, peaches, pears and cherries and place each in a container.

On Board Preparation: Preheat the oven to 325°. In a 13x9 baking dish, combine the drained fruit and set aside. In a small saucepan, combine the brown sugar, butter and mustard. Cook over medium heat, stirring constantly until smooth. Pour over the fruit and bake, uncovered, for 20 minutes or until thoroughly heated.
Serves: 8.

<u>Vegetables and Side Dishes</u>

Artichoke and Spinach Bake

40 ounces frozen chopped spinach
8 tablespoons butter
1 medium onion, chopped
1 pint sour cream
1/2 cup grated Parmesan cheese
1 teaspoon salt
28 ounces artichoke hearts, drained
6 ounces fried onion rings

Instructions

At Home Preparation: Cook the spinach according to package directions, drain very well, cool and place in a container. Chop the onion and place in a container. Grate the Parmesan and place in a container. Drain the artichoke hearts and place in a container.

On Board Preparation: Preheat the oven to 375°. In a skillet, melt the butter and sauté the onion. In a bowl, combine the sour cream, cheese, onion and salt. Add the spinach and mix well. In a 13x9 baking dish, line the bottom with the artichokes. Pour the spinach mixture over the artichokes and top with the French fried onions rings. Bake for 30 minutes.
Serves: 8.

Artichoke and Spinach Casserole

8 1/2 ounces artichoke hearts, drained
20 ounces frozen chopped spinach
8 ounces cream cheese
1 stick butter
8 slices bacon
1 cup grated Parmesan cheese
1/2 cup pecans, toasted

Instructions

At Home Preparation: Drain the artichokes, cut into quarters and place in a container. Thaw the spinach, squeeze out all moisture and place in a container. Cook the bacon, drain, cool, crumble and place in a container. Grate the Parmesan and place in a container. Toast the pecans until golden, cool, and place in a container.

On Board Preparation: Preheat the oven to 350°. Place the artichokes and spinach in a bowl. Melt the butter and cream cheese together (cream cheese will be lumpy) then mix with the spinach and artichokes. Spoon into an 8x8 baking dish. Sprinkle with the crumbled bacon and Parmesan. Top with the pecans. Bake about 30 minutes or until bubbly. *Serves: 4.*

Asparagus Gratin

- 3 pounds asparagus
- 1 cup sliced green onions
- 1 cup butter
- 1/2 teaspoon thyme
- 1/2 teaspoon rosemary
- 2 tablespoons chopped red bell pepper
- 1/2 teaspoon salt
- 1/2 cup Chablis
- 2 tablespoons grated Parmesan cheese

Instructions

At Home Preparation: Clean the asparagus spears and steam until tender yet still crisp, about 5 minutes. Immediately run under cold water. Pat dry and place in a container. Sauté the green onions in butter until just tender. Add the thyme, rosemary, red bell peppers and salt. Cool and place in a container.

On Board Preparation: Preheat the oven to 350°. Place the asparagus in a flat buttered casserole. Pour the wine over the asparagus. Spoon the onion mixture over the asparagus and sprinkle the cheese on top. Bake for 10 minutes until cheese melts and browns slightly.
Serves: 6.

Asparagus with Orange Butter

- 1/3 cup butter
- 2 tablespoons grated orange peel
- 1/4 cup orange juice
- 1 1/2 pounds asparagus
- 1 large orange

Instructions

At Home Preparation: Grate the orange rind and place in a container. Clean the asparagus, removing the woody ends and place in a container. Peel and section the orange and place in a container.

On Board Preparation: Combine the butter, orange rind and juice in a saucepan and bring to a boil. Reduce heat and simmer until reduced by half and slightly thickened, stirring occasionally. Set aside and keep warm. Cook the asparagus for 6-8 minutes or until crisp tender. Drain and place on a serving dish. Pour the orange sauce over and garnish with the orange sections.
Serves: 6.

Asparagus with Pecans

    1 1/2 pounds asparagus
      3/4 cup finely chopped pecans
        2 tablespoons vegetable oil
      1/4 cup cider vinegar
      1/4 cup soy sauce
      1/4 cup sugar
      1/4 teaspoon ground pepper

Instructions

At Home Preparation: Cut the woody ends from the asparagus. Steam in an asparagus steamer or in about 2 inches of water until bright green, about 6 minutes. Rinse under cold water and drain. Cool completely and place in a container. Chop the pecans and place in a container. Whisk together the oil, vinegar, soy sauce and sugar. Place in a container.

On Board Preparation: Layer the asparagus and pecans in an oblong dish. Pour the oil mixture over the asparagus and season with pepper. Marinate in the refrigerator for at least two hours or up to 2 days.
Serves: 4.

Asparagus with Wasabi Dressing

       24 ounces asparagus
      1/2 teaspoon salt
        1 bunch green onions
        2 tablespoons sesame seeds, toasted
        4 tablespoons ginger root
        4 tablespoons soy sauce
        1 medium lemon
        1 teaspoon wasabi
        3 ounces vegetable oil

Instructions

At Home Preparation: Wash and trim the asparagus, removing the woody ends and peeling the bottom of the spears. Cut each spear into 3 pieces about 1-1/2 inches and place in a container. Thinly slice the green onions, white part only and place in a container. Peel the ginger root, finely chop or grate and place in a container. Toast the sesame seeds, cool and place in a container.

On Board Preparation: Separate the asparagus stem pieces from the tops. Cook the stems in boiling salted water for 3-5 minutes or until crisp-tender. Remove and rinse under cold water. Drain and dry on paper towels. Add the tips to the boiling water and cook for 2 minutes, rinse with cold water, drain and dry. Make the dressing by adding the ginger root to the soy sauce in a bowl. Squeeze the juice from the lemon into the mixture and stir. Add 1/2 teaspoon wasabi, whisking well then add the oil and whisk again. Taste and add additional wasabi by whisking it in, to taste. Add the green onions and the asparagus stems and toss gently to coat. To serve, using a slotted spoon, place the stems on a plate and arrange the tips around the outside. Drizzle some of the dressing over the tips and sprinkle with the toasted sesame seeds.

Serves: 6.

Baked Mushrooms In a Sour Cream Sauce

> 1 pound sliced mushrooms
> 2 tablespoons butter
> 1 cup sour cream
> 2 tablespoons flour
> 1/4 teaspoon salt
> 1/8 teaspoon pepper
> 1/2 cup grated Cheddar cheese
> 1/2 cup grated Monterey Jack cheese

Instructions

At Home Preparation: If mushrooms are not purchased already sliced, wash, remove the stems, slice the mushroom. Grate the cheeses and place in a container. Sauté the mushrooms in butter and drain. Cool and place in a container.

On Board Preparation: Preheat the oven to 325°. Place the mushrooms in a small baking dish. In a small saucepan, combine the sour cream, flour, and season with salt and pepper. Heat slowly so as not to boil, stirring until sauce is smooth. Pour over the mushrooms and top with the cheeses. Bake for 15 minutes.

Serves: 4.

GALLEY TIP

Nuts will keep much longer if frozen. And, if you have to shell them, the job will be much easier.

Barbecued Sweet Potatoes

2 tablespoons ketchup
2 teaspoons ketchup
1 tablespoon Worcestershire sauce
1 tablespoon red wine vinegar
1 teaspoon mustard
1/2 teaspoon ground black pepper
1 pound sweet potatoes

Instructions

At Home Preparation: In a small bowl, combine first 6 ingredients and mix well. Place in a container. Peel and slice the sweet potatoes into 1/4-inch slices and place in a container.

On Board Preparation: Prepare the grill. Brush the potato slices on both sides with the ketchup mixture. Grill, turning frequently and brushing with remaining ketchup mixture until cooked through, about 4 minutes per side.
Serves: 4.

Recipe Notes
These are a great side dish with sandwiches, burgers or grilled chicken, steak or fish.

Blue Cheese Stuffed Portobello

4 tablespoons olive oil
1 large onion, sliced
3 cloves garlic, minced
1 tablespoon chopped fresh thyme
1/4 teaspoon salt
1/8 teaspoon freshly ground pepper
1 cup port
2 1/2 ounces spinach, coarsely chopped
4 medium Portobello mushrooms
2 ounces blue cheese

Instructions

At Home Preparation: Slice the onion and place in a container. Mince the garlic and place in a container. Chop the thyme and place in a container. Wash the spinach, pat dry with paper towels and coarsely chop. Wrap in paper towels and place in a perforated zip top bag. Gently wash the mushrooms and remove the stems, reserving for another use. Sprinkle the mushroom caps lightly with lemon (to prevent discoloration) and place in a container.

On Board Preparation: Heat 2 tablespoons of the olive oil in a large skillet until moderately hot. Add the onion and cook until soft and lightly browned, about 15 minutes. Add the garlic, thyme, salt, and pepper and cook for another 5-7 minutes. Add the port and cook until the liquid is reduced by about two-thirds, about another 10 minutes. Add the spinach and cook until wilted. Set aside in a mixing bowl. Wipe the skillet clean with a paper towel. Gently rub a spoon on the underside of the mushroom caps to scrape off the gills. Heat the remaining olive oil in the skillet until hot. Add the mushrooms, gill side up, and cook over medium-high heat for 2 minutes. Flip over and cook an additional 2 minutes. Flip again so they are gill side up. Season with salt and pepper. Top each with the onion mixture, pouring the juices over the mushrooms. Add 1 tablespoon water to the pan and simmer, covered, until the mushrooms are barely tender, about 5 minutes. Crumble the blue cheese on top, cover and cook just until the cheese melts, about 2 minutes.
Serves: 4.

Bourbon Baked Beans

4 pounds canned Boston baked beans
16 ounces crushed pineapple, drained
12 ounces chili sauce
1/2 cup strong brewed coffee
1/2 cup bourbon
1/4 cup firmly packed brown sugar
1 tablespoon molasses
3/4 teaspoon mustard powder

Instructions
Combine all ingredients in a Crock-Pot or other slow cooker. Cover and cook on high 2 hours; uncover and cook to desired consistency. Serve with a slotted spoon.
Serves: 10.

Recipe Notes
These are really easy and a big hit. Make ahead and reheat when you are ready to serve.

Broccoli with Blue Cheese Sauce

- 2 tablespoons butter
- 2 tablespoons flour
- 1 cup milk
- 3 ounces cream cheese
- 1/3 cup crumbled blue cheese
- 1 1/4 pounds fresh broccoli spears

Instructions
At Home Preparation: Wash the broccoli and cut into spears. Dry thoroughly and place in a container.

On Board Preparation: Steam the broccoli until just tender; keep warm. In a saucepan, melt the butter. Stir in the flour and heat until bubbly. Slowly add the milk, cooking over low heat until thickened. Add the cream cheese and blue cheese, heat to boiling, stirring constantly. Serve over hot broccoli.
Serves: 8.

Broccoli with Orange Sauce

- 2 large oranges
- 1 1/2 pounds fresh broccoli florets
- 1 teaspoon butter
- 1 small onion, chopped
- 2 teaspoons finely chopped crystallized ginger
- 8 ounces lemon yogurt

Instructions
At Home Preparation: Grate the orange rind and place in a container. Peel and section oranges, and place in a container. Wash the broccoli and cut into florets, dry and place in a container. Chop the onion and ginger and place each in a container.

On Board Preparation: Steam the broccoli over boiling water, and cook 3-4 minutes until crisp-tender. Melt butter in a nonstick skillet over medium-high heat. Add onions and ginger; sauté until tender. Remove from heat. Toss broccoli and onion mixture with orange rind and sections in a large bowl. Gently stir in yogurt. Serve immediately.
Serves: 6.

Carrots Flambé

  1 pound carrots
3/4 cup pistachio nuts, shelled
  2 tablespoons butter
1/2 teaspoon salt
1/4 teaspoon pepper
  2 tablespoons brandy

Instructions

At Home Preparation: Peel the carrots, slice on the diagonal and place in a container.

On Board Preparation: Steam the carrots until crisp-tender. Put the carrots, pistachios, and butter into a serving dish, stirring to distribute and melt the butter. Salt and pepper to taste. Sprinkle the brandy over all and flame.
Serves: 6.

Recipe Notes
Be sure to use the natural pistachios, not the dyed ones.

Carrots Normandy

  1 pound fresh carrots
1/2 teaspoon salt
1/4 teaspoon pepper
  7 ounces apple cider
1/2 large lemon
3/4 ounce butter
  2 dashes nutmeg
1/4 pint heavy cream
1/4 cup chopped fresh parsley

Instructions

At Home Preparation: Peel the carrots, cut into 1/4 inch diagonal slices. Cook in salted boiling water until just crisp tender, about 5 minutes. Drain, cool and place in a container. Chop the parsley and place in a container.

On Board Preparation: Place the carrots in a shallow pan with the cider, juice from the 1/2 lemon and butter. Season with salt and pepper and a little nutmeg. Bring to a simmer, cover and cook for 5 minutes. Uncover and continue cooking until all the liquid has evaporated and the carrots are nicely glazed. Add the cream and heat through, shaking the pan to coat the carrots. Sprinkle with the parsley before serving
Serves: 4.

Cauliflower Medley

- 1 cup white wine
- 1 cup chicken broth
- 1 tablespoon butter
- 1 medium head cauliflower
- 4 stalks celery
- 1 medium red bell pepper
- 1 medium onion
- 1/2 teaspoon salt
- 1/4 teaspoon pepper
- 1/4 cup pecans, toasted

Instructions

At Home Preparation: Wash the cauliflower, cut into 1-inch florets and place in a container. Cut the celery into 1/2-inch pieces, and the bell pepper into 1/4-inch julienne strips, and place each in a container. Dice the onion into 1/2-inch pieces and place in a container. Chop the pecans, toast them to lightly browned, cool and place in a container.

On Board Preparation: Place the wine, broth, butter and cauliflower in a saucepan and cook, covered, 10-15 minutes or until crisp-tender. Remove the cauliflower, leaving the liquid in the pan. Add the celery and cook covered for 2 minutes. Add the onion and cook 1 minute. Add the bell pepper and cook 2 minutes. Remove the vegetables. Bring the liquid to a boil and reduce to 1/2 cup. Return all the vegetables to the pan, reheat through and season to taste. Garnish with the toasted pecans.
Serves: 6.

Cauliflower with Dijon Sauce

- 2 medium heads cauliflower
- 2 tablespoons butter
- 3 tablespoons all-purpose flour
- 1 cup chicken broth
- 1 cup half & half
- 1/4 cup Dijon mustard
- 2 teaspoons lemon juice
- 1/2 teaspoon ground pepper

Instructions

At Home Preparation: Wash the cauliflower heads and break into florets. Steam the cauliflower until tender; drain, cool and place in a container.

On Board Preparation: In a saucepan, melt butter and stir in flour. Cook, stirring constantly for one minute. Add the chicken broth and half and half, heating to boiling, stirring constantly. Lower the heat and simmer for 5 minutes, stirring occasionally. Remove from heat and whisk in the mustard, lemon juice and pepper to taste. Reheat the cauliflower in the microwave until hot. Pour the sauce over the hot cauliflower.
Serves: 8.

Cinnamon Green Beans

1	tablespoon butter
1/4	cup chopped onion
1/4	teaspoon cinnamon
1 1/2	pounds fresh green beans
1/2	cup chicken broth
3/4	teaspoon salt
1/2	teaspoon pepper
2	tablespoons tomato paste
6	slices bacon

Instructions
At Home Preparation: Chop the onion and place in a container. Snap the ends off the green beans, wash, dry and place in a container. Fry the bacon slices until crisp, cool, crumble and place in a container.

On Board Preparation: Melt the butter in a saucepan and sauté the onion and cinnamon until the onion is transparent. Stir in the green beans, chicken broth and salt and pepper to taste. Heat to boiling, reduce heat and simmer 15 minutes or until beans are crisp-tender. Fold in the tomato paste and crumbled bacon.
Serves: 6.

GALLEY TIP
When cooking cauliflower, Brussels sprouts, cabbage, etc. put a little vinegar in the cooking water to cut down on the odor.

Citrus-Marinated Mushrooms

1/4 cup rice vinegar
2 tablespoons sugar
2 tablespoons fresh lime juice
1 tablespoon low sodium soy sauce
3/4 teaspoon crushed red pepper
1/4 teaspoon salt
4 cloves garlic, thinly sliced
1 teaspoon grated orange peel
2 teaspoons extra virgin olive oil
1 teaspoon dark sesame oil
1/2 teaspoon grated lime zest
1 pound mushrooms, halved
2 tablespoons chopped fresh parsley

Instructions

At Home Preparation: Combine the first 7 ingredients in a small saucepan. Bring to a boil and cook 1 minute or until the sugar dissolves. Remove from heat; stir in orange rind, oils and lime rind. Cool and place in a container. Clean and halve the mushrooms, sprinkle with a little lemon juice to prevent oxidation, and place in a container.

On Board Preparation: Combine the vinegar mixture and mushrooms in a large bowl and toss well to combine. Cover; refrigerate overnight. Just before serving, add the parsley and toss to combine.
Serves: 6.

Creamy Mashed Potatoes

5 pounds red potatoes, peeled
1/4 teaspoon salt
10 ounces Alfredo sauce
1/2 cup butter
1/2 teaspoon salt
1/4 teaspoon pepper

Instructions

At Home Preparation: Peel the potatoes and cut into 1-inch cubes. Cook the potatoes with the salt in boiling water to cover until tender, about 15-20 minutes. Drain thoroughly, and place in a container.

On Board Preparation: Stir the remaining ingredients into the potatoes and mash until smooth. Heat and serve.
Serves: 6.

Ginger-Curry Carrots

     1   pound baby carrots
    1/2 cup orange juice
     1   teaspoon minced garlic
     2   tablespoons sugar
     2   tablespoons butter
    1/2 teaspoon minced fresh ginger
    1/2 teaspoon curry powder

Instructions
At Home Preparation: Combine all ingredients except the carrots and place in a container.

On Board Preparation: Combine the carrots with the orange juice mixture in a medium saucepan. Bring to a boil, reduce heat to low, cover and cook 6-8 minutes. Serve hot.
Serves: 4.

Gingered Carrots and Beets

     1   pound carrots
     1   pound beets
     1   tablespoon butter
     3   tablespoons orange juice
     1   teaspoon finely grated fresh ginger
    1/2 teaspoon finely grated orange peel
     1   teaspoon salt
    1/2 teaspoon pepper

Instructions
At Home Preparation: Peel the carrots and cut on the diagonal in 1/4-inch slices. Steam about 5 minutes or until just crisp-tender. Be careful not to over cook. Run under cold water immediately, drain and pat dry and place in a container. Cover the beets with water in a pan and bring to a boil. Cook, covered, about 20 minutes or until a fork can be inserted easily. Peel, cool and slice in 1/4-inch slices and place in a container. Chop the fresh ginger and place in a container. Grate the orange peel and place in a container.

On Board Preparation: Melt the butter in a pan. Add the orange juice, ginger and orange peel. Add the carrots and beets, toss in the juice and season with salt and pepper. Heat through.
Serves: 6.

Gorgonzola Artichoke Hearts with Walnuts

      1/4 cup minced shallots
        2 large minced garlic cloves
      1/4 cup olive oil
       18 ounces frozen artichoke hearts
        2 tablespoons lemon juice
      1/3 cup crumbled gorgonzola cheese
        1 tablespoon minced fresh parsley
      1/2 cup halved walnuts

Instructions

At Home Preparation: Cook the artichoke hearts according to package directions. Place in a container. Mince the garlic and place in a container. Mince the parsley and place in a container. Toast the walnut halves, cool, and place in a container.

On Board Preparation: In a large skillet cook the shallots and garlic in the oil over medium heat, stirring constantly, for about 5 minutes. Add the artichoke hearts, raise the heat to medium-high and continue cooking until heated through. Add the lemon juice and remove from the heat. Add the Gorgonzola and toss until the cheese melts. Garnish with the minced parsley and walnut halves.
Serves: 6.

Green Beans Provencal

        2 pounds fresh green beans
       24 medium cherry tomatoes, halved
      1/2 cup chopped red onion
      3/4 cup chopped fresh parsley
      1/4 cup water
      1/4 cup white wine vinegar
        2 tablespoons grated Parmesan cheese
        2 tablespoons olive oil
      1/2 teaspoon dried thyme
      1/2 teaspoon pepper
        2 cloves garlic, minced

Instructions

At Home Preparation: Wash the green beans, pat dry, and cut into 1-1/2 inch pieces. Place in a container. Halve the cherry tomatoes and place in a container. Chop the onion and place in a container. Chop the parsley and place in a container. Drain and plunge into cold water then drain again. Combine the beans, tomatoes, and onion and place in a container.

On Board Preparation: Steam the beans, covered, for 8 minutes or until crisp-tender.   Combine the parsley and remaining ingredients in a small bowl and stir until well blended. Pour over the vegetables and toss gently to coat. Serve at room temperature.
Serves: 12.

Green Beans with Bacon

    1 3/4 pounds fresh green beans
      1/4 cup water
        8 slices bacon, chopped
        5 medium green onions, chopped
      1/2 teaspoon salt
      1/2 teaspoon pepper

Instructions

At Home Preparation: Place the beans and 1/4 cup water in a large microwave container. Cover with plastic wrap and pierce to vent. Microwave on high 4-7 minutes or until crisp-tender. Plunge into ice water immediately to stop the cooking process. Drain well, cool and place in a container. Cook the bacon in a large non-stick skillet over medium heat until crisp. Remove and drain on paper towels. Reserve 2 tablespoons of the drippings and place in a container. Cool the bacon, chop and place in a container.   Chop the green onions, white and light green parts only, and place in a container.

On Board Preparation: Put the reserved drippings into a skillet and heat over medium-high heat. Sauté the green onions about 1 minute. Stir in the green beans, salt and pepper and continue to sauté 2 to 3 minutes until thoroughly heated. Stir in the bacon.
Serves: 4.

GALLEY TIP
The juice of one lemon will yield about 1/4 cup juice.

Green Beans with Toasted Pecans

    2 pounds green beans, trimmed
    8 tablespoons butter, cut in pieces
  1/4 cup finely chopped shallots
  1/2 cup pecans, toasted
    2 tablespoons fresh lemon juice
  1/2 teaspoon salt
  1/4 teaspoon freshly ground black pepper

Instructions

At Home Preparation: Wash and trim the green beans. Bring a large pot of salted water to a boil. Add the green beans and cook until just tender, about 5 minutes. Plunge immediately into ice water to stop the cooking. Drain, cool, and place in a container. Chop the shallots and place in a container. Toast the pecans by placing them in a toaster oven at 350° being careful not to burn. Cool, coarsely chop, and place in a container.

On Board Preparation: In a large skillet over medium-high heat, melt the butter. Add the shallots and pecans and cook stirring until the butter turns a light brown and begins to smell nutty. Be careful not to burn. Add the beans and toss to coat. Cook until the beans are warmed through, about 3 minutes. Add the lemon juice and season with salt and pepper.
Serves: 8.

Grilled Balsamic Asparagus

    1 pound asparagus spears
    1 teaspoon olive oil
  1/4 teaspoon kosher salt
  1/8 teaspoon freshly ground black pepper
    1 tablespoon balsamic vinegar

Instructions

At Home Preparation: Wash, and prepare the asparagus by snapping off the woody ends. Place in a container.

On Board Preparation: Prepare the grill. Place the asparagus in a bowl and drizzle with the oil. Season with salt and pepper and toss to coat. Place the asparagus on a grill rack or vegetable grilling dish coated with cooking spray. Grill 2 minutes on each side or until crisp-tender. Place in a bowl and drizzle with the vinegar. Serve immediately.
Serves: 4.

Honey Glazed Carrots

1 1/2	quarts water
5	cups carrots, thinly sliced
3	tablespoons chopped fresh parsley
2	tablespoons honey
1/2	teaspoon salt
1/2	teaspoon grated orange peel
1/4	teaspoon freshly ground black pepper

Instructions

At Home Preparation: Wash, peel and slice the carrots. Place in a container. Chop the parsley and place in a container. Grate the orange rind and place in a container.

On Board Preparation: Bring the water to a boil in a medium saucepan. Add the carrots; cook for 20 minutes or until tender. Drain well. Place carrots and remaining ingredients in a large bowl; toss gently.
Serves: 8.

Horseradish Carrots

2	pounds carrots, peeled & sliced
1/2	cup mayonnaise
2	tablespoons minced onions
1 1/2	tablespoons horseradish
1/2	teaspoon salt
1/4	teaspoon pepper
1/2	cup crushed saltine crackers
2	tablespoons butter
1	tablespoon chopped fresh parsley
3	dashes paprika

Instructions

At Home Preparation: Peel and slice the carrots. Mince the onion and place in a container. Crush the saltines and place in a container. Chop the parsley (for garnish) and place in a container. Place the carrots in a pan with enough water to cover; cook until crisp-tender, about 10 minutes. Drain, reserving 1/4 cup of the liquid. Place the reserved liquid in a container. Cool the carrots and place in a container.

On Board Preparation: Preheat the oven to 325°. Place the carrots in a baking dish. Combine the reserved liquid, mayonnaise, onion, horseradish, salt and pepper; pour over the carrots. Sprinkle with the cracker crumbs and dot with butter. Sprinkle with parsley and paprika. Bake about 20 minutes or until heated through.
Serves: 8.

Lemon and Herb Grilled Vegetables

  2/3 cup olive oil
  1/3 cup fresh lemon juice
  1/3 cup dry vermouth
    2 tablespoons crumbled dried rosemary
    1 tablespoon crumbled dried thyme
  1/2 teaspoon sugar
  1/2 teaspoon sea salt
  1/2 teaspoon freshly ground black pepper
    4 servings zucchini, mushrooms, bell peppers, baby carrots, summer squash, etc.

Instructions
At Home Preparation: Mix all ingredients except the vegetables and place in a container. Clean and cut vegetables into bit size pieces and place each in a container.

On Board Preparation: Bring the marinade to room temperature. Pour over the prepared vegetables and let marinate for 30-60 minutes. Prepare the grill and grill the vegetables basting with the marinade while cooking.
Serves: 4.

Marinated Asparagus with Prosciutto

    2 pounds fresh asparagus
  3/4 cup vegetable oil
  1/4 cup white wine vinegar
    2 tablespoons Dijon mustard
    2 tablespoons honey
    2 teaspoons dried tarragon
  1/4 pound prosciutto

Instructions
At Home Preparation: Snap the tough ends off the asparagus; remove scales if desired. Cook, covered, in an asparagus cooker or in a small amount of boiling water 4 minutes or until crisp-tender; drain. Plunge into ice water to stop the cooking process; drain. Place in a container. Combine oil and next 4 ingredients and place in a container.

On Board Preparation: Shake the oil and vinegar mixture briskly. Pour over the asparagus; cover and chill at least 2 hours. Remove asparagus, reserving marinade and arrange on a platter. Top with prosciutto and drizzle with reserved marinade.
Serves: 8.

Marinated Green Beans

     4 cups fresh green beans
     1 medium onion, thinly sliced
     1 clove garlic, minced
        Marinade:
     2 tablespoons sugar
     1 teaspoon paprika
   1/4 teaspoon salt
   1/8 teaspoon pepper
     1 teaspoon oregano
   1/2 teaspoon mustard powder
     5 tablespoons wine vinegar
     4 tablespoons olive oil

Instructions

At Home Preparation: Cook the fresh green beans until crisp-tender. Drain and rinse with cold water. Pat dry and place in a container. Slice the onion and place in a container. Mince the garlic and place in a container. Mix together the dry ingredients for the marinade and place in a container.

On Board Preparation: Place the green beans, onion and garlic in a bowl. To the dry ingredients for the marinade, add the vinegar then add the oil, 1 tablespoon at a time, mixing well. Pour over the green bean mixture, cover, and refrigerate at least 2 hours or overnight. If serving hot, heat through over medium heat. This dish is also good served cold.
Serves: 6.

Recipe Notes

Substitute 32 ounces of canned, French cut green beans, well drained for the fresh if desired.

GALLEY TIP
Don't cry over chopped onions! Place the onion in the freezer for a few minutes before you chop it.

Marinated Vegetable Medley

1/3 cup white vinegar
1/3 cup balsamic vinegar
2/3 cup vegetable oil
2 cloves minced garlic
1 teaspoon salt
1 teaspoon sugar
1 teaspoon dried oregano
1 teaspoon dried basil
1/4 teaspoon freshly ground pepper
1 1/2 cups broccoli florets
1 medium onion, sliced
1/2 pound mushrooms, halved
1 pound carrot
14 ounces artichoke hearts, drained and halved
1 cup oil cured black olives, halved
1 cup celery, sliced
2 ounces pimientos, sliced, drained and chopped

Instructions
At Home Preparation: Mince the garlic and place in a container. Crush the oregano and basil in a mortar and pestle and place in a container. Clean the broccoli and cut into florets. Steam the broccoli until just crisp-tender; drain, cool and place in a container. Slice the onion and place in a container. Wash, dry and halve the mushrooms, sprinkle with lemon juice, and place in a container. Drain the artichoke hearts, halve and place in a container. Drain the ripe olives, halve and place in a container. Slice the celery into 1/4- inch pieces and place in a container. Drain the pimiento, chop and place in a container.

On Board Preparation: In a saucepan, combine the first 9 ingredients and bring to a boil. Reduce heat and simmer uncovered for 10 minutes. Combine all the vegetables except the broccoli in a large bowl, placing the broccoli in a separate bowl. (Marinating the broccoli separately keeps it a richer color.) Pour the hot marinade over the vegetables in each bowl. Stir gently or toss to coat. Cover and chill several hours, gently stirring or tossing occasionally. Drain the vegetables, combine the broccoli with the others and serve.
Serves: 6.

Onions in Gruyere Sauce

2 pounds boiling onions
1/2 teaspoon butter
1 tablespoon flour
2 cups milk
1 pinch ground cloves
1/4 teaspoon salt

    1/8 teaspoon pepper
      3 ounces Gruyere, thinly sliced
      2 tablespoons chopped fresh parsley

Instructions
At Home Preparation: Trim and peel the onions. Slice the Gruyere and place in a container. Chop the parsley and place in a container. Place the onions in a pot and cover with water. Bring to a boil and cook gently for 20 minutes. Drain, cool and place in a container.

On Board Preparation: Melt the butter in a large skillet. Add the flour and mix well. Gradually pour in the milk, stirring constantly, and bring to a boil over medium heat until thickened, about 15 minutes. Remove from heat and season with the cloves, salt, and pepper. Add cheese and stir until melted. Add parsley and stir. Add the onions and heat through over low heat.
Serves: 4.

Recipe Notes
If you want an extra-rich side dish, substitute one cup heavy cream for one cup of the milk.

Peanuty Sweet Potatoes

      4 cups sweet potatoes
      2 cups sugar
    1/4 cup creamy peanut butter
      2 cups milk
      4 large eggs, slightly beaten
      2 sticks butter
      1 teaspoon nutmeg
      1 teaspoon cinnamon
  1 1/2 cups crushed corn flakes
      1 cup firmly packed light brown sugar
      1 cup chopped Spanish peanuts

Instructions
At Home Preparation: If using fresh sweet potatoes, cook until tender, drain and cool and mash. If using canned sweet potatoes, drain and mash. Mix with the sugar and peanut butter and place in a container. Crush the corn flakes and place in a container. Chop the peanuts and place in a container.

On Board Preparation: Soften 1 stick of butter. Preheat the oven to 400°. Add the milk, eggs, softened butter, nutmeg and cinnamon to the sweet potatoes and mix well. Pour into a greased casserole and bake for 20 minutes. To make topping, melt the remaining butter and combine with the corn flakes, brown sugar and peanuts. Spread over the potatoes and bake and additional 10 minutes.
Serves: 8.

Peas and Cauliflower in Yogurt

3/4	pound fresh English peas
2	cups water
4	cups cauliflower florets
1/4	teaspoon salt
3/4	cup plain yogurt
3	tablespoons chopped fresh cilantro
1	tablespoon lemon juice
1/4	teaspoon ground cumin
1	dash white pepper

Instructions

At Home Preparation: Shell and wash peas. Wash the cauliflower and separate into florets. Chop the cilantro and place in a container. Bring 2 cups water to a boil in a large pan. Add the peas and cauliflower, cover and cook about 7 minutes or until crisp-tender. Drain well; place in a bowl with salt and toss. Place in a container.

On Board Preparation: Reheat the vegetables. Combine yogurt and remaining ingredients stirring well. Pour over the vegetables and toss well.
Serves: 4.

Peas and Prosciutto with Risotto

1	small onion
4	ounces prosciutto
1 1/2	pints chicken stock
1	sprig thyme
1	large bay leaf
3	ounces butter
7	ounces risotto
4	ounces dry white wine
4	ounces frozen peas
1/4	teaspoon salt
1/8	teaspoon pepper
1/2	cup shaved Parmesan cheese

Instructions

At Home Preparation: Chop the onion and place in a container. Cut the prosciutto into thin strips and place in a container.

On Board Preparation: Bring the stock to a boil with the thyme and bay leaf. Reduce heat to simmer. Melt the butter in a saucepan, add the onion and cook over medium heat until softened. Add the risotto and stir until the grains are coated with butter, about 2 minutes. Add the wine and stir until it is absorbed completely. Begin adding the simmering stock a little at a time, allowing the risotto to absorb before adding more, until half the stock has been added. Add the frozen peas and continue adding the rest of the stock until the risotto is al dente. Stir in the prosciutto and salt and pepper to taste. Remove from the heat and let rest for 2 minutes before serving, topped with the Parmesan shavings.

Serves: 2.

Potato and Tomato Casserole

1	pound potatoes
3	medium onions, thinly sliced
6	tablespoons butter
1/4	teaspoon salt
1/8	teaspoon pepper
1	large can tomatoes
1	teaspoon basil
1/8	cup chopped fresh parsley
2	cups bread crumbs
6	tablespoons butter
3	tablespoons grated Parmesan cheese

Instructions

At Home Preparation: Peel the potatoes and cook in salted boiling water until tender. Drain, cool and cut into thin slices. Place in a container. Slice the onions and sauté in the butter until soft and translucent. Cool and place in a container. Make the bread crumbs and place in a container. Grate the Parmesan and place in a container.

On Board Preparation: Preheat the oven to 350°. Put half the potato slices in a buttered casserole dish, layering with the onions and salt and pepper to taste. Put the tomatoes in a bowl, with the liquid and basil and mash. Pour half the tomatoes over the potato layer. Sprinkle with parsley. Repeat with another layer. Melt the extra butter and combine with the bread crumbs and Parmesan. Spread over the top of the casserole. Bake, uncovered for about 30 minutes until the top is golden brown.

Serves: 4.

GALLEY TIP

Don't ever soak vegetables after slicing unless you are going to use the liquid in the cooking process. Too much of the nutrients are lost in soaking.

Sherried Mushrooms

1/2   cup tomato sauce
1/4   cup olive oil
1/4   cup dry sherry
1/8   teaspoon cayenne pepper
   2   teaspoons mustard powder
1/4   teaspoon salt
1/8   teaspoon pepper
1/2   cup heavy cream
1 1/2   pounds mushrooms, quartered

Instructions

At Home Preparation: Clean the mushrooms, cut into quarters, sprinkle with a little lemon juice, and place in a container.

On Board Preparation: In a skillet, combine tomato sauce, olive oil, sherry cayenne pepper and dry mustard. Heat thoroughly over medium heat. Salt and pepper to taste. Cover and simmer over low heat for 3 minutes. Stir in the cream and mushrooms. Heat to boiling. Reduce heat, cover and simmer for 3 minutes.
Serves: 6.

Spicy Peas and Pecans

   4   slices bacon, chopped
1/2   cup chopped onion
  32   ounces frozen baby sweet peas, unthawed
1/2   cup water
   1   teaspoon Creole seasoning
   1   cup chopped pecans, toasted

Instructions

At Home Preparation: Chop the onion and place in a container. Chop the pecans and toast in a shallow pan in the toaster oven at 350°, stirring occasionally until just beginning to brown, about 10 minutes. Cool and place in a container.

On Board Preparation: Cook the bacon in a large skillet over medium heat until crisp. Remove and drain on paper towels, reserving 1 tablespoon drippings in the skillet. Stir the onions into the hot drippings. Reduce heat to medium-low and cook until lightly browned, about 15 minutes. Add the peas, 1/2 cup water and Creole seasoning. Cook 10 minutes, stirring occasionally until peas are tender. Stir in the bacon and pecans.
Serves: 8.

Spinach and Artichoke Casserole

    40 ounces frozen chopped spinach
    1/2 pound sliced mushrooms
    3/4 cup butter
    1/2 cup mayonnaise
      1 cup sour cream
      1 cup grated Romano cheese
  8 1/2 ounces artichokes, drained and quartered
      2 medium tomatoes, thinly sliced
    2/3 cup bread crumbs

Instructions
At Home Preparation: Wash and slice the mushrooms. Sauté the mushrooms in 1/4 cup of the butter until just tender. Grate the Romano cheese and place in a container. Drain and quarter the artichokes and place in a container. Slice the tomatoes and place in a container. Cook the spinach according to package directions, drain, cool and place in a container.

On Board Preparation: Preheat the oven to 350°. Combine the mayonnaise, sour cream and 2/3 cup of the cheese; stir in the spinach, mushrooms and artichokes. Butter a casserole dish and place the mixture in it. Arrange the tomato slices on top. Melt the remaining butter and stir in the bread crumbs and remaining cheese. Sprinkle over the top of the casserole; bake for about 30 minutes.
Serves: 12.

Recipe Notes
Use Hellman's mayonnaise for the best flavor.

GALLEY TIP
Mushrooms are fresh when the gills are not yet open.

Spinach in Parmesan Cream Sauce

    2 tablespoons butter
    1 cup onion, sliced
    2 teaspoons minced garlic
  1/2 cup all-purpose flour
2 1/2 cups half & half
1 1/4 cups grated Parmesan cheese
1 1/2 teaspoons Italian seasoning
    4 medium coarsely chopped fresh basil leaves
  1/2 teaspoon cracked black pepper
  1/4 teaspoon salt
  10 ounces frozen chopped spinach, drained
  1/2 cup bread crumbs
  1/2 cup grated Parmesan cheese

Instructions

At Home Preparation: Slice the onion and place in a container. Mince the garlic and place in a container. Grate the Parmesan and place in a container. Chop the basil and place in a container. Combine the 1/2 cup bread crumbs and 1/2 cup Parmesan and place in a container. Thaw and thoroughly drain the spinach and place in a container.

On Board Preparation: Preheat the oven to 350°. Melt the butter in a saucepan. Add the onion and garlic and sauté gently. Add the flour and cook 1 minute, stirring constantly. Gradually add the half-and-half and cook until bubbly, about 5 minutes. Remove from heat and stir in the cheese and seasoning. Combine with the spinach and spoon into a buttered baking dish. Sprinkle the top with the bread crumb mixture. Bake 30 minutes.
Serves: 4.

Spinach Sauté

    2 tablespoons olive oil
    1 clove garlic, minced
  1/4 cup chopped onion
    5 large mushrooms, sliced
    4 dashes lemon juice
  1/4 cup white wine
  10 ounces frozen chopped spinach
  3/4 cup grated Parmesan cheese
  1/4 teaspoon salt
  1/8 teaspoon pepper

Instructions

At Home Preparation: Mince the garlic and place in a container. Chop the onion and place in a container. Wash and slice the mushrooms, sprinkle very lightly with lemon juice and place in a container. Grate the Parmesan and place in a container. Cook the spinach according to package directions, cool, drain well and place in a container.

On Board Preparation: Sauté the garlic, onion and mushrooms in the olive oil until translucent. Stir in the wine and set aside. Add the cheese, sauté mix, salt and pepper to the cooked spinach, and heat through. Add the onion and mushroom mixture and stir.

Serves: 4.

Sweet and Sour Asparagus

2/3 cup white vinegar
1/2 cup sugar
  1 teaspoon whole cloves
  3 sticks cinnamon
  1 tablespoon celery seed
1/2 cup water
  2 pounds asparagus
  1 large egg, hard cooked

Instructions

At Home Preparation: Clean the asparagus, snapping off the woody ends, dry and place in a container. Hard boil the egg, cool, peel, chop and place in a container.

On Board Preparation: In a saucepan, mix the first six ingredients and bring to a boil. Place the asparagus in a flat baking dish and pour the boiling liquid over. Cover and refrigerate for 24 hours. To serve, pour off the liquid and garnish with the chopped egg.

Serves: 8.

Recipe Notes
Be sure to pick out the smallest diameter fresh asparagus for this dish!

Sweet and Sour Baked Beans

  1 teaspoon mustard powder
1/8 teaspoon garlic powder
1/2 teaspoon salt
1/2 cup wine vinegar
  4 large onions
  8 slices bacon
 30 ounces dry butter beans, cooked
 16 ounces canned baby lima beans, drained
 16 ounces canned red kidney beans, drained
 16 ounces canned baked beans
  4 slices bacon
3/4 cup packed brown sugar

Instructions

At Home Preparation: Slice the onions into rings and place in a container. Cook the 8 bacon slices until crisp, cool, crumble and place in a container. Drain the butter beans, lima beans, and red kidney beans and place in a container.

On Board Preparation: Preheat the oven to 350°. Combine the sugar, mustard, garlic powder, salt and vinegar in a bowl. In a skillet, add this mixture to the onion rings, cover and simmer for 20 minutes. Add the beans and crumbled bacon and mix well. Pour into a 3-quart casserole and arrange the 4 slices of (uncooked) bacon strips on top. Bake 1 hour.
Serves: 12.

Tomato Pie

    2 cups biscuit mix
  2/3 cup buttermilk
1 1/4 cups grated Parmesan cheese
    2 large tomatoes, seeded
    2 tablespoons all-purpose flour
    1 small sweet onion, minced
  1/2 cup chopped fresh basil
  1/2 teaspoon salt
  1/2 teaspoon freshly ground black pepper
  3/4 cup creamy mustard-mayonnaise blend

Instructions

At Home Preparation: Grate the Parmesan cheese and place in a container. Seed and thinly slice the tomato and place in a container. Mince the onion and place in a container. Chop the fresh basil and place in a container.

On Board Preparation: Preheat the oven to 400°. Lightly grease a 9-inch pie plate. Stir together the baking mix and buttermilk just until blended. With your hands, pat into the bottom and up the sides of the greased pie plate. Bake for 7 minutes, remove from the oven and sprinkle with 1/4 cup cheese. Toss the tomato slices with flour and arrange in layer over the cheese. Sprinkle with half of the onion, basil, salt and pepper. Repeat with another layer of the same. Stir together the remaining 1 cup cheese and the mustard-mayonnaise blend and spread over the top of the pie. Bake for 25 minutes or until lightly browned. Let stand 10 minutes before serving.
Serves: 6.

Two-Potato Mash

2	pounds sweet potatoes
1	cup sour cream
1/4	cup packed brown sugar
1/4	cup butter
1	teaspoon kosher salt
1/4	teaspoon cinnamon
22	ounces mashed potatoes, frozen or prepared
2 1/4	cups milk
1/2	teaspoon pepper

Instructions

At Home Preparation: Pierce sweet potatoes with a fork and arrange in a circle on paper towels in microwave. Microwave on HIGH for 12 minutes or until tender, rearranging after 6 minutes. Let stand for 5 minutes. Peel and mash. Add 1/2 cup sour cream, sugar, 2 tablespoons butter, 1/2 teaspoon salt and pepper. Stir until well blended. Place in a container. Melt the remaining 2 tablespoons butter. Combine the mashed potatoes with the milk, remaining 1/2 cup sour cream 2 tablespoons of melted butter, remaining 1/2 teaspoon salt, and pepper, stirring to combine. Place in a container.

On Board Preparation: Heat both the sweet potatoes and mashed potatoes in the microwave. Place the mashed potatoes in the serving bowl. Spoon the sweet potatoes in, swirling with a spoon just enough to slightly combine without blending completely. You should be able to see the contrast between the sweet and mashed potatoes swirls.
Serves: 12.

Index

Order Form

Fax Orders: 866 457-0424 (toll free). Please use this form.
Telephone Orders: 727 360-3222.
Online Orders: http://www.theyachtinggourmet.com
Postal Orders: MEM Publications, 5301 Gulf Blvd., B507, St. Pete Beach, FL 33706
Telephone: 727 360-3222

Name:_____

Address:_____

City: _____ State: _____ Zip: _____

Telephone: _____

Email: _____

The Yachting Gourmet $32.95   # of single copies _____

The Yachting Gourmet Twin Pack $58.95. # of double copies _____
(One for home and one for the boat! Save 10%.)

Sales Tax: Please add 7% for shipments to Florida addresses.

Shipping via Priority Mail:
        U.S. $5.00 for one book.
        $10 for 2-4 books.
        Additional copies, please call for shipping charges.

Payment: (Please check your payment choice.)

___Check enclosed. (Please allow 10 business days for personal checks or money orders to clear the bank once your order has been received.)

Credit Card payments accepted through the website or directly via PayPal (www.paypal.com). Please use the account marymask@yahoo.com to send payment. If ordering directly through PayPal please fax this order form indicating PayPal as your selected payment to 866 457-0424.

891890

Made in the USA